*"I was born not knowing
and have had only a
little time to change that
here and there."*

Richard Feynman, American physicist, 1918–1988

KNOW
IT ALL

THE
LITTLE BOOK
OF
ESSENTIAL
KNOWLEDGE

SUSAN ALDRIDGE
ELIZABETH KING HUMPHREY
JULIE WHITAKER

The Reader's Digest Association, Inc.
Pleasantville, NY/Montreal/London/Singapore

A Reader's Digest Book

This edition published by The Reader's Digest Association, Inc.,
by arrangement with Quid Publishing, Level Four,
Sheridan House, 114 Western Road, Hove, BN3 1DD, England
www.quidpublishing.com

For Reader's Digest
U.S. Project Editor: Fred DuBose
Canadian Project Editor: Pamela Chichinskas
Copy Editor: Barbara Booth
Project Designer: Jennifer Tokarski
Senior Art Director: George McKeon
Executive Editor, Trade Publishing: Dolores York
Associate Publisher, Trade Publishing: Rosanne McManus
President and Publisher, Trade Publishing: Harold Clarke

Library of Congress Cataloging-in-Publication Data

Aldridge, Susan.
 Know it all : the little book of essential knowledge / Susan
Aldridge, Elizabeth King Humphrey, Julie Whitaker.
    p. cm.
 Includes index.
 ISBN 978-0-7621-0933-3
1. Handbooks, vade-mecums, etc. 2. Encyclopedias and
dictionaries. 3. Questions and answers. I. Humphrey, Elizabeth
King. II. Whitaker, Julie. III. Title.
 AG105.A255 2008
 031.02--dc22
                                                    2008017437

We are committed to both the quality of our products and the
service we provide to our customers. We value your comments,
so please feel free to contact us.
The Reader's Digest Association, Inc.
Adult Trade Publishing
Reader's Digest Road
Pleasantville, NY 10570-7000

For more Reader's Digest products and information,
visit our website:
www.rd.com (in the United States)
www.readersdigest.ca (in Canada)
www.readersdigest.co.uk (in the UK)
www.rdasia.com (in Asia)

Printed in China

1 3 5 7 9 10 8 6 4 2

Chapter Eight

📖 Religion and Thought

Chapter Nine

🎨 Artistic Endeavor

Chapter Ten

❓ The Quizzes

Welcome!

Allow us to introduce *Know It All* and welcome you to the ranks of the better-informed—to wit, the self-assured folks who aren't at a loss for words when a conversation turns to the great painters or global warming or Eastern religions. We also hope you'll agree that filling your memory bank with snippets of general knowledge is its own reward. For one thing, much of the basic information that helps us make sense of the world can sometimes get lost in today's never-ending barrage of information. For another, exposure to names, places, and events that have secured a place in history can pique your curiosity and make you want to learn more.

Easy Does It

Know It All makes it easy for you to absorb things you might have forgotten, or never learned, or have simply been shouldered aside by the constant stream of "content" from electronic media and the Internet—all without the dry biographies, lists of dates, or baffling scientific jargon that glaze your eyes over faster than you can say, "Huh?" Instead, you'll find simple, everyday language describing the places, people, and phenomena that have shaped the world. Our goal is to bring you "just the facts" in a concise and entertaining way—not that we don't add the occasional tidbit of trivia for the fun of it. Increasing the fun quotient are the quizzes following each of the nine chapters, plus a "final exam" at the end.

The uniform structure of *Know It All*—a total of two pages per subject, split over nine chapters—allows you to browse though the book at your leisure. (Would you like to quickly bone up on the stars above before joining your astronomy-major pal for lunch? Turn to page 20. Need to know who built the Taj Mahal and why? Go to page 215.)

Special Features

Throughout the book, different kinds of special features pop up here and there—knowledge in an even smaller nutshell.

- **In the Know** sidebars focus on a single related subject. For example, in "Reptiles: On Land to Stay" (pages 66–67), an In the Know sidebar relates the story of Tu'i Malila, a tortoise that may have lived longer than any animal on record.

- **Key Player** sidebars shed light on some of the movers and shakers who changed history—among them Alexander the Great and Charles Darwin.

- **Conversation Starter** sidebars put forth interesting snippets of knowledge and ask questions likely to spur debate—from rising sea levels to the choice of *Time* magazine's Person of the Year.

- **In Fact . . .** sidebars are catchalls for all kinds of facts, most of them lesser known, but fascinating nevertheless. Do you know the difference between solar flares, prominences, and sunspots?

- **Test Yourself** quizzes offer 32 pages of challenging questions to try by yourself, or with family members or friends who've read the book—or perhaps who think they "know it all" already. When it comes to giving your brain cells a workout, an hour or so of quizzing beats video games any day!

Nine Intriguing Chapters

Your "subjects of study" are divided into nine chapters, all chock full of stories and facts and the "greats" of world history.

 Understanding the Universe starts with the birth of the cosmos, pilots you through our solar system, and ends by exploring the amazing atom.

 The Story of the Earth surveys our planet from its very core to the upper atmosphere, with spreads on minerals and gems, volcanoes, climate change, and more.

 The Story of Life takes a look at everything from plants and birds and mammals to life forms under the sea —not to mention the species *Homo sapiens* (us).

Exploring the World runs from the first civilizations to voyages of discovery to history-changing periods such as the Renaissance and the world's great revolutions.

 Invention and Discovery considers more than just Edison's lightbulb. It starts with the birth of agriculture and ends with the International Space Station.

Conflicts of the Modern Age begins with the American Civil War and progresses to wars of the twentieth century: from World Wars I and II to the prolonged conflicts in Vietnam, Afghanistan, and the Balkans.

 The Structure of Society looks at forms of government, world population, iconic leaders of the last century, and economics—the study of the financial and mercantile systems that make the world hum.

 Religion and Thought looks into the world's religions, ancient mythologies, and examines the four branches of philosophy.

 Artistic Endeavor peers into the realm of the arts and architecture and profiles some of the greatest creative geniuses of all time.

What You Can Gain

In a sense, the complete *Know It All* package—the easy-to-absorb presentations of subjects as varied as the first terrestrial animals and the atomic bomb; the informative sidebars; and the stimulating plethora of quizzes—is akin to the stone that causes the surface of a lake to ripple: The more you learn, the more you want to know.

Curious about the monarch or artist or gemstone or animal you read about in the book but had never heard of? Look him, her, or it up online, or spend a couple of hours in your local library. With *Know It All* as your springboard, you can find out where the path leads. Who knows? A detour could lead you to something so fascinating you'll want to read everything on the subject.

Your reward? Finding new interests, feeling more self-assured, and holding your own in conversations with people from all walks of life. Not a bad return on a small book of 256 pages . . . .

Chapter One

Understanding the Universe

Gazing up at the star-studded heavens inspires
awe like little else. The starry sky also prompts
eternal questions about the nature of the universe.
How did it all begin? How does it work? What is our
place in it, and are there other living beings out
there? This chapter considers these questions and
a few more. In addition, it introduces you to some of
the scientists whose groundbreaking insights
put us on the road to investigating the
mysteries of the universe.

The Cosmos:
An Explosive Birth?

"How did it all begin?" In the scientific realm the answer to the never-ending question of how the universe began is far from simple. Today's reigning theory posits a so-called Big Bang, which estimates the starting point at 14 billion years ago. But like every cosmological theory, the Big Bang has its limits.

The Big Bang theory states that all matter and energy were once contained in compressed primordial matter—an area of infinite density no bigger than a dime. This unimaginable situation—in which time and space and the laws of physics as we now understand them did not apply—is known as a "singularity."

It's easy to imagine that the Big Bang was some kind of super-explosion, a Hollywood spectacular on an infinitely larger scale. Yet cosmologists say this was not so; for a start, there would have been no bang, because there were no sound waves. Instead, the event is believed to have been more like a smooth but incredibly fast expansion.

The birth of time We don't know what happened between the Big Bang and the tiny time afterward known as the "Planck time"—after physicist Max Planck—but below are some key later events.

The Birth of an Idea

The theory of an expanding universe was proposed in the 1920s by Russian mathematician Alexander Friedmann and Belgian physicist (and priest) Georges Lemaître. The first evidence to support it was found by American astronomer Edwin Hubble in 1929. Hubble was measuring the velocities of stars in 46 galaxies and saw that the light they emitted was shifted toward the red end of the spectrum. This "red shift" meant that they were all moving away from our solar system and from one another. That they were moving apart implied they must once have been closer together, supporting the concept of an explosive origin.

More evidence in support of the theory came in 1964, when the American radio astronomers Arno Penzias and Robert Wilson discovered a puzzling background

Time after the Big Bang	10^{-35} seconds	1 second	3 minutes
Event	Massive inflation begins.	Matter begins to "freeze out" in the form of atomic nuclei of hydrogen and helium.	The production of new atomic nuclei stops.

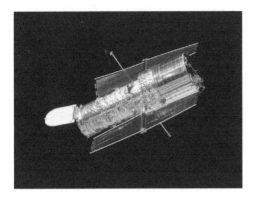

The Hubble Space Telescope is positioned above the Earth's atmosphere to search out evidence for such theories as the Big Bang.

noise from a distant area of the sky. At first they thought it was caused by radio interference or pigeon droppings on their antenna. But scientists at Princeton University concluded that the noise resulted from radiation left over from the Big Bang—radiation that has been called the "afterglow of creation."

Problems with the Theory

Although widely accepted, the Big Bang theory has major problems. The amount of matter evident in the universe couldn't produce the gravity required to create galaxies, and the universe is still accelerating.

In response, scientists have suggested that up to 90 percent of the matter in the universe is actually "dark matter" that cannot be seen and that "dark energy"—estimated to comprise three-quarters of the universe—is causing the continued acceleration. Both dark matter and dark energy have yet to be detected, but projects such as NASA's Joint Dark Energy Mission (target launch 2015) will explore these theories.

1 million years	100 million years
Stable hydrogen atoms form.	The first star begins to shine.

Newton's Laws: Why Things Move As They Do

Why does an apple fall down, not up or sideways? What keeps the Moon in orbit, not flying off into space? When Isaac Newton connected the dots between an apple and the Moon, he discovered the force of gravity. His law of universal gravitation and his three laws of motion opened the door to the modern age of science.

In his most famous work, *Philosophiae Naturalis Principia Mathematica* (1687), Isaac Newton set down the laws that form the basis of modern physics. In the *Principia* he made clear the workings of gravity and the characteristics of motion. Though best known for his mathematical leaps forward in the book, Newton was a powerhouse of ideas, making significant advances in other fields, including optics and the study of light. Today his laws of motion remain mostly unchallenged.

What Goes Up . . .

Newton's law of universal gravitation states that all objects in the universe are attracted to all other objects. Newton calculated that the force of the attraction—gravity—between two objects is equal to the mass of each object multiplied by a gravitational constant and divided by the square of the distance between the objects. Whew! Basically, this means that larger masses exert the stronger attraction (why apples fall toward Earth's gravitational center) but the force of gravity is reduced by distance (why the Moon doesn't hurtle toward Earth or some other larger celestial body).

The mass of the Earth is so much greater than that of the objects upon it (be they tennis balls, parachutes, or birds) that the force of attraction is large. Accordingly, objects fall if gravity is the only force acting on them. Yet when a ball is struck by a tennis racket, for example, it moves in an arc influenced by the force of the hit, air resistance, and gravity. Unless the shot is returned, it will soon fall to the ground.

Conversation Starter Want to lose weight? Try moving to another country. Weight depends on mass and gravity. Because the Earth isn't a uniform sphere, gravity varies slightly over the planet. So you'll be slightly lighter in Cape Town than you would be in Rome, but not by much.

The Laws of Motion

Newton went on to describe in his three laws of motion a framework for the mechanics of the universe.

The first law, or law of inertia, states that objects will remain at rest or in uniform motion in a straight line unless acted on by an external force. For instance, if you set a marble rolling it will eventually stop because of friction and air resistance. Yet a marble set on a frictionless surface in a vacuum would keep rolling forever.

Newton's second law states that the force of acceleration of an object is equal to the mass of the object times the acceleration (meters per second per second). Take a compact car and an SUV with the same engines and put the pedal to the metal. The lighter-weight compact will accelerate faster than its heavier big brother, and this is in accord with Newton's second law.

Key Player

Sir Isaac Newton
1643–1727

Brilliant, wild-tempered, and hypersensitive to slights, Newton was known for his prolonged grudge matches with other great men. And as master of the British mint, he happily tracked down counterfeiters and had them thrown into jail.

Newton's third law, the one most people remember, is that for every action there is an equal and opposite reaction. In other words, if two objects are in contact, then they exert equal and opposite forces on one another. An example of this is the recoil that is experienced when firing a gun, as the force propelling the bullet outward is also exerted back through the stock of the gun.

Newton's discoveries are generally regarded as the launching point for modern cosmological sciences. His mathematical laws of gravitation and motion made it possible for the first time to calculate and predict the movement of planets. His law of gravitation could be challenged only by another genius, and that didn't happen until 1905, when Einstein unveiled his theory of relativity.

The Milky Way: Billions of Stars Strong

Surely the first humans must have looked up and wondered about the pale swath of light that drapes across the night sky. We know it as the Milky Way. Its name comes from the Greek tale of Hera, the queen of Olympus, who spread drops of breast milk across the heavens. We now know that each of those mythical droplets is one star in 100 billion.

Every star occupies its own galaxy—a cluster of stars, dust, and gas held together by gravity—and astronomers classify these galaxies by shape: spiral, barred spiral, elliptical, and irregular. The dust and gas of a galaxy are together known as nebulae, and they are the stuff from which stars are born.

Our star, the Sun, is part of the Milky Way galaxy—so called because it appears as a faint band of light in a clear night sky—which was first studied by the British astronomer William Herschel in the 1780s.

No one knows how many galaxies are in the universe, but there is a huge variety, ranging in size from thousands to hundreds of thousands of light-years across. [A light-year is the distance light can travel in a year, 5.88 trillion miles (9.46 trillion km).]

Most galaxies occur in groups of anything from a handful to many thousands. The distance between each galaxy within a cluster is immense, and most galaxies are moving away from one another. However, vast and spectacular collisions between galaxies can occur; in fact, the Andromeda Galaxy is heading straight for our Milky

A spiral galaxy has a pinwheel shape with arms curling out from a densely packed central core. It is further classified according to how tight the spiral is.

A barred galaxy has evolved from a spiral galaxy and has an oblong of stars passing through a center from which the spiral arms emerge.

An elliptical galaxy contains a lot of dust and may be spherical, oval, football, or lens-shaped.

An irregular galaxy fits none of the other categories and often has no particular form.

Way. But you needn't lose any sleep over it: Its estimated arrival time is approximately 3 billion years from now.

The Life of a Galaxy

The first galaxies probably formed about 2 billion years after the Big Bang, when gas began to cool and coalesce under the force of gravity.

Astronomers believe that most galaxies had formed by about 7 billion years after the Big Bang, with those that rotated faster becoming spiral galaxies, and the slower ones becoming elliptical.

In some galaxies the nebulae composed of gas and dust are still giving birth to stars. This occurs in the spiral arms of a galaxy, and the blue stars in the outer reaches are in fact younger than the yellow ones, which are closer to its center.

The Heart of a Galaxy

The stars within a galaxy rotate around its core, with those that are farther away moving more slowly than those close to the center.

Galaxies with particularly dense cores are known as "active galaxies," and the gravity at the center sucks dust, gas, and even stars in, emitting large amounts of energy. The centers of spiral galaxies are a strong source of X-rays, and it is thought that they may even contain incredibly dense black holes.

IN THE KNOW

Sometimes known simply as "the galaxy," the Milky Way is a spiral galaxy containing a mixture of around 100 billion old and young stars; at its center is a huge black hole. The Sun is a middle-aged star about 30,000 light-years from the core, on the spiral arm located in the constellation of Orion. The 30-plus galaxies, including the Milky Way, that make up the Local Group are among an estimated 125 billion galaxies.

The Milky Way has a pinwheel shape with arms curling out from a densely packed central core.

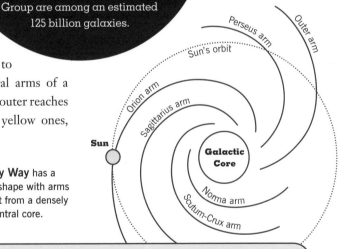

Conversation Starter The Milky Way is one of a group of some 30 galaxies known as the Local Group. Its diameter is about 100,000 light-years, and the distance from Earth to the Andromeda Galaxy, our nearest neighbor, is more than 2 million light-years. Talk about a long commute!

Constellations: Ancient Legends in the Stars

The ancient Greeks and Romans looked at the stars and saw their mythical figures outlined in the heavens. Navigators later learned how to use these so-called constellations as directional aids, the most vital being the North Star, or Polaris.

When you look at the night sky, it appears as a horizon-to-horizon upturned bowl. Astronomers use the traditional constellations to construct star maps for both the northern and southern hemispheres. An observer standing at either pole of the Earth sees only the stars of that hemisphere. At lower latitudes, however, some of the stars from the other hemisphere are visible on the horizon.

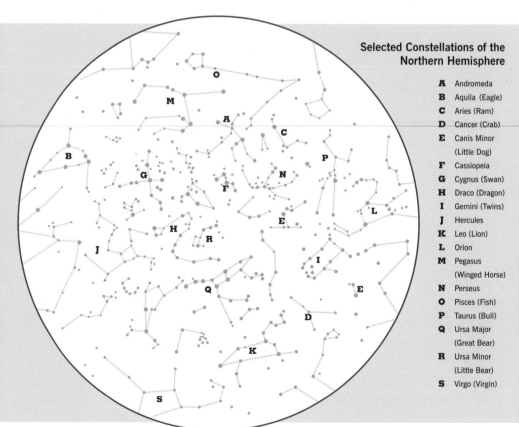

Selected Constellations of the Northern Hemisphere

- **A** Andromeda
- **B** Aquila (Eagle)
- **C** Aries (Ram)
- **D** Cancer (Crab)
- **E** Canis Minor (Little Dog)
- **F** Cassiopeia
- **G** Cygnus (Swan)
- **H** Draco (Dragon)
- **I** Gemini (Twins)
- **J** Hercules
- **K** Leo (Lion)
- **L** Orion
- **M** Pegasus (Winged Horse)
- **N** Perseus
- **O** Pisces (Fish)
- **P** Taurus (Bull)
- **Q** Ursa Major (Great Bear)
- **R** Ursa Minor (Little Bear)
- **S** Virgo (Virgin)

Navigating the Night Sky

The stars you see at night change with the time of year and your location. However, it is possible to make sense of the night sky with a few pointers. For example, the "handle" of the Big Dipper—seven of the stars in the Great Bear—points directly at Polaris, the North Pole star. In the southern hemisphere no obvious star marks the celestial South Pole, but the Southern Cross can be seen as an arrow pointing toward it.

Each star also has a two-part name: the name of its constellation and a Greek letter denoting its brightness; alpha is the brightest, so Alpha Centauri is the brightest star in the Centaurus constellation. Ancient names for stars include Sirius (Alpha Canis Majoris, or the "Dog Star"), the brightest star in the sky.

Proper Motion

The change of position of individual stars in our galaxy is referred to as "proper motion," which is detectable only by accurate measurements made through telescopes and stays invisible to the naked eye over a human lifetime. Proper motion dictates that some 200,000 years from now, the Big Dipper and other constellations will have dispersed and be no more.

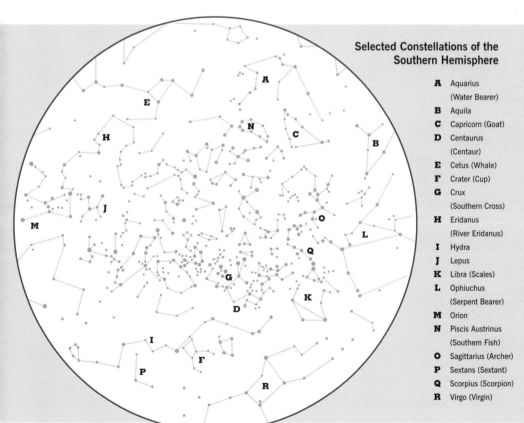

Selected Constellations of the Southern Hemisphere

A Aquarius (Water Bearer)
B Aquila
C Capricorn (Goat)
D Centaurus (Centaur)
E Cetus (Whale)
F Crater (Cup)
G Crux (Southern Cross)
H Eridanus (River Eridanus)
I Hydra
J Lepus
K Libra (Scales)
L Ophiuchus (Serpent Bearer)
M Orion
N Piscis Austrinus (Southern Fish)
O Sagittarius (Archer)
P Sextans (Sextant)
Q Scorpius (Scorpion)
R Virgo (Virgin)

The Science of the Stars

The night sky is a breathtaking sight. And the pinpoints of light become even more amazing when you realize that each of the 2,000 stars visible to the naked eye is actually an immense ball of gases radiating vast amounts of energy—the result of the tumultuous thermonuclear reactions burning within its core.

When you look up at the sky, all of the stars that you see lie within our galaxy, the Milky Way. Stars in other galaxies are too far away to see with the naked eye, as are countless stars within the Milky Way itself.

The Vastness of the Universe

The incomprehensibly large distances between stars mean that miles or kilometers will not suffice when measuring them, so light-years are used. This measurement is the distance that light travels in one year in a vacuum. [The speed of light is 186,282 miles (299,792 km) per second and 5.88 trillion miles (9.46 trillion km) per year.]

The Sun, our nearest star, is just 8 light-minutes away from Earth, while Alpha Centauri, the nearest star to the Sun, is so distant that it takes the light it throws out some 4.3 years to reach us. Many visible stars are so remote that when you look up at them, you are actually looking hundreds of years into the past.

The brightness of a star depends not only on how luminous it is but also its distance from the Earth. One of the brightest stars in the sky, Sirius, is 20 times brighter than the Sun and is also relatively close to us at a distance of just 8.7 light-years. However, while other stars may burn a thousand times brighter, they still appear to be fainter because of their remoteness.

Grouping Stars

Stars rarely occur in isolation; they exist as families: pairs, triplets, and even larger groups. Stars born from the same nebula

Conversation Starter The closest star to the Sun, known as Alpha Centauri, lies in the southern part of the sky. But it is actually a pair of yellow stars that rotate around each other every 80 years. When viewed by the naked eye from Mother Earth, they look like a single star.

will often cluster in groups of dozens or even hundreds. Some relatively young stars, like the Pleiades, form loosely bound open clusters, while very old stars form denser globular clusters, which orbit near the center of the galaxy that they inhabit.

The Life and Death of a Star

A star is born when disturbances within a nebula—a cloud of dust and gas in space—cause it to collapse. As the mass contracts, gravity pulls the nebula into a ball of gas and it becomes a protostar. As it grows ever hotter, the protostar triggers thermonuclear reactions that turn hydrogen into helium, causing the young star to radiate energy in the form of heat and light.

The Crab Nebula is the remnant of a supernova that took place around 900 years ago. Despite occurring over 6,500 light-years away, the exploding star was so bright that it was visible even during the daytime. The Crab Nebula is still expanding rapidly.

When it has reached a relatively stable state, a star enters the main, or most active, phase of its life cycle. The energy of a star comes mostly from the fusion of hydrogen nuclei within its core at temperatures of millions of degrees. As a star ages, the thermonuclear reactions use up its hydrogen fuel, and eventually it begins to swell, cool, and become a red giant. Then the star's outer layers begin to drift away, leaving a small, dense, hot, luminous core known as a white dwarf.

Going Supernova

A different fate awaits the brightest, heaviest stars: When they reach the red-giant stage, they undergo a supernova—a spectacular explosion that flings most of their matter out into space. In a galaxy such as our Milky Way, a supernova happens on average once every 50 years, and the shockwaves may disturb gas clouds and in turn trigger the birth of a new star.

Once a supernova has shot the outer layers of a red giant into space, an incredibly dense core is left. The core, thought to consist mostly of neutrons, is called a neutron star. As the star shrinks, its core spins faster and faster, and some stars give out beams of radio waves that, like a lighthouse's rotating beam, seem to pulse regularly—the reason these stars are called pulsars.

A neutron star may shrink even more to form a black hole—an area of such extreme density and gravitational pull that even light cannot escape it.

The Sun: Our Own Star

Without the gigantic nuclear reactor we call the Sun, our small blue planet would be just another barren piece of space debris. Although in cosmological terms the Sun is no more than average in size and age, it's our very own star, and we can't live without it.

The Structure of the Sun

It may look like a solid yellow sphere, but the Sun, like other stars, is made up mainly of hydrogen and helium gas. The core of the Sun is so hot that hydrogen atoms are stripped of their electrons and exist only as nuclei. Fusion between hydrogen nuclei at these high temperatures creates helium nuclei and also releases vast amounts of energy that we see as light and feel as heat.

Although the Sun doesn't have a solid surface like Earth's, its visible surface is known as the photosphere. Here it is much cooler than at the core, where the temperature is around 27,000,000°F (16,000,000°C). The composition of the surface layer is about 73 percent hydrogen, 25 percent helium, plus traces of heavier elements, including carbon and iron. Above the photosphere is the solar atmosphere, which itself has several subdivisions. The outermost layer is the corona, the halo of ionized gas visible only during a solar eclipse.

The Death of the Sun

Our Sun began burning as a star about 4.57 billion years ago, and it is estimated that its hydrogen fuel will run out in another 1.5 billion years. The Sun's diameter is about 100 times greater than that of the Earth, but it's not large enough to explode in a supernova when it dies. If scientists' predictions turn out to be accurate, in about 5 billion years' time the Sun will swell to become a red giant (see "The Life and Death of a Star," page 21), encompassing the current orbit of the Earth and the other inner planets. It will then lose most of its matter and contract until it becomes a white dwarf.

Chromosphere

Convection Zone

Radioactive Zone

Core

Photosphere

Corona

A solar eclipse, visible from France in 1999, shows the haze of the Sun's corona extending into space.

Auroras

An aurora is a beautiful display of glowing light of all colors, which takes place high in the Earth's upper atmosphere. It is caused by the emission of light when a stream of atomic particles coming from the Sun, known as the solar wind, collides with the molecules of the upper atmosphere. Auroras are most commonly seen near the magnetic poles of the Earth: the Aurora Borealis, or northern lights, in the North; and the Aurora Australis, in the South.

Exceptional auroral displays are connected to increased solar activity, as greater numbers of solar flares and prominences cast more particles into the solar wind. Solar eruptions that occur in the direction of the Earth can result in light shows unusual in their intensity, duration, and even location, often being reported far closer to the equator than normal.

Typically, an aurora takes the form of a fluctuating curtain of color against the night sky. It's hardly surprising that the phenomenon's ethereal beauty has inspired fabulous folklore and tales—none more fitting than the Norse legend holding that the Northern Lights were in fact Bifrost, a bridge between the mortal world and that of the gods.

In Fact...

- **Sunspots** are dark patches of relatively low temperatures on the Sun's surface. Although they may look small, they are actually many times bigger than the Earth. Not permanent, sunspots have a short life span of between a few days and several weeks.

- **Solar flares** are massive explosions that are apparently related to sunspots, because they tend to occur nearby. A flare will easily release as much energy as millions of hydrogen bombs but will last only for a few minutes.

- **Solar prominences** are longer lived than sunspots, although they last for only a matter of months. Prominences form a cloud stretching from the Sun's surface for thousands of miles into space, sometimes in a giant tongue-shaped loop.

The Solar System: Our Planetary Neighborhood

You could think of the eight planets that orbit the Sun as our celestial neighbors, alike in fundamental ways but also very different. Jupiter is the biggest on the block, and Mercury is the smallest, and a number of "dwarf planets" clamor to join the club.

The solar neighborhood includes the terrestrial planets Mercury, Venus, Earth, and Mars; the gas giants Jupiter, Saturn, Uranus, Neptune; and the newly designated "dwarf planet" Pluto.

The farther away the planet is, the longer it takes to orbit the Sun. The Earth derives its year from one complete orbit, while the nearest planet, Mercury, takes just under three months and Neptune as long as 165 years. Each planet also spins on its own axis, and one full rotation gives the length of that planet's day. Most planets, save Mercury and Venus, have at least one satellite, or moon, and other stars likely have solar systems.

Mercury

Mercury, closest to the Sun, is less than half the size of the Earth. A rocky ball with almost no atmosphere, its temperature ranges from 870° to –300°F (465° to –184°C). The *Mariner 10* probe flew past Mercury in 1974 and revealed that its surface is pitted with large meteorite craters.

Venus

The next planet out, Venus (the "evening star"), shines brightly at twilight. Shrouded in clouds of sulfuric acid, its atmosphere is mainly carbon dioxide. The *Mariner 2* space probe explored Venus in 1962 and found that its surface temperature averages 847°F (475°C), the hottest in the solar system. Venus is a lesson of sorts, since its high temperature is an extreme example of global warming caused by carbon dioxide.

Earth

Explored in detail in Chapter 2, Earth is the only planet in the solar system known to have the liquid water at its surface necessary for a temperate climate and life as we know it.

Mercury   Venus   Earth   Mars

Jupiter

Mars

Often called the red planet, Mars is the only other planet in the solar system that could potentially support life as we define it. Surface exploration has revealed that plentiful hematite, an ore of iron, is the source of Mars's red color. Its surface also has many volcanoes, canyons, and intriguingly, markings that look like dried-up riverbeds.

Jupiter

The biggest and brightest planet, Jupiter consists of helium converted to liquid by extreme gravitation. Violent storms churn up the gas clouds that wreath the planet, and the planet sports a distinctive red storm spot about 15,000 miles (24,000 km) long.

Saturn

Saturn is distinguished by its large rings, which are made up of millions of rock and ice particles and visible with a good pair of binoculars. It is covered by clouds of ammonium hydrosulphide, and notably it is thought to radiate more energy out into the solar system than it receives from the Sun.

Uranus

Uranus was the first planet to be discovered by telescope, by William Herschel in 1781. Its atmosphere is made up of hydrogen, helium, and frozen methane, which accounts for its blue color.

Neptune

The existence of Neptune was predicted in 1843 by the English astronomer John Adams and independently by French mathematician Urbain Le Verrier in 1846. Both men noted that Uranus behaved as if a neighboring planet was distorting its orbit, and Neptune was duly located in September 1846.

Like Uranus, Neptune is an intense blue, and its atmosphere is composed mostly of hydrogen, helium, and methane.

IN THE KNOW

Looking at these pages, you might well note the absence of Pluto, the disowned stepchild of the planets. Well, this is because a separate classification of "dwarf planets" was created in 2006, and this now includes Ceres (formerly classified as an asteroid), Pluto (formerly considered a true planet), and Eris (which was discovered in 2003, identified in 2005, and was what prompted the reconsideration of planetary classifications).

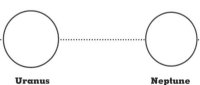

Saturn

Uranus

Neptune

Comets, Meteors, and Other Celestial Visitors

Space is full of stuff, and now and again some of the stuff tips its hat at us as it passes by. But when a meteor or other celestial visitor penetrates the Earth's atmosphere, the results can be spectacular and sometimes catastrophic.

Comets: Dirty Snowballs

A comet is an icy body that includes rocky, metallic, and carbon-based material in a core sometimes described as a "dirty snowball." Individual comets are rarely seen, mainly because many of them spend much of their time near the edge of the solar system, orbiting the Sun in an elliptical path that may take over a million years to complete. Some comets, however, have a far shorter orbital period, such as Enke's comet, for example, which takes only 3.3 years to circumnavigate the Sun.

When a comet does become visible, it is often spectacular. As it nears the Sun, it warms up, and some of the ice in its core vaporizes to form a cloud and a tail. In fact, this tail gives the comet its name, which derives from the Greek for hair. The cloud, or "coma," and tail are often bright enough to be seen with a telescope or even the naked eye, and every year a dozen or so comets become visible. Some have been known to astronomers for some time—such as Hale-Bopp and Halley's comets, both of which are named for their discoverers—while others are new discoveries.

Although comets are now generally appreciated for the beautiful spectacle that they are, in history they were often taken to be portents of doom. In fact, the Bayeux Tapestry, which depicts the Norman invasion and conquest of Britain in 1066, features the appearance of Halley's comet, possibly as an omen of King Harold's death.

IN THE KNOW

There is much speculation about whether a large asteroid could actually hit the Earth. Certainly there was a major catastrophe of some kind 65,000 years ago that wiped out the dinosaurs and many other animals. Could it happen again? Well, NASA scientists are keeping an eye out for what they call "near-Earth objects" and are looking hard at A99942 Apophis, an asteroid that is likely to pass close to Earth in 2029 and again in 2036.

Meteors and Shooting Stars

A meteor is a metallic, rocky, or carboniferous object, sometimes as small as a dust particle, which generally burns up before actually reaching the Earth. Meteors can be seen as flashes of light in the night sky, giving rise to their popular name, shooting stars, though they are nothing of the kind. The orbits of comets leave a trail of dust in their wake—the comet's tail. Sometimes the Earth will pass through a portion of the tail, giving rise to a spectacular show called a meteor shower, where dozens of meteors flash in a dramatic light display.

Meteorites are quite different from meteors. They are bits of asteroids that actually enter the Earth's or another planet's atmosphere and crash into the surface. Some are big enough to create a crater where they fall, and the pocked surface of the Moon provides an easily viewed record of the impact of large meteorites.

Asteroids

An asteroid is a minor planet, or planetoid, that orbits the Sun in the same plane as Earth. Made of rock and metal, most are probably debris from the formation of inner planets. In our solar system most orbit in a belt in the 342 million-mile (550 million-km) gap between Mars and Jupiter and are too faint to be seen with the naked eye.

The first and largest asteroid to be discovered is known as Ceres, and it was first

Key Player

Edmond Halley
1656–1742

An English astronomer, Halley was famous for producing the first atlas of stars in the southern hemisphere. He was also an expert on comets, realizing that they orbited the Sun and calculating the orbits of 24. Halley claimed that comets observed in 1531, 1607, and 1682 were one and the same and that the comet appeared at 76-year intervals. He was right, and what we know as Halley's Comet, last seen in 1986, will circle back in 2062.

thought to be a new planet. It is about one quarter the size of the Moon and was discovered in 1801 by the Italian astronomer and Theatine monk Giuseppe Piazzi. Ceres, with a diameter of 621 miles (1,000 km), has since been reclassified as a dwarf planet (see page 25), one of perhaps many among the 18,000 asteroids in the belt that have been discovered so far.

The orbits of comets, are elliptical unlike those of the planets and asteroids (the shaded areas denote asteroid belts). The size of their orbits determines how often they will be seen.

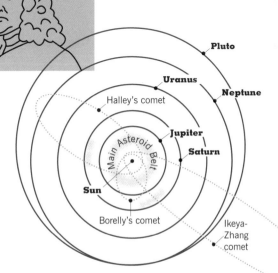

Time and Space: It's All Relative

As a junior clerk at the Swiss patent office, Albert Einstein reviewed other people's ideas and contemplated Newton's laws of gravitation and motion. And by 1905 he was ready to change the way we think about time, space, and the universe.

By around 1900 a few inexplicable chinks were showing in the armor of Newtonian physics. Sir Isaac's law of universal gravitation didn't quite explain the orbit of the planet Mercury, for example. More precise astronomical instruments were revealing other anomalies that no one could account for, until a 26-year-old patent official named Albert Einstein published three papers and introduced the concept of relativity. Einstein theorized that space and time are not fixed, that they can be squeezed or stretched and depend on the point of view of an observer. He also introduced the idea that space and time are not separate but rather aspects of a single construct known as space-time.

Bending Time

Einstein's conclusion to his extraordinary theory was that the speed of light is a constant, the same for everyone regardless of whether they are stationary or traveling toward or away from the source. Lightspeed is fixed at an astonishingly fast 186,282 miles (299,792 km) per second, and nothing can travel faster.

Based on his amazingly counterintuitive leap of logic, Einstein reasoned that if the speed of light is constant, then the passage of time would depend on your movement. This means the passage of time can differ slightly for different people, and even for clocks.

Testing Time

Another consequence of Einstein's theory is that during acceleration, an object's mass increases, its size decreases, and the passage of time relating to it slows. We don't notice these changes, because the effects are negligible until we approach the speed of light, which explains our firmly held perceptions

IN THE KNOW

Einstein was in California when Hitler came to power in 1933, and he never moved back to Europe. In response to the threat of Nazism, Einstein helped initiate the Manhattan Project and America's research into the nuclear bomb. However, when he realized the potential for destruction that had been unleashed, Einstein spent much of the rest of his life arguing for nuclear disarmament. The great scientist died in 1955 at the age of 76.

of space and time as immutable. However, the effects of relativity can be measured even at very low speeds. For example, if two atomic clocks—devices that are accurate to a few billionths of a second per day—are synchronized and a clock is sent on a return flight to the other side of the world, there will be a tiny difference between the times shown on the traveling clock and the clock that never left home.

This effect means that astronauts return from space having aged a tiny fraction less than their Earthbound colleagues.

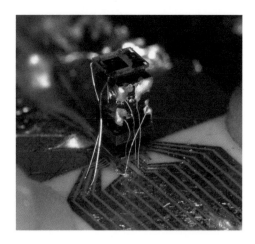

The World after Einstein

The publication of Einstein's theories led to a revolution in science called quantum physics.

This has required an even more dramatic rethinking of our concepts of space and time and raises some mind-blowing ideas, including the possibility of particles, or even small objects, existing in two places at once.

One practical product of quantum physics is the quantum computer, some of the calculations of which appear to take place in a parallel universe! Perhaps most strangely of all, quantum physics even

Key Player

Albert Einstein
1879–1955

Contrary to myth, Einstein wasn't the patron saint of underachievers, though he did leave school at 17. In the same year, he renounced his German citizenship and moved to democratic Switzerland to finish his studies. He always valued childhood, recalling his intense curiosity, at age five, about a compass and "what lay deeply hidden" behind the visible object.

An atomic clock can be used to demonstrate the theory of relativity. This U.S. National Institute of Standards and Technology chip-scale atomic clock is so accurate that it would neither gain nor lose a second if it ran for more than 60 million years.

accepts the possibility of particles moving backward in time.

If that all sounds too weird for you, then don't worry; the American physicist John Wheeler once said: "If you are not completely confused by quantum mechanics, you do not understand it."

The Amazing Atom: Protons Plus

The idea that everything is made up of tiny particles we can't see goes back to ancient Greece. Scientific investigation has disclosed what makes up atoms, how they function, and how they interact to create the universe's immense diversity.

It wasn't until the early nineteenth century that atomic theory based on empirical study was put forward as an explanation for various chemical observations. The theory was that of physicist John Dalton, the first of three famous physicists who would probe the atom's secrets. Dalton's analysis showed that the proportion of different elements in compounds is always the same. He found that compounds were made of spherical entities called atoms, and each type of element had its own type of atoms, differing in weight. Atoms joined together in groups to form molecules.

Inside an Atom

Once thought to be the smallest particles, atoms are now understood to consist of many far smaller "subatomic" particles. It is this subatomic structure that determines an atom's characteristics and the element to which it belongs. An atom consists of a nucleus of protons and neutrons, which is orbited by a cloud of electrons. However, it is possible to further divide protons and neutrons, and it is then that we reach the limit—what are now thought of as the "fundamental" or "elementary" particles. These fundamental particles are divided into two groups: particles of matter, known as fermions; and particles of force, called bosons.

This much simplified outline is the basis of the Standard Model, the dominant theory of particle physics. In describing how the various particles of force and matter behave, it also underpins the characteristics of the different elements, the molecules that they form, and the way that these behave. In fact, this model describes much of the universe that we live in and how it works.

Conversation Starter The first person to postulate that matter is composed of tiny invisible particles in motion was the Greek philosopher Democritus. His fifth-century BCE writings were lost, but his theory of atomism (from *atomon*, or "uncuttable") inspired modern atomic science.

The electron, a tiny negatively charged particle, and the proton, a larger positively charged particle, were discovered in the late nineteenth and early twentieth centuries. In 1911 the New Zealand-born physicist Lord Rutherford, who would become known as the father of nuclear physics, carried out an experiment firing positively charged alpha particles at a thin gold foil. To his astonishment, most of the particles passed through the foil—suggesting that the atoms making it up were composed mostly of empty space. The occasional particle bounced back, repelled by the protons in the nuclei of the gold atoms where most of an atom's mass is concentrated.

Later the Danish physicist Neils Bohr proposed that the electrons, which surround the nucleus, are arranged in distinct orbits—like the planets in the solar system—with a fixed energy. Still, it is an electromagnetic force, not gravity, that keeps electrons and protons together. For his work, Bohr was awarded the Nobel Prize in 1922.

The Character of Atoms

Lying at the heart of an atom, protons give it much of its character. Because the nucleus of an atom contains protons and neutrons (discovered in 1932 by Sir James Chadwick), both are now known as "nucleons." The number of protons within the nucleus determines the element to which it belongs, while the number of neutrons determines its isotope. Although the isotope of an atom is far from inconsequential, the number of protons is much more important in determining the atom's properties.

Positive Attraction

The reason that the number of protons plays such an important part in deciding the character of an atom is that their positive charge attracts enough electrons to give the atom a neutral charge overall. When two or more atoms come into contact, it is the positive charge of the protons in their nuclei that attracts the various atoms' electrons into a combined "molecular orbit," bonding them into a molecule.

This propensity for an atom to interact and bond (or not) with certain other atoms bestows it with unique characteristics.

The key role of the proton is recognized in each element's atomic number. An atom of hydrogen has a single proton and an atomic number of one; a helium atom with two protons has an atomic number of two, and so on.

● protons

● neutrons

○ electrons

Now that you've read all about the universe, it's time to see if you understand it. The following questions will test your knowledge on everything from the vastness of the universe to the tiniest subatomic particles.

The Cosmos: An Explosive Birth?

1 What did Penzias and Wilson discover in 1964?

a) *radiation left over from the Big Bang*

b) *light pollution*

c) *a new galaxy*

2 At what time after the Big Bang did the first star begin to shine?

3 What is the name given to the interval between the Big Bang and the point at which a time line of events can be started?

4 In what year did Hubble find evidence for the Big Bang?

5 How much of the matter in the universe might be dark matter?

Newton's Laws: Why Things Move As They Do

1 What makes an apple fall from a tree?

2 How many laws of motion did Newton put forward?

3 What other field of physics was Newton involved in?

4 Which Newtonian law explains the recoil of a gun?

The Milky Way: Billions of Stars Strong

1 What are the three main components of a galaxy?

2 What are the four types of galaxies?

3 True or False: A yellow star is older than a blue one.

4 How many stars are in the Milky Way?

a) *10 million*   b) *100 million*

c) *impossible to say*   d) *100,000 million*

Constellations: Ancient Legends in the Stars

1 The brightest star in the sky has three different names. What are they?

2 In which larger constellation will you find the Big Dipper?

The Science of the Stars

1 What unit is used to measure the distances between stars?

2 Which element is transformed into helium, thereby providing the energy of a young star?

3 What does a red giant turn into as it dies?

The Sun: Our Own Star

1 How much bigger in diameter than the Earth is the Sun?

   a) *10 times*   b) *100 times*
   c) *1,000 times*   d) *1,000,000 times*

2 What is the more popular name for the Aurora Borealis?

The Solar System: Our Planetary Neighborhood

1 Which planet is also called the evening star?

2 Which is the biggest planet in our solar system?

   a) *Jupiter*   b) *Saturn*
   c) *Neptune*   d) *Uranus*

3 Apart from Earth, which planet could have the potential to support life?

4 What are Ceres, Eris, and Pluto known as?

Comets, Meteors, and Other Celestial Visitors

1 How long does it take Enke's comet to go around the Sun?

2 A meteorite is a chip off what celestial object?

   a) *a star*   b) *the moon*
   c) *an asteroid*   d) *a comet*

Time and Space: It's All Relative

1 The speed of light is approximately

   a) *186 million miles per hour*
   b) *186,000 miles per minute*
   c) *186,000 miles per second*

2 According to relativity, when astronauts return from space, are they

   a) *older than*   b) *younger than*
   c) *the same age as*

they would have been if they had stayed at home?

3 In which year did Albert Einstein die?

The Amazing Atom: Protons Plus

1 Name the three main subatomic particles.

2 What is an element's atomic number?

Chapter Two

The Story of the Earth

We live on a planet that is spinning through space. A world where the air, the waters, and even the ground beneath our feet are constantly in motion. This chapter looks at the home we call Planet Earth—how it came into being, the forces that shape and shake the land and the oceans, and the materials of which our world is made.

The Formation of Planet Earth

Once, the Earth was thought to be just a few thousand years old, but scientists now date its origins to more than 4.5 billion years ago, when a cloud of cosmic dust, battered by supernovae, began to spin. Out of this celestial chaos came all the bits and pieces that formed the solar system, including our Earth, the third planet from the Sun.

For the first half a billion years or so of Earth's life, the pieces of matter that shared its orbit kept colliding with it, adding to it, imparting energy, and keeping it in a molten state. Under the influence of gravity, the heavier elements sank toward the center of the Earth, and the lighter material floated to the surface, resulting in a layered structure.

At this stage this spinning molten ball had no water or atmosphere, but as the Earth grew, its increased gravity attracted gases, including water vapor, that remained on the surface—and as it cooled, a crust formed about 4.1 billion years ago.

Evidence from moon rock suggests that the next 300 million years were a period of intense bombardment as chunks of interplanetary junk, including meteoroids, asteroids, and comets, battered the planet. These impacts would have released steam from within the Earth's crust and may even have brought ice on the surface of comets. They also continued to add to the Earth's mass. This period, the Late Heavy Bombardment, increased the Earth's mass until it ended about 3.8 billion years ago.

The oldest rock formations found on Earth date from this period. Current theory suggests that preceding crusts were

4.54 billion years
The Earth forms from spinning space dust and is added to as other detritus collides with it.

4.54–4.2 billion years
Although still a molten ball, the Earth develops a layered structure as heavy elements sink and lighter ones float.

4.1 billion years
The Earth begins to form a crust, while the gases start to collect to make up its atmosphere.

3.8 billion years
The end of the Late Heavy Bombardment signals the end of the Earth's formative phase.

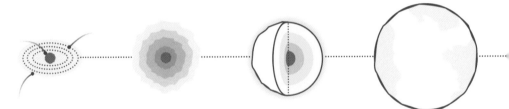

destroyed by the intense and sustained bombardment. When this finished, the crust then re-formed, and the Earth's oldest rock formations date from this time.

The Structure of the Earth

In broad terms the Earth consists of four concentric layers. At the center is an inner core, which is composed mainly of iron and nickel, with a diameter of about 1,520 miles (2,440 km). The size of the Earth and the gravitational forces at its center are such that, despite a core temperature of some 6,700°F (3,700°C), the pressure is sufficiently high to keep this inner core in a solid state.

The next layer out is a 1,240-mile (2,200-km)-thick outer core of liquid metal. The thickest layer, called the mantle, lies between the outer core and the Earth's crust. The mantle, which is roughly 1,775 miles (2,855 km) thick, is composed of silicate rocks, which are rich in iron and magnesium, in a semi-molten state.

The Earth's crust—ranging from 3–40 miles (5–70 km) in thickness—also consists of silicate rocks. The thinner parts of the crust have a composition similar to the mantle, while the thicker parts are richer in aluminum, potassium, and sodium.

IN THE KNOW

It is the rotation of the Earth's liquid metal outer core around its solid metal inner core that gives rise to the planet's magnetic field.

The Earth's Layers

The innermost layer of the Earth is its solid inner core, made of iron and nickel. This is surrounded by a molten outer core, and then a mostly solid layer of mantle. On top of this is the crust, which is very thin by comparison, measuring 3–40 miles (5–70 km) thick.

Inner Core (1,520 miles / 2,440 km diameter)
Outer Core (1,240 miles / 2,200 km thick)
Mantle (1,775 miles / 2,855 km thick)
Crust (3–40 miles / 5–70 km thick)

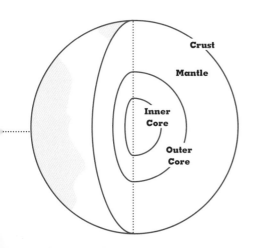

Crust
Mantle
Inner Core
Outer Core

Water World: The Earth's Oceans

Water, water everywhere. Planet Earth is the wet blanket of the solar system—literally; about 70 percent of the Earth's surface is covered by more than 1,400 billion billion tons of the stuff. In fact, all life depends on this enormous ocean reservoir, despite the fact that close to 98 percent of it is undrinkable.

There are several likely sources for the water found on Earth. Some was probably present from the time the planet was forming. But until Earth grew large enough to have sufficient gravity, any atmosphere, including water vapor, was carried away on the solar wind (a stream of high-energy particles that is emitted by the Sun).

Water Retention

When the Earth had reached about 40 percent of its present mass, water vapor released through volcanic action and from water-containing minerals began to be retained in the atmosphere. A significant proportion of the planet's water also may have arrived on asteroids and, to a lesser extent, comets.

The Early Ocean

As the planet cooled, the water vapor in the atmosphere condensed, pooling in the lowest areas of the Earth's irregular crust and forming the ocean. The steady movement of the tectonic plates and continental landmasses (see pages 42–43) has changed the shape and position of the world ocean over time, and this process continues.

Because the crust is thinnest at the ocean floor, it is the most geologically active part of the Earth's surface and is undergoing constant regeneration. Very few parts of the seabed are older than 170 million years—extremely young in geological terms.

In contrast, the contents and total volume of the world's oceans may have been relatively constant for the last 3 billion years. Evidence points to an early ocean with low

Conversation Starter With so much seawater available, desalinating it makes good sense. But the costs of producing and distributing desalted water on a grand scale remain prohibitive today. A cheap natural-energy source—solar power—could be the answer in the future.

The world's oceans encompass more than a dozen seas. In the North Pacific, for example, lie the Sea of Japan and the South China Sea. In the North Atlantic are Hudson Bay, the Gulf of Mexico, and the Caribbean Sea.

oxygen levels, but the salinity, or concentration of salts (mainly sodium chloride), may not have altered greatly.

Salt was initially dissolved from minerals in the Earth's crust beneath the ocean, and since then salt has entered the ocean through the erosion of minerals on the land by water that flows into the sea. You might expect salinity to increase over the eons, but processes—including the formation of salt deposits, chemical reactions with other minerals, and the deposition of salt in sedimentary rock—keep salt levels roughly in balance. However, in the Red Sea—a stretch of water between North Africa and the Arabian Peninsula—evaporation is high and the flow of water slow, making salinity higher.

The Blue Planet

Far from being separate entities, the oceans and the land are intimately related through phenomena such as erosion, climate, and the water cycle (see pages 48–49). Waves and currents remove and deposit material along the coasts. Evaporation and subsequent rainfall leach rocks and minerals into the oceans. The depositing of this material alters the course of rivers and the shape of coasts and estuaries.

The ocean itself is a huge heat sink, lessening temperature fluctuations over the whole planet and driving global weather systems. An issue of current concern is that the effects of global warming may include rising sea levels, which could significantly alter the planet's weather.

One World, One Ocean

Excluding rivers and lakes, all the world's surface water is interconnected, so it is possible to talk of a single "world ocean." However, it is usually divided into at least three named areas: the Atlantic Ocean, the Pacific Ocean, and the Indian Ocean. The waters around the North and South polar regions are sometimes referred to as the Arctic and Southern oceans, respectively.

Partially enclosed or geographically definable areas of the ocean are generally called seas, bays, and gulfs.

Earth's Atmosphere: A Coat of Many Layers

Earth's invisible coating of gases gives us the air we breathe and defends us against outside forces that would make life on the planet impossible. The atmosphere is a multilayered shield fending off dangerous radiation, extreme temperatures, and flying objects from space. It rewards us, too, with blue-sky days and starry, starry nights.

The atmosphere is composed of five main layers. From the ground up, these are the troposphere, the stratosphere, the mesosphere, the thermosphere, and the exosphere. The exosphere, the outer layer, has no definite outer edge; gases here become increasingly thin until they merge into space.

The Essential Ozone Layer

The ozone layer can be found in the lower part of the stratosphere, around 9–22 miles (15–35 km) above the surface of the Earth. Relatively high concentrations of ozone are present in this layer, though the amounts are still very small. The ozone layer is vital for our health

because it absorbs harmful ultraviolet rays from the Sun. Pollution has caused ozone levels to fall, and holes in the layer also appear in spring and early summer in polar regions. The main cause of ozone depletion is chemicals like CFCs (chlorofluorocarbons), which are aerosol propellants that are now banned in many places.

The Troposphere

The troposphere is the lowest layer of the atmosphere and the only one in which living things can breathe. It contains about 80 percent of the gas in the atmosphere and is sometimes referred to as the "weather layer" because all weather occurs here. In this layer, air rises and sinks, winds are generated, and clouds form. The troposphere extends to about 12 miles (20 km) high at the equator and 6 miles (10 km) at the poles.

The Stratosphere

The stratosphere lies between
approximately 6–12 miles (10–20 km)
and 31 miles (50 km) above the Earth's
surface. Temperatures here vary from
−76°F (−60°C) at the bottom to just
above freezing at the top. The
stratosphere contains the ozone layer.

Thermosphere

The top of the thermosphere layer
is about 400 miles (640 km) above
the Earth. Temperatures here are
high because the air molecules
absorb radiation from the Sun.
The temperature increases with
height, reaching 3,630°F (2,000°C)
at the top of the layer.

Mesosphere

The top of the mesosphere
is about 50 miles (80 km) above the
Earth's surface. Temperatures decrease in
this layer and can be as low as −148°F
(−100°C) at the very top. Meteors
entering the atmosphere generally burn
up in the mesosphere.

Exosphere

The exosphere is the top layer of the
atmosphere, lying about 500 miles
(800 km) above the Earth's surface.
The air here is very thin, and gas
molecules float in and out of space
because there is no boundary between
the exosphere and outer space.

On Shifting Ground: Plate Tectonics

We can't feel it, but the ground under our feet is always in motion. Earth's continents sit on plates that are always jockeying for position. Over eons the slow movement of tectonic plates dramatically realigns great landmasses, pushing up mountain ranges, carving out ocean trenches, and shaking us up with earthquakes and volcanic eruptions.

The Continental Jigsaw

As early as the seventeenth century, it was noted that the coastlines of some continents, particularly those of Africa and South America, fitted together like a jigsaw puzzle. In the late 1900s the presence of remarkably similar fossils and geology on matching coasts led to the theory that all the continents were once part of a single landmass, Pangaea, which had since moved apart. German astronomer and meteorologist Alfred Wegener put forward the theory of continental drift to explain the movement of landmasses. While there was plenty of geologic evidence to support the theory of continental drift, there was no satisfactory explanation as to why it should happen, so Wegener's theory was largely ignored.

Fresh Evidence

In the 1950s studies revealed that magnetic rocks of different ages within continents were magnetized in different directions. This meant that their orientation in relation to the poles must have changed over time—new evidence for the theory of continental drift. The great breakthrough came when studies of the seabed found that new crust was being formed along ridges in the ocean floor, pushing apart the masses on each side. To explain how the crust could incorporate new material, it was initially proposed that the Earth was getting larger, but the discovery of "subduction zones," where the edge

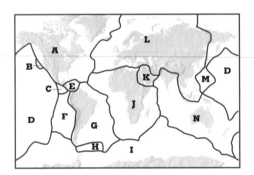

Continental Plates of the World
The above map of the world shows the arrangement of the world's tectonic plates. Note the correlation between these boundaries and those parts of the world with active volcanoes and frequent earthquakes.

A North American Plate
B Juan De Fuca Plate
C Cocos Plate
D Pacific Plate
E Caribbean Plate
F Nazca Plate
G South American Plate
H Scotia Plate
I Antarctic Plate
J African Plate
K Arabian Plate
L Eurasian Plate
M Philippine Plate
N Indian-Australian Plate

of one plate of the Earth's crust was actually being pushed beneath another and becoming molten again, completed the picture. Wegener's continental drift theory was accepted as the theory of plate tectonics.

This theory helps answer many questions about geology and the fossil record. Most important, it explains the process behind volcanic and seismic activity, for it's at plate boundaries that most volcanic eruptions and earthquakes occur.

What's Happening?

The lithosphere—the outer rocky layer of the Earth's crust and upper layer of the mantle—floats on the mantle's lower layer, the semisolid asthenosphere. The lithosphere consists of several major and minor plates, some including continental land masses, that move relative to each other. The plates meet at three kinds of boundaries, as shown at right.

Convergent plate boundaries, or destructive boundaries, are where plates meet "head on." When this involves an oceanic plate, subduction (sinking) occurs and one oceanic plate slides beneath the other, leaving an ocean trench. On land the result can be a collision that causes the land to buckle and rise. The mighty Himalayas were formed and continue to grow in this way.

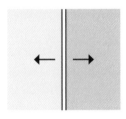

Divergent plate boundaries occur where molten basalt pushes up through the Earth's crust, probably as a result of convection currents within the Earth's mantle, and forces the plates apart. This kind of boundary is also called a constructive boundary because new crust is formed. Divergent boundaries form ocean ridges.

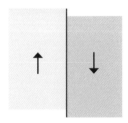

Transform boundaries occur where two plates move sideways against each other. This is sometimes called a sliding boundary, but because of the huge pressures and the friction between the plates, rather than sliding smoothly they tend to build up enormous tension and then suddenly move past each other with a jolt.

In Fact...

Pangaea, a single massive supercontinent, is thought to have existed some 250 million years ago. It is unlikely to have been the first, and over the eons landmasses may have repeatedly united and then moved apart. This sequence has now been reconstructed in detail. How fast (or slowly) do the continents move? At a speed comparable to the rate of growth of your fingernails.

Rocks and Fossils: Earth's Upper Crust

The Earth's crust is like an enormous parking lot covered with a great variety of rocks—some that we see and others below the surface. Different types of rock are composed of different minerals and form in different ways—some very quickly in conjunction with volcanic action and others through the slow process of sedimentary buildup.

Igneous Rock

Igneous rocks, like basalt and granite are formed as molten magma pushes up through the Earth's crust and cools and solidifies. Studying these rocks helps us understand the structure and behavior of the Earth's tectonic plates because igneous rocks form mainly at plate boundaries.

Igneous rock that has hardened beneath overlying rock cools slowly and tends to have an obvious crystalline structure. Granite is such an "intrusive," or plutonic, rock, and it makes up the cores of the world's major mountain ranges.

When magma hardens above the crust, it cools quickly and forms "extrusive," or volcanic, rocks such as lava, basalt, or pumice. These mostly form where tectonic plates are being pushed apart.

Devil's Tower, Wyoming, is a tall formation of igneous rock left when the softer sedimentary rock around it eroded.

More than 90 percent of all rock is igneous, and some 700 types have been identified, most lying beneath other rocks.

Sedimentary Rock

About three-quarters of the Earth's surface is covered by sedimentary rocks formed by the deposition and compression of chunks and particles of minerals. Sedimentary rocks are formed in three main ways.

Most common sedimentary rocks are formed when particles of material that has disintegrated due to weathering are deposited elsewhere. Under the pressure of successive layers, the particles gradually form into rock such as fine-grained siltstone, coarser sandstone, or conglomerates (rounded particles), and breccia (angular particles) that comprise grains of up to an inch (2.5 cm) in diameter.

Sandstone is a sedimentary rock. Here you can see its different layers.

Some sedimentary rock is biological in origin. Limestone, for example, is formed from the calcareous (calcium-rich) skeletons of marine organisms such as coral, foraminifera, and mollusks deposited in their billions on the seabed. The chalk that makes up the White Cliffs of Dover is a form of limestone. The Niagara escarpment on the Canadian/American border is a limestone outcrop. Although harder than most sedimentary rocks, limestone is relatively easily eroded, and most of the world's major cave systems have been created by the action of water on limestone.

Sedimentary rock can also be formed by the precipitation, or solidification, of chemicals that are dissolved in water. For example, the evaporation of seawater can lead to the formation of halite (rock salt) and gypsum (a calcium compound).

Metamorphic Rock

Metamorphic rock is formed by the heating and compression of pre-existing rocks. Metamorphic means "changed in form." The pre-existing rock may be igneous, sedimentary, or even another metamorphic rock. The process occurs as a result of tectonic activity, when colliding plates create enormous pressures or when intrusive magma heats and transforms the rock

Marble is an example of metamorphic rock. Its swirls are caused by impurities.

around it. The nature of metamorphic rock will depend on the initial rock, the temperature, and the pressure the rock is subjected to. Slate and marble are examples of metamorphic rock.

Fossilization

Fossils are found mainly in sedimentary rock because the depositing of layers provides the right conditions. The sediment keeps out oxygen and prevents the once living material from decomposing. A process of permineralization then occurs, in which empty spaces in the tissue are filled with water rich in minerals that gradually replace the original structure. Most fossils consist of hard tissue like bones and teeth, but sometimes soft tissue, such as skin, can also be fossilized.

Fossil fish display what was once living tissue that has been replaced by minerals.

Earth's Climate: What Gives?

The Earth's average temperature has fluctuated greatly throughout its history. Today we worry about polar ice caps and glaciers melting more quickly than ever before. Still, there have been times in the past when ice and snow were virtually absent from the planet. Could we be headed for another iceless age?

The term ice age sometimes refers to periods when ice sheets were more extensive than usual. But these times are more accurately called glacials, and they occur within an ice age; the periods between glacials are called interglacials. We are now in an interglacial in what is probably the Earth's fourth great ice age. What has distinguished the last 200 years is the melting of ice at apparently unprecedented rates as the temperature of the Earth gradually grows warmer.

Climate Change

In the early nineteenth century the Swiss-German geologist Jean de Charpentier suggested that the Alpine glaciers he had been studying had at one time been far larger. Later a Swiss-American geologist, Louis Agassiz, built on Charpentier's notion and proposed that Earth at one time had been completely covered by ice.

Ice Ages Past . . .

Since then, scientific advances have contributed to our understanding of the Earth's ice ages, and it is now thought that the first major ice age occurred some 2 billion years ago. Another ice age, 850 to 630 million years ago—probably the most severe—may have covered the entire globe in ice, a frosty scenario known as "Snowball Earth."

The end of that ice age seems to have coincided with the evolution of a great many tiny organisms, although whether there is a causal link between these events and what they might be remains a matter of debate.

Conversation Starter Sea levels rise as warmer temperatures result in melting ice and thermal expansion of the oceans. We can pray that the average global rise predicted by scientists—3.5–34.5 inches (9–87.5 cm) over the next century—is as close as possible to the lower end.

Then, between 400 and 300 million years ago, another ice age struck, and the planet was again plunged into a cold period, known as the Karoo Ice Age, named for the glacial till (sediment) found in the Karoo hills of South Africa.

The Franz Josef Glacier in New Zealand exhibits a cycle of retreats and advances, at one time advancing as fast as 28 inches (70 cm) a day.

. . . and Present

The current ice age began some 40,000,000 years ago, reaching its coldest period about 3,000,000 years ago. The last glacial period (often referred to inaccurately as an ice age) ended about 10,000 years ago, and the first human civilizations began to flourish shortly after. How global warming will affect Earth's cooling and warming cycles—and, more urgently, sea level as glaciers and the polar ice caps melt—is the pressing issue of our age.

The Global Greenhouse

Without the greenhouse effect, a natural process that heats the Earth's surface and atmosphere, our average temperature would be a frigid 0°F (–18°C)—ensuring a permanent ice age, to say the least. The warmed globe radiates what is called "infrared radiation," most of which should travel through atmospheric layers to space. With the advent of the Industrial Revolution in the late 1700s, more and more infrared radiation began to be absorbed by naturally occurring greenhouse gases,

IN THE KNOW

In December 2007, 187 nations—including the United States—agreed that industrial and developing nations alike should do what they could to stem global warming. The agreement, forged at a forum in Bali before commitments made under the 1997 Kyoto Protocol expire, advances the United Nations' goal of putting a binding pact on climate change in place by the year 2009.

including carbon dioxide (CO_2). The increase of average concentrations of CO_2, from about 280 parts per million in 1700 to about 380 parts per million in 2005 is the major cause of global warming.

In 2007 the Intergovernmental Panel on Climate Change (IPCC) asserted that human activities—including the use of fossil fuels—was "very likely" the catalyst for global warming.

Some scientists estimate that the Earth's temperature will rise by as much as 9°F (5°C) by 2050, while others heatedly disagree. What isn't in dispute is that the world's ice is in a literal meltdown. For instance, the largest single block, the Ward Hunt Ice Shelf in the Arctic, lasted some 3,000 years before it started to crack in 2000; a mere two years later it was split through and is now breaking apart.

The Never-Ending Water Cycle

To survive, every living thing on Earth depends on water, and our planet is the ultimate recycler. The "hydrologic cycle" is a constant interchange among the atmosphere, living things, and surface waters, all powered by the Sun. Even slight variations in the cycle, whether natural or man-made, can turn forests into deserts and arid plains into seas.

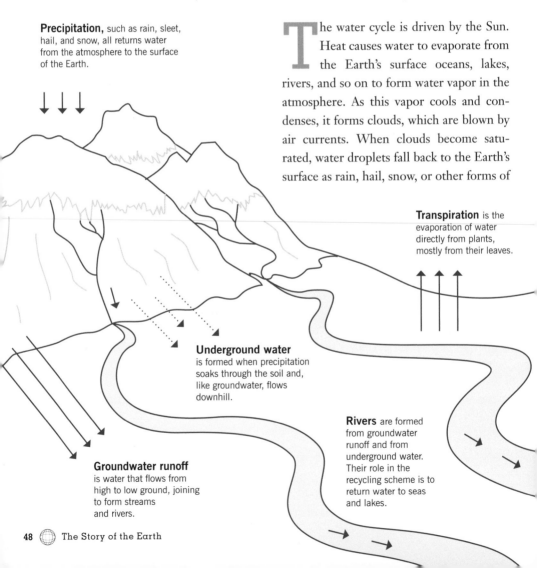

Precipitation, such as rain, sleet, hail, and snow, all returns water from the atmosphere to the surface of the Earth.

The water cycle is driven by the Sun. Heat causes water to evaporate from the Earth's surface oceans, lakes, rivers, and so on to form water vapor in the atmosphere. As this vapor cools and condenses, it forms clouds, which are blown by air currents. When clouds become saturated, water droplets fall back to the Earth's surface as rain, hail, snow, or other forms of

Transpiration is the evaporation of water directly from plants, mostly from their leaves.

Underground water is formed when precipitation soaks through the soil and, like groundwater, flows downhill.

Rivers are formed from groundwater runoff and from underground water. Their role in the recycling scheme is to return water to seas and lakes.

Groundwater runoff is water that flows from high to low ground, joining to form streams and rivers.

precipitation. This water eventually runs above or below ground into the continental networks of streams, rivers, and lakes that feed into the seas.

The Thirst for Freshwater

Many species, including humans, depend on freshwater to survive. But it's rarer than you might think, comprising only 3 percent of the Earth's water, and most freshwater is frozen in glaciers and the polar ice caps.

Heat energy from the Sun drives the water cycle, causing evaporation.

Wind helps move water around the cycle, for example, blowing clouds formed over sea back over land.

Evaporation occurs when the Sun heats water at the Earth's surface—in lakes, rivers, and seas—causing it to become water vapor and enter the atmosphere.

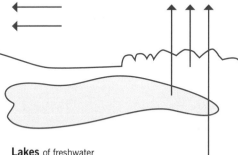

Lakes of freshwater form when river water and groundwater runoff gather in natural basins.

Oceans contain the vast majority of the Earth's water, forming marine habitats. The great majority of evaporation occurs from seawater.

Groundwater runoff in agricultural areas can contain fertilizers, which may have negative effects on an ecosystem if polluted waters leach into lakes, rivers, or oceans. This increase in chemical nutrients in the water (known as eutrophication) can cause excessive plant growth and algal blooms that deplete oxygen levels and make it harder for aquatic life to survive.

Acid rain is precipitation that has an unusually high level of acidity. The increased acidity is caused mostly by burning fossil fuels such as coal and gasoline, which release sulfur dioxide and oxides of nitrogen into the air. These mix with water in the air to create acids.

Acid rain increases the acidity of lakes and rivers, harming aquatic creatures and plants. It also has a detrimental effect on forests, depleting the soil of nutrients needed for growth and germination, damaging leaves and needles, and reducing the trees' ability to withstand cold.

In some cases acid rain has caused so much damage that whole forests have died. Particularly hard-hit regions include eastern Europe, eastern Canada, and the north-eastern United States. Many governments have now introduced legislation to reduce fossil-fuel emissions.

Minerals and Gems: Treasures of the Earth

People have forever been captivated by precious metals, crystals, and gemstones, from ostentatious shows of wealth such as diamonds and sapphires mounted on rings to practical uses—gold sheaths on stereo-system plugs, for example. How do these precious materials form? Where are they found? Why are they so highly prized?

The wealth of nations is often tied to the richness of their mineral deposits. Some parts of the world are richer than others, giving rise to disputes among countries over the rights to extract minerals from certain areas. One such spirited dispute centers around who gets the right to exploit the minerals of Antarctica.

Precious Metals

Rocks that contain extractable minerals are known as ores. These ores are usually found in "veins"—cracks in the rock where hot fluids once flowed and left rich deposits behind. The ores are mined and processed to produce pure, precious metals such as platinum, gold, silver, titanium, copper, and iron.

Gold and silver have been prized for ages. Both gold- and silversmiths from ancient Egypt and other early civilizations forged works of art from these precious metals. The quest for gold drove the conquistadors of Spain to the shores of the New World and sent prospectors across America and Canada to California, Alaska, and the Yukon in the "gold rushes" of the nineteenth century. In Australia, too, miners rushed to locations where they thought gold might be found, and many who came up empty-handed turned to opal mining instead.

For all its wealth of mythology, gold does not qualify as the Earth's most precious metal. That distinction belongs to platinum, which is worth twice as much as gold.

IN THE KNOW

If you get birthstones mixed up, read on. January is garnet; February is amethyst; March is aquamarine; April is diamond; May is emerald; June is pearl; July is ruby; August is peridot or carnelian; September is sapphire; October is opal; November is topaz; and December is turquoise. What's yours?

Smelting is the term used for the process of extracting a metal from its ore by heating and melting.

Crystals

The Greek root for the word crystal, *kryos*, means icy cold. In fact, in ancient days it was believed quartz was made up of water that had frozen so solid that it would never thaw out.

Crystallization occurs when a liquid compound is cooled, or when evaporation leaves particles laid out in a regular pattern.

No two crystals are exactly alike. Crystallographers recognize 32 main classes of crystals, classifying them by the kind of symmetry they display. These classes are grouped into seven lattice systems (shapes), among them cubic and hexagonal. Variations within the lattice systems include needlelike shapes, long prisms, and grapelike formations. Most crystals do not form as single crystals but rather as aggregates of many.

Key Player

Friedrich Mohs
1773–1839

The hardness of a particular mineral results from the arrangement of its atoms, and minerals vary widely. In 1812 German geologist Friedrich Mohs devised a scale to define the hardness of minerals. He arranged 10 minerals on a scale from 1 (softest, talc) to 10 (hardest, diamond).

Gemstones

Gems such as opal, ruby, and sapphire are natural crystalline minerals that can be cut and polished. They are commonly found in "geodes," cavities created by gas pockets within rock that was once molten.

Gems owe their value to their beauty and durability, and also to their rarity. From the earliest times, humans have used gems in the finest jewelry but also for practical purposes. For example, the hardness of diamonds (the hardest natural material known) makes them suitable for tipping drill bits.

Some countries' economies are founded on the extraction of particular gems. South Africa, for example, is the world's leading diamond exporter, while the finest emeralds are to be found in Colombia.

Quartz is a very common mineral, and as such it has little value. Regardless, it is known for its extraordinary prism shapes.

Ruby is a gemstone that occurs in a variety of red hues. The cut of the ruby that is shown here is appropriately known as "brilliant."

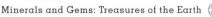

Volcanoes: Builders and Demolishers

Everyone has seen the immense forces unleashed by volcanoes on television or in the newspapers—not to mention disaster movies starring volcanoes busy blasting molten rocks high in the air and coughing up glowing rivers of lava. In the real world, what geological forces cause these spectacular eruptions?

The majority of volcanoes are found at the borders between the Earth's tectonic plates. Where a collision between two plates causes one to slide under the other and melt, the resultant volcano can be extremely violent. Eruptions tend to be much quieter where plates are separating and a volcano forms as molten rock comes to the surface through the gap.

Other volcanoes form away from the plate margins in areas known as hot spots. These are the result of streams of hot mantle called plumes, which force their way through the Earth's crust. On the seabed, repeated eruptions can form a string of volcanic islands as the crust moves steadily over the hot spot. For example, the Hawaiian Islands were formed in this way, as were some islands in the Caribbean Sea.

Volcanic landscapes can have an awesome beauty and are a major tourist attraction on the Big Island of Hawaii and countries such as Japan and New Zealand. The heat generated by volcanic activity can cause water below and above ground to become hot, creating spectacular hydrothermal (hot water) features such as geysers, steam vents, hot springs, and bubbling mud pools. In some cases the hot water can be put to good use—in Iceland, for instance, as much as 40 percent of the country's electricity comes from hydrothermal power.

IN THE KNOW

Kilauea, in Hawaii, is one of the most active volcanoes. The last major eruption lasted from 1983 to 2005. Then, lava flows destroyed hundreds of buildings in the community of Puna and added almost 600 acres to the coastline. A U.S. Geological Survey (USGS) online "volcanocam" tracks Kilauea's ongoing activity day by day.

Types of Volcanoes

A volcano's shape (see opposite page) depends largely on the type of lava produced when tectonic plates collide or separate. When the plates collide, thick, sticky lava is created and cools to form a steep cone-shaped volcano that may add mass with each eruption. When plates separate, the lava is generally thin and runny, creating a large, gently sloping volcano.

Two Famous Eruptions

Mount Vesuvius, in Italy, is an exceptionally active volcano. Its most violent (and best-known) eruption began on August 24, 79 CE when it spewed rock and ash for two days and destroyed the Roman cities of Herculaneum and Pompeii. Thick layers of ash hid the cities for almost 1,700 years. When they were excavated in the eighteenth century, archaeologists discovered that vacancies in the cementlike ash once held bodies. The vacancies were later used to create plaster casts of the victims' dying poses.

One of the largest volcanic eruptions in modern times occurred when Krakatoa, in Indonesia, blew its top in August 1883. The explosion generated the loudest sound in recorded history and was heard as far away as 3,000 miles (4,800 km). More than 36,000 people were killed in the blast, and two-thirds of the island was destroyed.

Krakatoa is still active. Although there have been frequent eruptions in recent decades, none of them have been anywhere near as powerful as the earthshaking blast of 1883.

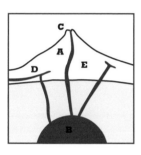

A Main conduit
B Magma chamber
C Crater
D Secondary conduit
E Layered ash and lava

Composite volcanoes are tall, conical volcanoes of alternating layers of lava and volcanic ash. They are also known as stratovolcanoes. Examples include Mount Fuji in Japan and Mount Vesuvius in Italy.

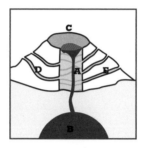

A Main conduit
B Magma chamber
C Crater
D Secondary conduit
E Layered ash and lava

Shield volcanoes form when runny lava called basalt erupts and spreads over a large area to form a gently sloping volcano. This type of volcano often has many side vents.

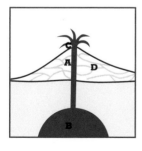

A Main conduit
B Magma chamber
C Crater
D Layered ash and lava

Cinder cone volcanoes are steep-sided volcanoes with layers of volcanic ash. Each time the volcano erupts, another layer is added. Examples include Parícutin in Mexico and Sunset Crater in Arizona.

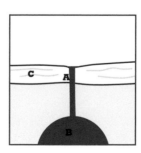

A Main conduit
B Magma chamber
C Basalt plateau

Fissure volcanoes form when runny lava flows out along a crack in the Earth's surface. The lava cools to form a plateau, such as the Deccan plateau in India.

The Destructive Power of Earthquakes

Nature holds in store few more destructive examples of her immense power than earthquakes and their associated tsunamis. The violent shaking of an earthquake and the towering waves of a tsunami can cause thousands of deaths—a terrifying demonstration of the powerful forces at play in the Earth's crust.

The great tectonic plates that make up the Earth's crust are gradually moving against each other. But instead of moving smoothly, tension builds up until there is a sudden movement and release of energy—in the form of seismic waves—causing the ground to shake. This is an earthquake.

The point in the crust at which this occurs is called the focus, and the point on the Earth's surface lying directly above the focus is more familiarly known as the epicenter.

Thousands of small earthquakes occur around the world annually. Most can be detected only by sophisticated seismometers and do no damage. Many earthquakes are more serious, however. On average, 18 major earthquakes (measuring 7–7.9 on the Richter scale) and one great earthquake (measuring 8 or greater) occur every year (see opposite page).

IN THE KNOW

It has long been reported that some creatures behave strangely before an earthquake. In 1975, many animals in the Chinese city of Haicheng began acting up. The authorities knew that Haicheng was vulnerable to earthquakes and evacuated the city. Days later, a large quake struck, but while many buildings were destroyed, there were few casualties.

Where in the World?

More than 80 percent of the world's largest earthquakes occur along the Pacific Ring of Fire, a 25,000-mile "horseshoe" around the basin of the Pacific Ocean. The Ring is also home to 452 volcanoes, more than half the world's active and dormant cauldrons. In a great earthquake, the ground shakes and sometimes even ruptures. Within just a few seconds an entire city may be flattened as buildings, bridges, and roads collapse. Fires may break out due to damaged gas and electrical supplies. Earthquakes can also cause landslides and avalanches, and underwater quakes can cause tsunamis (see opposite page). The loss of life can be massive, especially in densely populated towns and cities, where people become buried under falling debris. Even those who survive the initial impact often succumb to diseases afterward.

The Richter scale was devised by U.S. scientist Charles F. Richter at the California Institute of Technology in 1935. It measures the magnitude of an earthquake on a scale from 1 (minor) to 10 (beyond devastating).

The five most severe earthquakes ever recorded are:

- Chile, May 22, 1960—9.5 on the Richter scale, killing 1,655 people.

- Prince William Sound, Alaska, March 28, 1964—9.2 on the Richter scale, killing 131 people.

- Sumatra, Indonesia, December 26, 2004—9.1 on the Richter scale; subsequent tsunamis killed 227,898.

- Kamchatka, Russia, November 4, 1952—9.0 on the Richter scale; because of its remoteness, the number of casualties remains unknown but is thought to be low.

- Off the coast of Ecuador, January 31, 1906—8.8 on the Richter scale, killing 1,000 people.

The deadliest earthquake ever recorded killed 830,000 people in Shensi, China, on January 23, 1556. It is believed to have measured about 8 on the Richter scale.

Deadly Waves

Earthquakes that occur beneath the sea can cause gigantic seismic sea waves known as tsunamis (Japanese for "great harbor waves"). The waves travel as fast as 500 miles (800 km) an hour. In deep water, the waves may be small and barely detectable as they travel across the ocean (see top diagram below). As a tsunami approaches the shoreline, however, it grows in height and energy (see bottom diagram below). Its effects on the land can be devastating.

On December 26, 2004, the most destructive tsunami in history hit the coastlines of a number of countries in Asia, killing nearly 250,000 people. Since then, more sophisticated tsunami-warning systems have been put in place around the world, in the hope that such a large-scale disaster can be avoided in the future.

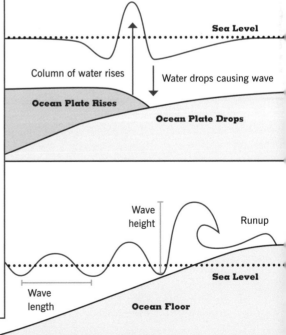

Now that you have stretched your mind back to the very birth of the planet and have looked at everything from the inexorable creep of continents to the amazing explosive power of volcanoes, how much can you remember? It's time to test yourself.

The Formation of Planet Earth

1. When did the Earth come into existence?

   a) *4,540 years ago* b) *454,000 years ago*
   c) *4,540,000 years ago* d) *4.54 billion years ago*

2. What causes the Earth's magnetic field?

3. From what is the Earth's inner core composed?

Water World: The Earth's Oceans

1. What percentage of the world's surface is covered by water?

   a) *60 percent* b) *70 percent*
   c) *80 percent* d) *90 percent*

2. What are the world's three major oceans?

3. True or False: The Earth's crust is generally thinner underneath the ocean than it is on land.

4. What is the process of turning seawater into freshwater known as?

Earth's Atmosphere: A Coat of Many Layers

1. Name the five main layers of the atmosphere.

2. What does a barometer measure?

3. Which two gases make up 99 percent of the Earth's atmosphere?

   a) *nitrogen and sulfur dioxide*
   b) *oxygen and carbon dioxide*
   c) *nitrogen and oxygen*
   d) *neon and ozone*

4. How do CFCs (chlorofluorocarbons) harm the atmosphere?

On Shifting Ground: Plate Tectonics

1. What kind of tectonic plate boundary has created the Himalayas?

2. A convergent plate boundary is also known as a creative boundary or a destructive boundary?

3. All the Earth's continents were once united in a giant supercontinent. What was this called?

Rocks and Fossils: Earth's Upper Crust

1 What is the term for rock that has been formed by the deposition of mineral particles?

2 Metamorphic rock such as slate and marble is formed by what processes?

Earth's Climate: What Gives?

1 How many major ice ages has the Earth endured?

   a) *2*   b) *3*
   c) *4*   d) *5*

2 How long ago did the first major ice age occur?

3 What was the world's largest ice shelf, before it started to crack in 2000?

The Never-Ending Water Cycle

1 What percentage of the world's water is freshwater?

2 What is the main cause of acid rain?

3 What is transpiration?

   a) *evaporation from rivers*
   b) *evaporation from lakes*
   c) *evaporation from plants*
   d) *evaporation from oceans*

Minerals and Gems: Treasures of the Earth

1 Crystal comes from the Greek word *kryos*. What does it mean?

2 How many classes of crystals are there?

3 Which country is the world's largest exporter of diamonds?

   a) *Canada*   b) *Switzerland*
   c) *South Africa*   d) *Australia*

Volcanoes: Builders and Demolishers

1 Which Roman cities were destroyed when Mount Vesuvius erupted in 79 CE?

2 Name four different shapes of volcanoes.

3 In which country would you find the Krakatoa volcano?

The Destructive Power of Earthquakes

1 What do you call a gigantic seismic sea wave?

2 What prompted the Chinese authorities to evacuate the city of Haicheng before the 1975 earthquake?

3 Where was the deadliest earthquake ever recorded?

Chapter Three

The Story of Life

Life on Earth is marvelously complex, and from its earliest origins billions of years ago, it has evolved to fill a myriad of niches in Earth's ecosystems. This chapter takes a look at how life has evolved into the forms that populate today's planet and notes the crucial role played by DNA. You'll also get acquainted with the basics of sea life, insects, reptiles, birds, mammals, and plants—and with a few extinct creatures, the likes of which we will never see again.

The Birth of Life on Earth

Life on Earth is ancient. So ancient, in fact, that even though it took around a billion years for the first forms of life to emerge after the planet itself had formed, evidence of life can be traced back to an astonishing 3.5 billion years ago. Humans arrived on the scene about 200,000 years ago—practically seconds in the great scheme of things.

Evidence of the presence of water—an absolute prerequisite for life as we know it—can also be found in 3.8-billion-year-old sedimentary rocks in Isua, West Greenland. The Earth's composition, though not its geography, was probably much the same then as it is now, but its atmosphere was very different, and this must have affected how life emerged.

It was originally assumed that the atmosphere was a mixture of methane, ammonia, hydrogen, and water vapor, but now some experts think that nitrogen rather than ammonia, and carbon dioxide rather than methane, were the major components. What is almost certain is that there was no oxygen at the time, although this is essential for many life-forms, including humans, today.

IN THE KNOW

Trying to reconstruct the events of 3.5 billion years ago needs not just science but a dash of imagination, too. The period between the start of the universe and the first life on Earth allows the possibility that life evolved elsewhere. Fred Hoyle and Chandra Wickramasinghe have developed the idea of "panspermia," that life on Earth was "seeded" by microbes from space. Indeed, organic compounds such as amino acids have been found in interstellar dusts, meteorites, and comets.

The First Steps

Carbon, hydrogen, and nitrogen form the backbone of biological molecules such as DNA, proteins, and carbohydrates. They assemble themselves into living cells in three stages. First, nucleotides and amino acids are assembled. These then join together into DNA and protein, which are long chains of the simpler units.

A theory put forth by organic chemist Alexander Graham Cairns-Smith, a Scot, holds that clay may be the key to DNA. Clay crystals, formed from silicates, trap molecules to their surfaces. The properties of the silicate surfaces modify the molecules. The new molecules free themselves from their clay environment and replicate independently, creating new living organisms from nonliving matter spontaneously.

Conversation Starter When in the 1950s American scientists Miller and Urey showed that the building blocks for life could emerge from a primordial soup, some chemists were led to joke, "Mix some ammonia and methane in a test tube and leave it in the Sun for a week. Then shout down the tube, 'Is there anybody there?'"

Self-replication (DNA, RNA) and catalysis (enzymes) then helped get life started and kept it going. These two biochemical processes are essential to the activities of cells today and must have been present, in some primitive form at least, from the start. One more essential was some kind of protective barrier—a primitive cell wall—that kept the polymers together so they could do their work rather than just diffusing.

Meanwhile, experiments by the Russian biochemist Aleksandr Oparin (1894–1980) showed how primitive cells might have formed through self-assembly of protein molecules into a kind of shell that allowed substances to pass in and out through a membrane. Oparin was one of the first scientists to have a vision of life emerging from an oxygen-free "primordial soup."

In 1953 Stanley Miller and Harold Urey, working at the University of Chicago, combined methane, hydrogen, ammonia, and water and ran electric current through the solution to simulate the lightning storms believed common on the early Earth. After one week 10 to 15 percent of the carbon (originally methane) had formed organic compounds like those that gave rise to life.

A Timeless Question

This picture raises many questions. Shock waves from meteors and comets, lightning, and intense ultraviolet light from the Sun may have combined with many other disturbances to spark life on the planet. Or it may be that the so-called primordial soup was formed in niches on the ocean floor called hydrothermal vents—the result of biochemical reactions among the minerals found in the vents. Whatever the reason, how life began is a question for the ages.

Hydrothermal vents on the ocean floor are one possible locus for the birth of life on Earth. Scientists first discovered a hydrothermal vent, or "smoker," off the coast of South America in 1977—a hot spring at a depth of 1.6 miles (2.5 km). Many other vents are now known to exist.

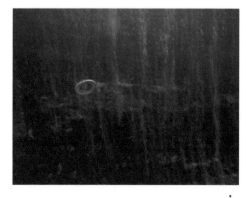

Insects and the Diversity of Life

Although they might not be as obvious to the eye as mammals in a field or birds in the air, insects make up a whopping 80 percent of the world's animal species. About a million known species have been listed, demonstrating the rich diversity of life on Earth—and entomologists speculate that 10 times that many species may exist.

Insects, which belong to the phylum Antropoda, are found everywhere on Earth—mainly on the land and in the air rather than in the sea. It's thought that what we call bugs evolved around 400 million years ago. They move on six legs and many can fly, even though their veined wings appear too light to support them.

Insects fulfill many ecological needs and form crucial links within their ecosystems. For example, they pollinate plants and scavenge on (and thereby recycle) the nutrients locked up in dead animals and plants. Some also produce products that are useful to humans, including honey, wax, and silk, and are therefore farmed.

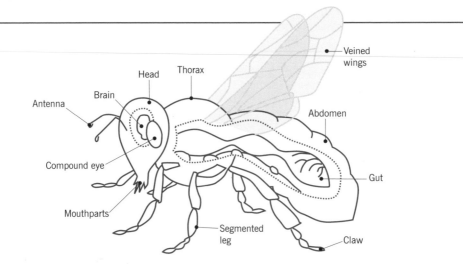

While the anatomy of insects varies, they have some common characteristics. Their segmented bodies have an external skeleton and are divided into a head, thorax, and abdomen. The head contains a brain and possesses a pair of compound eyes, three pairs of mouthparts, and a pair of antenna. Three pairs of legs are attached to the thorax, as is a pair of veined wings, while both the thorax and the abdomen contain the basic respiratory, nervous, and digestive systems.

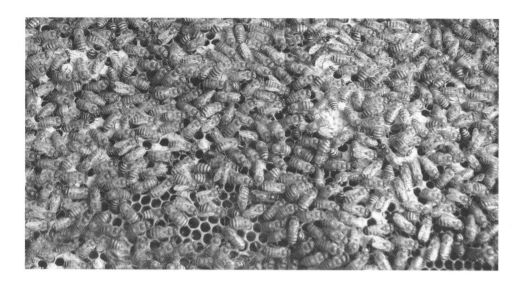

The Social Life of Bees

Bees live in communities populated by three different types of bee. The queen, whose sole function is to reproduce, may lay up to 1,500 eggs in one day and lives for one to three years. She has a more developed body because, as a newly hatched larva, she was fed only the protein-rich jelly produced in the glands of worker bees (hence the name of the beauty product "royal jelly"). The queen's stinger isn't barbed, enabling her to sting repeatedly and survive.

The drone is a male born of an unfertilized egg—his only purpose is fertilizing the Queen. He has huge eyes and no stinger.

Thinning Swarms? In 2007, honey bee colonies died off by the hundreds of thousands in North America and Europe, with everything from drought to cell phone towers theorized as the cause of this "colony collapse disorder." Then, in 2008, a likely culprit was identified: Israeli Acute Paralysis Virus. Whatever the cause, scientists are working apace to restore health to insects so vital to our ecosystem.

Worker bees are infertile females with stingers that are pulled from the body when used, causing death. A colony has as many as 80,000 workers, which produce both wax and honey and live for about six weeks. Worker bees communicate with an elaborate system of dance that signals the location of food sources to their hive mates.

Conversation Starter Insects might be tiny, but there are so many of them that ants and termites alone are believed by some scientists to account for as much as 20 percent of the world's combined mass of all creatures, known as the animal biomass.

Beneath the Waves: The Life Aquatic

Only 150 years ago, naturalists had no idea of the rich biodiversity of the seas. Because deep oceans are dark and cold, it was assumed that nothing could survive there. Today, modern technology gives us a far greater understanding of what lives beneath the waves.

The first clues came from broken underwater telegraph wires. When they were hauled up, all manner of unusual and previously unknown creatures clung to them. In light of this, the British navel vessel H.M.S. *Challenger* was assigned to carry out the first worldwide oceanographic survey in 1872–1876. It found thousands of specimens, many never seen before.

A Wet Planet

Water covers about 70 percent of the Earth's surface, and the oceans provide more than 170 times the living space as land, air, and freshwater put together. This ranges from the shallows of the seashore to the greatest depths. At 35,798 feet (10,911 m), the deepest known point is in the Marianas Trench in the northwestern Pacific Ocean, deeper than Mount Everest is high.

Seawater is salty and has remained at roughly the same composition for millions of years. This makes it a relatively easy environment for plants and animals to adapt to, compared to freshwater and dry land. In fact, it is believed that living creatures on Earth actually emerged from the sea.

The oceans are in constant motion. Cold, dense seawater sinks into the ocean floor, heats up in the basalt there, loses density in the heat, and then rises back up. Currents on the surface, driven by the wind, cool as they head toward the poles, gaining density.

Those waters flow into the ocean basins, where they mix extensively. With the differences among the waters muted, the oceans of the Earth become a great global system that transports heat and matter around the globe.

The surface temperature of water varies from 104°F (40°C) in tropical waters to 27°F (−1.9°C)—freezing, for seawater—in the Arctic and Antarctic. The depths of the oceans are very cold, even in tropical regions, at 32°–37°F (0°–3°C).

IN THE KNOW

Whales, the largest animals in the seas, are mammals, breathing with lungs. There are two suborders: the baleen whales, which do not have teeth and filter feed on plankton; and the toothed whales, which feed on fish and squid. Toothed whales have the remarkable ability to navigate the ocean by an inborn radar of sorts.

Life in the Depths

Animals exist at all levels of the sea, but their numbers decrease with increasing depth. Sea life also exists as distinct communities at the same depths over very wide areas of the ocean. Although life below the waves is diverse, land holds more species than does the marine environment. Scientists estimate that millions of animal and plant species are yet to be discovered. But of the more than 2,000,000 already identified, aquatic species account for only about 10 percent.

Continental Shelf		
Epipelagic Zone (The Sunlight Zone)	660 ft.	200 m
Mesopelagic Zone (The Twilight Zone)		
	3,300 ft.	1,000 m
Continental Slope	6,600 ft.	2,000 m
Bathypelagic Zone (The Midnight Zone)		
	9,900 ft.	3,000 m
	13,100 ft.	4,000 m
Abyssopelagic Zone (The Abyss)	16,300 ft.	5,000 m
Continental Rise		
	19,700 ft.	6,000 m
Ocean Basin		
	23,000 ft.	7,000 m
	26,300 ft.	8,000 m
Hadopelagic Zone (The Trenches)		
	29,600 ft.	9,000 m
Trench	32,800 ft.	10,000 m
	36,100 ft.	11,000 m

The Sunlight Zone

Like life on land, sea life depends upon plants and photosynthesis. But photosynthesis in the sea can happen only where the sunlight penetrates. Most sea plants are minute single-celled algae called phytoplankton, and many tiny herbivores feed directly on them, in turn becoming food for larger predators.

The Twilight Zone

In deeper waters, sunlight only partially permeates, and there is not enough to support photosynthesis. In order to see in such darkness, animals rely on very large eyes or produce their own light through bioluminescence.

The Midnight Zone

Sunlight cannot penetrate the midnight zone, so there are no plants. The water here is cold, and in order to conserve energy, many fish move very slowly, although large creatures such as squid and octopuses, and the whales that hunt them, can be found here.

The Abyss

At this great depth, most creatures are blind because of the complete lack of light, and the water temperature is near freezing. Although life here is relatively scarce, the abyss is home to many weird creatures capable of surviving the crushing pressures.

The Trenches

Deeper still than the abyssal waters are the deep-water trenches and canyons. Relatively little is known about life in these largely unexplored depths, but it does persist in simple forms such as starfish and tube worms.

Reptiles:
On Land to Stay

The early amphibians that evolved into frogs and toads and salamanders were the first animals able to breathe both underwater and on land. But it was the amphibians' reptilian descendants that became the first full-fledged land animals.

Four groups of reptiles survive today—lizards and snakes; turtles and tortoises; crocodiles; and the lonely tuatara, a "living fossil" found only in the South Pacific.

Lizards and Snakes

Lizards greatly outnumber their reptile relatives, and their species are the most diverse. They range in size from the formidable Komodo dragon of Southeast Asia, which grows to a length of 10 feet (3 m), to the dwarf gecko of the West Indies, a mere ¾ inch (2 cm) long.

Snakes probably evolved from burrowing lizards and are grouped as two main kinds. Pythons and other constrictors coil around their prey and squeeze them until they suffocate. Biting snakes kill with their fangs—all the easier if, as with rattlesnakes and cobras, their fangs release venom.

Turtles to Crocs

While lizards and snakes have scales, the bodies of turtles and tortoises are encased in hard shells. The main difference between turtles and tortoises boils down to water. Turtles spend all or part of their lives underwater, whether in wetlands or the ocean. Tortoises are landlubbers, wading into water only to clean themselves or drink. Tortoises also have extraordinarily long life spans, with some living 150 years or more.

Crocodiles' raised eyes and nostrils enable them to float low in the water, and a system of valves allows them to snatch prey underwater without sucking water into the lungs. They inhabit tropical and subtropical waters the world over, and the rare gavial crocodile is found only on the northern Indian subcontinent. The other species of the crocodile family, alligators and caimans, are limited to the Americas.

IN THE KNOW

Tu'i Malila (King Malila), a tortoise that died in the island kingdom of Tonga in 1965, is one of the longest-lived animals on record. He was presented to Tonga's royal family by Captain James Cook in 1774 when Cook made his second voyage to the Pacific. Tu'i Malila was a radiated tortoise, a type named for the radiating yellow marks on their shells. His shell is now on display in Tonga's capital city of Nuku'alofa.

The Four Orders of Reptiles

The largest order of reptiles has close to 8,000 species, while the smallest has a grand total of two.

Squamata (lizards and snakes) are by far the largest reptile order, with about 7,900 species. Lizards account for about 5,000 of these, and snakes for virtually all of the rest. The handful of other species belong to the amphisbaenid (worm lizard) suborder.

Testudines (turtles and tortoises) number between 300 and 400 species, some of them highly endangered. The 300-odd species of turtle spend most of their time in the water; sea turtles live in the ocean and can migrate great distances. Tortoises, with roughly 50 species, are land-dwelling herbivores (plant eaters).

Crocodilia are the largest reptiles yet are the closest living relatives of birds. The *Crocodylis* (crocodile) genus has 12 species, while the *Alligator* genus has only two: the Chinese alligator and the American alligator of the southeastern United States. The South American Caiman genus has five species, while the *Gavialis* genus is represented by the Indian gavial alone.

Sphenodontia have two non-extinct species of tuatara, which flourished 200 million years ago but were declared endangered in 1895. Now confined to islands off the coast of New Zealand, these 2½-foot (80-cm) lizardlike reptiles take their name from the Maori word for "peaks on back."

Birds and Life on the Wing

From the majestic bald eagle to the tiny hummingbird, the assortment of life in the air is mind-boggling. In the seas and on the land, birds such as the penguin and ostrich also occupy their niches. Amazingly, all 10,000 or so species, regardless of shape or size, trace their roots back to a common ancestor that lived some 150 million years ago.

Birds range in size from the tiny bee hummingbirds, just 2½ inches (6.2 cm) long, to the giant flightless birds like the ostrich and emu that can stand taller than a man. Throughout this vast range, around 1 in 10 bird species is thought to be endangered.

Grouping Birds

The classification of birds is complicated. Ornithologists make a big distinction between flightless birds, like the ostrich, and those that can fly. The latter comprises 24 groups called orders. The Passerines, which include the sparrow and many other common garden birds, account for more than one half of all bird species. But there are also the waterfowl, gulls, woodpeckers, kingfishers, owls, penguins, and doves/pigeons. Traditionally, birds are classified on the basis of anatomy (wing shape, beak shape, and so on), but DNA evidence from living birds is increasingly used to refine the relationships between different species.

The Characteristics of Birds

Feathers are a unique feature of birds; they enable flight, attract mates, and also protect and insulate a bird's body. A bird has a light but strong skeleton, which is also well adapted to flight.

Birds lay hard-shelled eggs, and the young, after hatching, generally require a prolonged period of parental care.

Birds have beaks but no teeth; however, the shape of each species' beak is usually well adapted to how and what it eats, whether, for example, insects, seeds, or pollen. Indeed, it was the differing shapes of birds' beaks that gave Darwin his first ideas on evolution.

IN THE KNOW

The cassowary found in the rain forests of northern Australia and New Guinea is an odd bird indeed. The large black-feathered body of this flightless bird dwarfs its long blue neck, making it seem that the cassowary and platypus may have been products of the same designer. This emu cousin stands up to 6 feet (1.8 m) tall, its head topped with a hornlike crest, or casque.

How Birds Fly

Most birds are efficient flying machines. The shape of their "airfoil" wings controls lift, stability, and thrust.

The air moving over the top of the wing moves faster than the air moving underneath it, creating a pressure difference and giving a "lifting" force. In addition, a bird propels itself by flapping its wings; in the case of hummingbirds, fast enough to be able to hover. On the other hand, some birds such as albatrosses and eagles are able to soar, gliding on air currents and flying for long distances without flapping their wings.

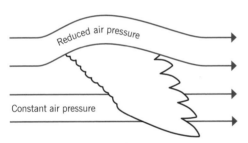

The shape of a bird's wing enables it to gain lift from the flow of air as shown above; while the internal structure, combined with strong chest muscles and feathers, allows it to power its flight.

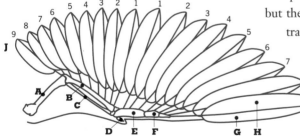

A Humerus
B Ulna
C Radius
D Pollex
E Carpometacarpus
F Second digit
G Outer vane
H Inner vane
I Primary remiges
J Secondary remiges

Amazing Migrations

The first bird migrations were noted about 3,000 years ago; however, not all species migrate, and those that do not are known as resident birds.

Migratory birds, such as swallows, undertake risky journeys to take advantage of more abundant food supplies, and more appropriate breeding grounds at different times of year. Some travel only short distances, but the sooty shearwater, a seabird that migrates between New Zealand and the north Pacific, makes an amazing round-trip of some 40,000 miles (64,000 km) a year.

The Secrets of Birdsong

Birds make two kinds of vocal sounds with their simple voice box. The "call" seems to serve the purpose of an alarm, begging for food or signaling to other birds, while the "song" is for attracting a mate or guarding territory. Not all birds can sing, however.

The best way to experience birdsong is to listen to the "dawn chorus," which generally starts an hour or so before dawn breaks. The birds tend to start singing in a set order. The purpose of the dawn chorus is not clear, but the air is colder at this time and sound travels faster, so the songs may just be more obvious. Many birds are also social animals, communicating through calls and song, and the dawn chorus may be an important feature of this sociability.

Mammals:
A Class of Their Own

We are mammals, and so are most of the other animals we see on land. In common with almost all the other creatures that make up the class Mammalia, humans are warm-blooded, have a spine, grow hair, sweat, and give birth to live young that females feed with milk. Humans and other mammals also share some of the same genes.

Mammals are vertebrates. That is, they have a backbone like the other vertebrates: birds, fish, amphibians, and reptiles. Many mammals are big, dominant, and conspicuous, but their numbers are fewer than those of other vertebrates. Around 5,400 different mammal species are known, compared to 10,000 bird species, 7,000 reptile species, and 28,000 species of fish.

What's a Mammal?

Mammals use lungs to breathe and have a heart with four chambers. They have a spine, a brain, and a nervous system. The outer part of the brain is enlarged in humans and other primates, a development that has been linked to both intelligence and consciousness. Mammals are also warm-blooded, possessing the ability to keep their body temperature constant through several bodily mechanisms that keep them warm or cool them down.

Mammals have evolved several different ways of moving around within their varied habitats. Heavy mammals such as elephants, hippopotamuses, and rhinos, for example, have developed a way of moving, known as graviportal, which involves splaying their digits around their limbs for support. At the other end of the spectrum, tree-dwelling mammals have extremely mobile limbs and may even, like New World monkeys, have a prehensile tail that can be used as a fifth hand.

Key Player

Gaylord Simpson
(1902–1984)

In 1945 George Gaylord Simpson suggested a new system of mammalian classification with respect to bodily features. Simpson said, of biology "Life is the most important thing about the world, the most important thing about life is evolution."

In the Sea and in the Air

The first mammals appeared on Earth around 265 million years ago, at a time when dinosaurs, which were reptiles, ruled. When the dinosaurs became extinct, mammals took over and filled many niches. Although many mammals have become extinct, the class has endured, and in many ecosystems is at the top of the food chain.

Not all mammals live on land. Three mammalian groups are aquatic: sirenians (dugongs and manatees, fully aquatic mammals inhabiting rivers, estuaries, swamps, and other wetlands); pinnipeds (seals and walruses, who evolved from a bearlike ancestor); and cetaceans (whales, dolphins, and porpoises, all noted for their high intelligence). Pinnipeds give birth and nurse their young on land, but cetaceans cannot cope out of deep water.

Meanwhile, in the air, bats are the only true flying mammals. Some mammals, including some species of squirrels, have the capacity to glide and can be highly mobile in an aerial environment.

What Mammals Eat

Unlike other animals, a young mammal depends on its mother for nourishment for an extended period of time. Such nurturing allows time for learning and is one reason mammals evolved so successfully.

Once they reach maturity, mammals are quite versatile in what they eat. There are four types, classified by diet:

- Herbivores, such as cows, horses, camels, and elephants, eat plants.

- Carnivores, such as dogs, tigers, lions, cats, whales, and dolphins, eat meat.

- Omnivores, such as humans and some bears, eat a mixed diet of both plants and meat.

- Insectivores, such as aardvarks and anteaters, eat insects.

In Fact...

The blue whale is the world's biggest mammal; they usually grow to a size of about 80 feet (24.5 m) long, and the biggest ever seen was 94 feet (28.5 m) and weighed 174 tons. The blue whale is also the world's loudest mammal; its whistle reaches 188 decibels and can be heard for several hundred miles around. (A human reaches up to 70 decibels.) Blue whales live in the Antarctic, North Atlantic, and North Pacific oceans.

The bumblebee bat is the world's smallest mammal, and its habitat is in western Thailand along the River Kwai. It is an endangered species and, as the name suggests, is about the size of a bee—around 1.2 inches (3 cm) long—and weighs about 0.07 ounces (1.98 g).

Homo Sapiens and the Origins of Us

All that is left of our earliest ancestors is a handful of fossils discovered in Africa. From these meager remains, researchers have pieced together the amazing story of the emergence of *Homo sapiens*—human beings—a mere 200,000 years ago.

In 2001–2002 the earliest human ancestor fossil ever discovered, a skull dating back some 7,000,000 years, was found in Chad: a specimen of the hominid (early human) species *Sahelanthrophus tchadensis*, nicknamed Toumai ("hope of life" in the Goran language of Chad).

To modern eyes this creature would look more ape than human, yet it had two characteristics that suggest the human race had already begun to carve out a path separate from that of its mammalian relatives. First, its canines were less sharp and prominent than those of the apes. More evocatively, there is evidence of Toumai and his (or her) contemporaries walking on two legs rather than four, since the position and orientation of the hole where the spinal cord passes into the skull suggests that *Sahelanthrophus* walked upright and looked straight ahead.

The location of the skull in Chad suggested that the hominid species occupied a wider expanse of Africa than previously believed. However, it has yet to be established that *Sahelanthrophus* is actually the earliest form of hominid. Another candidate is *Orrorin tugenensis*, a species discovered in 1974 (with additional fossils uncovered more recently) in the Tugen Hills of northern Kenya. The teeth, jaws, and limb-bone fossils date back 5,800,000 years, and the structure of the hip joint is evidence that these hominids walked upright.

The Next Step

The next major stage in human evolution was the emergence of the *Australopithecus* species. These hominids walked on two legs, and their teeth look distinctly human. Yet their brains were still small when compared to those of modern humans. One

Key Player

Lucy

Lucy is an almost complete skeleton of an *A. afarensis* hominid discovered by Donald Johansen and Tom Gray in 1974. Lucy's discovery allowed a much deeper understanding of the way early humans walked.

important example is *A. afarensis*, an example of which—the skeleton known as Lucy—was discovered in the Afar region of Ethiopia and dates back 3,000,000 years.

The Emergence of *Homo Sapiens*

With the appearance of the *Homo* genus, the most recent stage in human evolution, some of the characteristics that set us apart from other species (other than walking on two legs) become apparent. *Homo habilis*, a species dating to about 2,000,000 years ago, was discovered in the Olduvai Gorge, Tanzania, by Louis and Mary Leakey in 1964. *H. habilis* is distinguished from preceding archaeological discoveries by the species' much larger brain and the presence of tools alongside its fossils. This newfound mental capacity, combined with the ability to grip an object with the thumb and forefinger (a power lacking in apes), gave rise to the nickname of *H. habilis*: Handy Man. Thanks to the ability to use tools for hunting, this species was able to prosper and broaden its geographical range.

The next species, *Homo erectus* ("Upright Man"), lived from 2,000,000 to 200,000 years ago and was the first to spread out of Africa and into Asia. The presence of burned bones next to *H. erectus* fossils suggests these early humans knew how to control fire and use it for cooking. *H. erectus* then evolved into the modern human, *Homo sapiens* (*sapiens* is Latin for "wise" and refers to how humans from then on used their brains to develop language and culture). *H. sapiens* skeletons found in Ethiopia date back 150,000 to 200,000 years, and reconstructions show a less apelike face than its predecessors. This species spread to the Middle East, then through Asia, Europe, and North and South America.

The final transition to modern humans was Cro-Magnon man (*H. sapiens sapiens*), who lived 40,000–10,000 years ago. Humans of today look more or less the same as Cro-Magnons, in spite of the vast differences in our lives.

Unlocking the Mystery

The lineage of hominids who eventually evolved into humans has been drawn and redrawn time and again. Until a few years ago, for example, the species *Ramapithecus* was considered a part of our direct heritage to humans but is now known to be a branch that parted from our evolutionary tree.

The key to unlocking the mystery of how humans replaced Neanderthals and other species may lie in our ability to analyze our own DNA. In other words, the answer may well be in our genes.

IN THE KNOW

Neanderthal Man (*Homo Neanderthalis*) is our extinct cousin, not ancestor. He was much like us, so why did he vanish 30,000 years ago? American anthropologists Philip Lieberman and Edmund Crellin found the Neanderthal voice box to be less complex—and our ability to speak and develop language might have given us the edge.

Charles Darwin and the Story of Evolution

When naturalist Charles Darwin set out on his five-year voyage on H.M.S. *Beagle* in 1831, it marked the beginning of a revolution in biology. At the time, people generally believed that all the species had continued without change since the beginning of life on Earth; however, Darwin's discoveries were set to change that forever.

What Darwin saw on the remote Galapagos Islands, off the western coast of South America, suggested something radically different. These 10 rocky islands have a similar climate, but they are separated from one another by deep and fast water and are undisturbed by strong winds.

What struck Darwin was that each island had its own set of plants and animals, including finches, tortoises, and thrushes. He was also aware of the work of Thomas Malthus on competition among humans for resources including food, and Darwin came to the conclusion that variation among and between species would sometimes produce members of a species that were particularly well suited to their environment. These individuals would be more likely to survive and leave offspring, propagating the same genetic traits that helped them survive. For instance, imagine a family of mice with differing coat colors living in woodland. Those whose coat blends in best will be more likely to avoid predators, survive longer, and have more offspring to which they will pass on the color of their coat. This means that the next generation will have more mice of this color and is an example of how the "survival of the fittest" drives evolution via natural selection. Darwin eventually published his ideas in a book *On the Origin of Species by Means of Natural Selection* in 1859.

The Speed of Change

The rate of evolution is very slow for most large animals, but it does vary greatly, depending on the nature of the species and

IN THE KNOW

Evolution is a theory in the scientific sense of the word, meaning it has repeatedly passed the "scientific method" test. The scientific method involves 1) observation of a phenomenon; 2) formulating a hypothesis to explain the phenomenon; 3) using the hypothesis to predict the results of new observations; and 4) experiments by several independent, qualified scientists. A hypothesis borne out by experimentation comes to be regarded as a scientific theory.

the environmental pressure it is under. A modern example is the evolution of antibiotic resistance by bacteria. In this case, when bacteria are exposed to an antibiotic that kills some but not all of them, the next generation will have a higher percentage of the resistant bacteria. And because bacteria reproduce every 20 minutes or so, it is not long before a generation evolves that is completely insensitive to a particular antibiotic. This is what happened recently with the spread of bacteria like MRSA (Methicillin-resistant Staphylococcus aureus) in hospitals.

Evolution's Roots

Darwin really had no idea of the biological mechanisms of evolution. It was the Austrian botanist and monk Gregor Mendel who, around the same time, began to create an experimental basis for the theory. He carried out experiments with pea plants in his monastery garden, noting how characteristics such as flower color, height, and seed shape were inherited.

Pea plants generally reproduce by self-pollination, and in doing so, they produce very similar daughter plants. However,

Key Player

Charles Darwin
1809–1882

Darwin published the journal of his voyage in the *Beagle* in 1839 and did a great deal of reading and thinking before publishing his ideas on evolution. He discussed his thoughts with the geologist Charles Lyell and the botanist Joseph Hooker, while the naturalist Alfred Russel Wallace worked along similar lines and wrote a book dedicated to Darwin in 1869, publishing the tome *Darwinism* in 1889.

Mendel interrupted this natural process, choosing instead pairs with different characteristics and then cross-pollinating them.

From these experiments, Mendel observed that there was no blending of characteristics—a seed came out either wrinkled or smooth, not somewhere between. From this he developed the idea of the gene as an indivisible unit of inheritance, writing of it in 1865. Mendel's groundbreaking discovery attracted little attention in the scientific community until nearly a century later, when scientists revealed DNA as the stuff those genes were made of.

Over the course of 23,000,000 years, *Pronconsul hamiltoni* was followed by *Australopitcus afarensis*, *Homo habilis*, *Homo erectus*, and *Homo sapiens*—modern man, or us.

DNA and Genetics: The Stuff of Life

Why do you look like your parents but not your boss? Why do your grandparents see their parents in your features? The answers lie among the contents of the nuclei of virtually all living cells. Every plant, animal, and human inherits a combination of DNA from its parents . . . a mixture of characteristics that makes us unique.

The cells of animals and plants contain a central structure called a nucleus. Within the nucleus, and visible through high-powered microscopes, are threadlike structures called chromosomes, which carry genetic information in the form of genes—the functional units of inheritance.

A chromosome consists of a spiraling scaffold of protein molecules on which is wound a strand of DNA (deoxyribonucleic acid), the chemical that makes up a gene. Believe it or not, the DNA in a human cell measures around 4 feet (1.5 m) long and contains about 30,000 different genes, and it is these genes that determine your characteristics.

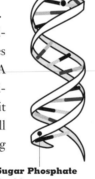

Base Pairs

Sugar Phosphate Backbone

Adenine ▭▬ Thymine

Guanine ▬▭ Cytosine

The Structure of DNA

DNA's chemical structure allows it to act as a chemical code that carries genetic information. All of the information it contains is found on a long string of a mere four chemical "letters": A (for adenine), C (cytosine), G (guanine), and T (thymine).

Each gene is composed of a stretch of DNA containing a thousand or so of these letters. DNA is in effect the set of blueprints for the proteins that carry out our biochemical functions—extracting energy from glucose, for example, and breaking down toxins.

The double helix of DNA is now famous. A model of beautiful simplicity, it uses just four chemical letters to write the instructions to make your body.

1869

Friedrich Miescher discovers a mysterious new acid in the nuclei of white blood cells in pus, later identified as deoxyribonucleic acid (DNA).

1928

Fred Griffith uncovers the existence of a "transforming principle" that transfers genetic instructions between bacteria—but he can't identify it.

1944

Oswald Avery announces that genes are made up of DNA, not protein as previously believed, and that DNA is Griffith's "transforming principle."

Key Players

James Watson	Francis Crick	Maurice Wilkins
b.1928	*1916–2004*	*1916–2004*

Chicago native Watson entered college at age 15 and completed his Ph.D. at 22. Unlike many prodigies, his flame never dimmed. One of his earliest theoretical breakthroughs, that the chemical components of DNA are paired, was key to mapping the double helix. An outspoken man, Watson drew criticism for comments about colleagues in his 1968 memoir.

With a background in mathematics and physics, Crick was the perfect complement to James Watson, the molecular biologist. The two men collaborated to build models of DNA molecules out of metal plates and rods to simulate the self-replicating property that underpins DNA's function. Along with Watson and Maurice Wilkins, he was awarded the Nobel Prize in 1962.

Born in New Zealand and educated in England, Wilkins worked on the Manhattan Project during World War II. He later conducted X-ray studies of DNA with a team that included England's chemist and crystallographer Rosalind Franklin, an expert in X-ray defraction photography. Wilkins and his team went on to provide visual evidence for the model of DNA.

1953

Francis Crick and James Watson publish the "double helix" structure of DNA.

1974

First experiments in genetic engineering, transferring DNA between different organisms, are conducted at Stanford University.

2003

The Human Genome Project, launched under James Watson in 1990, deciphers the human genetic code. Further research is still ongoing.

The Kingdom of Plants

From the houseplant by your window to the swaths of rain forest in the Amazon Basin, life on Earth depends upon plants and their ability to turn energy from the Sun into food. It goes without saying that plants are wholly unrelated to animals and bacteria, and they vary from simple algae and mosses to a vast array of flowering plants and trees.

Photosynthesis is the key to plant life. The chlorophyll that plants contain absorbs wavelengths of visible light from the Sun and uses it in a chain of bio-chemical reactions that turn carbon dioxide and water into sugars. The by-product is oxygen. You can even view this process by growing pondweed in a glass tank set in a window with full sun exposure—the plant will give off bubbles of oxygen.

The basic photosynthetic cycle is driven by energy from the Sun and uses water and carbon dioxide to create carbohydrates that fuel a plant's growth, giving off oxygen as a by-product.

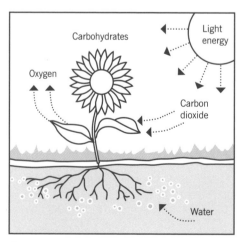

Carbohydrates

Light energy

Oxygen

Carbon dioxide

Water

The Uses of Plants

Plants have a vast range of uses, from foods and structural materials to medicines. Plants cultivated for the purpose of harvesting seeds, roots, and leaves or other parts for some kind of economic use are known as crops; cereals—botanically, types of grass with edible grains—are the most common.

Of course, we also consume many other plants in the form of fruits, vegetables, nuts, and seeds. Foods like sugar, spices, and vegetable oils are also plant-based.

Plants are also the source of our most basic materials. Cotton and flax provide natural textiles, and the cellulose in plants gives rayon and viscose. Wood is used to make everything from houses and furniture to paper and is our most elementary fuel. Interest in using cellulose and starch from corn to make biofuels like bioethanol is increasing apace. Even coal and oil are created from the long-dead remains of plants—the reason they're known as fossil fuels.

Humankind has long relied on medicinal plants and herbal remedies. Many modern drugs, including aspirin, morphine, quinine, and the anti-cancer drug Taxol come from plants. Soap, waxes, latex, turpentine, and other common household items are also the gift of the plant world.

Many plants are cultivated for aesthetic reasons. Cut-flower arrangements beautify the home, and bouquets and sprays celebrate or comfort at weddings and funerals. Flowerbeds and trees and shrubs are the tools of home landscaping, and home vegetable gardening is more "green" than ever.

Botanical gardens exist for both the scientific study of plants and the pleasure of visitors. Here, people get close-up views of plant specimens of every stripe—showpieces of Earth's amazing plant kingdom.

The Sex Life of Plants

Plants reproduce by bringing together male and female "gametes" in a process of pollination, which is helped along by the wind or bees and other flying insects.

The male sexual organ of a plant (the stamen) produces pollen that is transferred to the female sexual organ (the stigma). The result is a fertilized seed that goes on to germinate and develop into a new plant.

The anatomy of a flower is crucial to a plant's reproduction. Unlike most animals, many have both male and female sexual organs. Pollen is transferred from the anther of one plant's stamen to the stigma of another plant. From here it moves down the pollen tube and fertilizes the ovule. The transportation of pollen is often carried out by insects, which are attracted to a flower by its scent and brightly colored petals.

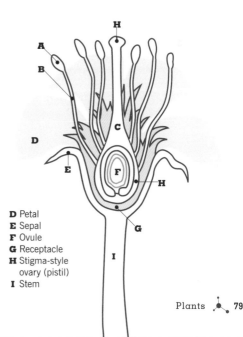

A Anther (bulbous end of stamen)	**D** Petal
	E Sepal
	F Ovule
B Filament (stem section of stamen)	**G** Receptacle
	H Stigma-style ovary (pistil)
C Pollen tube	**I** Stem

The Ecological Balancing Act

Ecology once referred only to the study of animal habitats. Today, it describes the study of the threatened ecosystems, or biomes, on which the survival of life on Earth depends.

Relationships within the whole of the biosphere—the mantle of life that covers the Earth—are too complex for detailed study, so earth scientists have broken them down into ecosystems, also known as biomes and plant formations. No "official" breakdown has been established, but ecosystems are generally divided into five broad habitats: forest, grassland, desert, marine, and freshwater. Within a particular ecosystem, animals and plants of a single species are called a "population," and the term "niche" describes how that species responds and relates to other species, given the ecosystem's resources.

Energy and Carbon

Change is the nature of ecosystems, yet change wrought by human activity can be drastic. Anything disrupting the flow of energy and the carbon cycle it powers can throw nature out of balance.

The marine and freshwater ecosystems are two of the "reservoirs" necessary for carbon exchange, or the carbon cycle. In the atmosphere, "carbon" means carbon dioxide (CO_2), essential to life. Unlike energy, carbon will recycle through ecosystems over and again by way of the food chain.

The food chain relies on the Sun to transfer energy from one link of the chain to the next.

- The first link, "producers" (green plants), use the Sun's radiant energy to make the carbon compounds on which life depends.

- The second, "primary consumers" (plant eaters), eat the producers and break down the plants' carbohydrates and proteins to obtain energy.

- The third, "secondary consumers" (carnivorous predators), obtain their energy by eating the primary consumers.

- The fourth, "decomposers" (bacteria, fungi, ants, and worms), feed on the carcasses of predators and return the broken-down organic material to the soil. This carbon-based material is recycled by the producers, or plants, and the food chain has come full circle.

The food chain represents the interdependence of all living things as the very key to survival, so it's no wonder that ecology has caught the world's attention.

Ecosystems Today

Many ecosystems around the globe are facing degradation or unsustainability. Among the contributing factors are rapid population growth, climate change, acid rain, water shortages, and the extinction of plant and animal species. Here's a look at the five broad ecosystems and how they are faring.

Forests—Covering about a third of Earth's land surface, forests contain around 70 percent of the carbon found in living things. Tropical and temperate forests have been logged and burned for wood and farming (more than half of the Earth's original forests have disappeared), but depletion is slowing because of worldwide concern.

Grasslands—Grasslands provide food and habitats for many bird and wild herbivore (plant-eater) species. In North America, some 97 percent of tall-grass prairie grasslands succumbed to agriculture or urbanization. Twenty to 40 percent of grasslands elsewhere have been converted to cropland, though up to 75 percent of South America's have disappeared.

Tundra—The coldest of all biomes, tundra is frozen ground that won't support trees or mammals. Yet when the permafrost—a frozen layer of soil from 3–10 feet (0.9–3 m) deep—melts in summer, thousands of species of insects breed and draw migrating birds. Warmer temperatures are causing the permafrost to melt, and the resulting wetlands emit methane gas and carbon dioxide that speed climate change.

Marine—Oceans cover about three-quarters of Earth's surface. Marine algae and phytoplankton supply much of the oxygen—and absorb much of the carbon dioxide—in the atmosphere through photosynthesis. Several species of algae and phytoplankton are endangered.

Freshwater—Plants and animals in the lakes, rivers, and wetlands of the freshwater ecosystems are adapted to the low-salt concentration in these waters. Many freshwater ecosystems have been depleted or eradicated by pollution and overfishing.

Lost Forever: A Guide to Extinction

Extinction is evolution's downside—for the unsuccessful species at least—as the survival of the fittest also means the death of the unfit. It's hardly a new phenomenon: Indeed, the Earth has witnessed a constant stream of extinctions, studded by major extinction events. Humankind has also been responsible for the death of many species.

Extinction becomes inevitable once the last few members of a species become incapable of reproducing, whether through age, lack of fitness, or the lack of another to breed with.

In 1796, naturalist and zoologist Georges Cuvier of the National Museum of Natural History in Paris introduced the idea of extinction. He had been puzzled by fossil findings that didn't correspond to any known animal. Cuvier's eye for fossils was so extraordinary he was able to reconstruct a whole mammal skeleton from just a single bone. "Life on this earth has often been disturbed by dreadful events," he said, referring to his belief that a series of natural catastrophes, such as volcanoes, massive floods, and meteor strikes, had wiped out certain species and left others to take their place.

IN THE KNOW

The Zoological Society of London recently released the first known footage of the long-eared jerboa, a rodent which looks like a mouse-sized kangaroo with enormous ears, hopping about in the Gobi desert. The rodent, whose legs are specially adapted for jumping like a kangaroo, is easily recognized by ears that are about a third bigger than its head. The jerboa is threatened by the domestic cat and is listed as endangered on the World Conservation Union's "Red List."

A History of Extinction

Extinction is common, at least over the whole history of evolution, although it was rare before humans dispersed out of Africa. From then on, the rate of extinctions rose dramatically.

While living fossils (species that have survived unchanged for hundreds of millions of years) still exist today, only a thousandth of the species that have ever existed remain. As some single species have become extinct, so mass extinctions have also taken place.

The so-called Cretaceous–Tertiary extinction event—which was perhaps triggered by asteroid impacts or extraordinary volcanic activity—occurred some 65,000,000 years ago and wiped out innumerable species, including, some scientists believe, the dinosaurs.

Some 784 species are known to have become extinct in the current epoch, which began some 10,000 years ago. According to the International Union for the Conservation of Nature and Natural Resources (IUCN), this may be a huge underestimate. What is more, global warming is likely to accelerate the rate of extinctions as habitats change and disappear because of climate change. Only a tiny fraction of species at risk, including rhinos and Bengali tigers, make it onto endangered-species lists, meaning many species become extinct without public notice.

The Ethics of Extinction

The success of the human species has been the cause of a large number of extinctions. While early humans may have driven some species extinct, only relatively recently has the concept of extinction (thanks to George Cuvier) come up, and along with that an ethical debate.

Extinction is generally thought of as being a bad thing, especially where it has been brought about by human activity. But this is not always the case. Tropical-disease experts have suggested bringing about the extinctions of malaria-carrying mosquitoes, and the World Health Organization talks of destroying the last remaining stocks of the deadly smallpox virus, which would be the first ever deliberate extinction of a species.

At the other extreme, cloning has been suggested as a way of reviving extinct species using DNA extracted from fossil bones. Extinct species have yet to be cloned, but the idea was used in the popular 1993 film *Jurassic Park*.

Mammoths were a number of elephant-like mammal species that went extinct between 11,000 and 4,000 years ago. It is thought that the main causes were climate change, as the world warmed up after the last ice age, and overhunting by humans.

Dodos were a flightless relative of the modern pigeon and a native of the island of Mauritius. The dodo moved slowly and nested on the ground, making itself and its eggs vulnerable to the cats, dogs, and rats that Western explorers brought with them. The dodo went extinct in the mid–late seventeenth century.

Passenger pigeons, a type of wild pigeon, were once the most common birds in North America. Vast flocks once darkened the skies, but hunting in the mid–late nineteenth century destroyed the population. The last one died in captivity in 1914.

Thylacines, also known as Tasmanian tigers, were a carnivorous marsupial. The last one died at the Hobart Zoo in Tasmania's capital city in 1936. The tigers' demise came when significant numbers were shot to prevent them from killing livestock. They had vanished earlier from mainland Australia in the face of indigenous hunters and competition from wild dogs.

Looking as far back as the beginning of life itself, this chapter has covered everything from the incredible diversity of insects to the origins of modern humans. Test how much you can remember about life in its many forms.

The Birth of Life on Earth

1. How old is life on Earth?

2. What is the name for the theory that life on Earth was seeded by microbes from space?

Insects and the Diversity of Life

1. What are the three main divisions of an insect's body?

2. What percentage of the world's animal species do insects represent?

   a) *50 percent*   b) *60 percent*
   c) *70 percent*   d) *80 percent*

3. What percentage of the world's biomass do ants and termites combined make up?

   a) *20 percent*   b) *30 percent*
   c) *40 percent*   d) *50 percent*

Beneath the Waves: The Life Aquatic

1. Name the five marine zones.

2. Where is the deepest part of the ocean?

3. True or False: At its deepest point the ocean is deeper than Mount Everest is high.

Reptiles: On Land to Stay

1. What are the four orders of reptiles?

2. True or False: Alligators and caimans can be found only in Africa.

Birds and Life on the Wing

1. All birds can trace their heritage back to a common ancestor. How long ago did it live?

2. The shape of a bird's wings helps it fly because

   a) *the air pressure above it is reduced*
   b) *the air pressure below it is reduced*

3. How far do some sooty shearwaters migrate in a year?

   a) *20,000 miles (16,000 km)*
   b) *30,000 miles (24,000 km)*
   c) *40,000 miles (32,000 km)*
   d) *50,000 miles (40,000 km)*

Mammals: A Class of Their Own

1 What is the world's largest mammal?

2 What is the world's smallest mammal?

3 Name the four classifications of mammals by diet.

Homo Sapiens and the Origins of Us

1 Of what species is the ancient skeleton nicknamed Lucy?

2 True or False: Modern humans (*Homo sapiens*) evolved from Neanderthals.

3 How old is the earliest *Homo sapiens* skeleton known?

   a) *2,000 years*   b) *20,000 years*
   c) *200,000 years*   d) *2,000,000 years*

Charles Darwin and the Story of Evolution

1 During which century did Charles Darwin live?

2 What was the name of the ship upon which Darwin traveled to the Galapagos Islands?

3 What is the full title of Charles Darwin's most famous book?

DNA and Genetics: The Stuff of Life

1 How is the structure of DNA most commonly described?

2 In what year was the structure of DNA published?

The Kingdom of Plants

1 What are the names of the male and female sex organs of plants?

2 The process of photosynthesis converts light energy, water, and carbon dioxide into energy and what by-product?

The Ecological Balancing Act

1 Name the four major links in the food chain.

2 Approximately what proportion of the Earth's land is covered by forest?

Lost Forever: A Guide to Extinction

1 When was the idea of extinction first introduced?

2 In which year did the last passenger pigeon die?

   a) *1814*   b) *1914*
   c) *1941*   d) *It's still alive*

Chapter Four

Exploring the World

Over the course of just a few thousand years, humankind has grown from scattered bands of hunter-gatherers to a global population of billions. Along the way, it has developed language and numbers, formed complex societies, built great cities and monuments, and founded empires—all the while pushing back the frontiers of the unknown. This chapter brings you the story of humankind's intellectual, cultural, and geographical explorations.

Out of Africa: A Guide to Human Migration

From the start, human beings have been on the move. Modern DNA evidence strongly supports the theory, first suggested by Charles Darwin, that humankind originated in Africa. Then about 100,000 years ago, humans and their bipedal predecessors began migrating northward. Thanks to archaeological research, we can now map our distant ancestors' slow, steady spread to all parts of the globe.

Studies of human DNA from today's populations have revealed that modern humans, *Homo sapiens*, arose in Africa between 200,000 and 140,000 years ago. The earliest modern human skulls discovered so far are about 130,000 years old and come from the Omo river basin in Ethiopia.

All the dates that follow can be disputed, but archaeological evidence suggests that early humans first migrated north about 100,000 years ago, and human skulls of that period have been discovered at Qafzeh in Israel. It appears these people either returned to Africa or became extinct, since no sign of further settlement has been found.

The Seminal Group

About 50,000 years ago, the world entered its last great glacial period—a time when sea levels were relatively low and allowed easier human passage between landmasses. At this time, a small population of modern humans left Africa and crossed the Red Sea into Arabia. Genetic evidence suggests that the ancestors of all non-African peoples came from this small group.

Migration down through the Americas is thought to have only taken a few thousand years, with the tip of South America reached some 11,000 years ago.

Subsequent generations moved along the Arabian coast to Iran and from there into the Indian sub-continent. From India, *Homo sapiens* appears to have taken two main migratory routes. One group traveled along the southeast Asian coast, reaching Australia approximately 45,000 years ago. The other group migrated northwest toward Europe.

Coming to America

When the western hemisphere was populated is a matter of debate, but many believe it occurred some 17,000 years ago when a population crossed the Bering Strait from Siberia into Alaska on a land bridge that existed at that time. *Homo sapiens* spread out and displaced rival hominids to become the first global hominid species of all time.

Europe was populated by a migration from India around 45,000 years ago. *Homo sapiens* displaced the existing Neanderthals, although humans took several millenia to reach the whole continent.

The first settlement of America is most likely to have been via a land bridge across the Bering Strait some 17,000 years ago.

Migration through Asia along the coast from the Middle East reached India, a major point of settlement from where further waves of migration originated, both to Europe and Southeast Asia.

The first humans evolved in Africa, and from here they set out to populate the rest of the world in two waves, the latter of which was about 50,000 years ago.

Australia and New Zealand were populated around 45,000 years ago by Aborigines and 1,000 years ago by Polynesians, respectively.

The First Civilizations: Three Giant Leaps

Early humans were hunter-gatherers, always searching for food. Things changed when they discovered how to cultivate the land and domesticate animals: Agriculture required settling down. Settlements became towns, then cities—and around 5000 BCE, some Middle Eastern cities produced the first distinctive cultures we know as civilizations.

The Sumerians

The earliest-known civilization is that of Sumer, dating from about 5000 BCE. The Sumerians built cities in the fertile area between the Tigris and Euphrates rivers in Mesopotamia (modern Iraq). Their most famous city was Ur.

Sumerians lived in houses made of mud bricks, grew crops, and kept domestic animals. Irrigation and the invention of the plow made farming more productive. The stone potter's wheel used by the Sumerians evolved into the wagon wheel. They also invented writing; their pictographs progressed to "cuneiform," a wedge-shaped script. The people believed in many gods and goddesses, and each city had a temple devoted to its patron deity—monumental, stepped-brick towers called "ziggurats."

The Sumerians were ruled by a succession of kings who, when they died, were buried in royal tombs with their servants and possessions. At first, Sumer was divided into a number of independent city states, but around 2330 BCE, the Sumerian cities were conquered and united under the control of Sargon, king of Akkad. This early empire collapsed circa 2193 BCE, to be followed eventually by Babylon as the dominant power in Mesopotamia.

IN THE KNOW

One of the earliest literary works comes from Mesopotamia. The *Epic of Gilgamesh* is a long poem, and its most complete form was preserved on 12 clay tablets. Though there's little historical evidence for his adventures, Gilgamesh was a real king of Uruk, in southern Mesopotamia, during the first half of the third millennium BCE.

The Egyptians

The world's second-oldest civilization arose along the River Nile in Egypt. About 5000 BCE, farming communities began to appear around the banks of the river, and in time these settlements developed into two kingdoms: Upper (Southern) and Lower (Northern) Egypt. Around 3100 BCE, Upper and Lower Egypt were united under the pharaoh Menes.

A succession of dynastic pharaohs ruled Egypt as god-kings for the next 3,000 years. A unified Egypt thrived under dynastic rule, and its culture flourished. The first two ruling dynasties foreshadowed the rich Old Kingdom period of 2700–220 BCE, when the pyramids were built. The last dynasty was the thirteenth, which was toppled by the Persians in 343 BCE after Nectanebo II lost a key battle.

Later occupied by the Macedonians, Egypt saw its influence and power wane. By the death of Cleopatra in 30 BCE, Egypt had fallen under Roman control.

The Indus

Another river civilization emerged in the Indus river valley in what is now Pakistan. Dating from about 2500 BCE, the Indus civilization was dominated by two great cities—Mohenjo-daro and Harappa. Both were built along a similar plan and supported populations of about 40,000 each.

A large citadel of mud and bricks lay to the west of each city and contained public buildings including a public bath and a ventilated granary. Below the citadel lay the town, covering more than a square mile (2.6 sq km). City streets were straight and frequently over 30 feet (9 m) wide. Many houses were built around courtyards and stood two stories tall. The cities had advanced drainage systems: Waste flowed through pipes to sewers under the main streets and then to soak-pits. Such sophisticated drainage was unknown anywhere else until Roman times.

For reasons that are still unclear today, the Indus culture went into decline around 1900 BCE and was eventually overcome by Indo-European invaders, the Aryans, about 200 years later.

Conversation Starter Thousands of small, ornate clay seals, or stamps, discovered in Indus cities bear hieroglyphic writing that has resisted deciphering. Until someone breaks the code, their messages remain one of history's most tantalizing mysteries.

Great Empires of the Ancient World

Civilizations live and expand; empires conquer and rule. The chief characteristic of a great empire is its capacity to control and defend vast territories and diverse populations through strong, central administration. Imperial rule can be ruthless and cruel or benign, but human history thus far teaches that even great empires don't last forever.

In ancient Mesopotamia, the Akkadian empire was succeeded by the Babylonians and the mighty Assyrians. Across the centuries, alliances were formed and broken as powers in the region fought and connived to become top dog. In the end, these early efforts at imperialism gave way to history's first great empire—the Persian.

Persia's Rise

In the ninth century BCE, the Medes, an Indo-European tribe, began entering what is now Iran. Allied with Babylon, they destroyed Nineveh, the Assyrian capital city, in 612 BCE and seized the Parsa, or Persian, region. The tables turned when the Persians, under King Cyrus II, subdued the Medes and proceeded to take territories from Anatolia (in modern Turkey) to Egypt to northern India. The Persians excelled at both warfare and propaganda, terrifying enemies with the prospect of engaging the

IN THE KNOW

In the third century BCE, China was divided, until, in 221 BCE, Ch'eng, king of Ch'in, defeated his rivals and unified the country. When he died, Ch'eng was buried in a tomb surrounded by more than 7,000 life-size terracotta warriors. This army was rediscovered in 1974 and is now a World Heritage site.

Immortals—an elite fighting force of 10,000. After 200 years, however, the Persian empire was broken up in just three years (333–330 BCE) by another determined empire builder, Alexander the Great.

Greece Fights Back

The Greeks and the Greek-speaking Macedonians proved to be Persia's bête noir. Cyrus managed to get a foothold in Ionia in 546 BCE. But when Persia's King Darius attempted to seize Athens in 490 BCE, the Greeks bested his armies in the epic battle of Marathon. Victories at Salamis in 480 BCE and at Plataea a year later secured Greek independence.

Organized into fractious city states, the Greeks were finally united by King Philip II of Macedon. Philip was assassinated before he could carry out his vow to eliminate the Persian threat. That task fell to his son, Alexander, who defeated the Persians and extended his empire around the Mediterranean, from the Spanish coast to Egypt, across all of Mesopotamia and eastward beyond the Indus river valley.

Greece itself wasn't a territorial empire, but it was the intellectual, scientific, and cultural center of the ancient world—an empire of the mind. Though not Greek, Alexander had been tutored by Aristotle, and the young king carried Greek culture and thought wherever his conquering armies went.

The Roman Empire

The Roman empire can be traced to a small, enigmatic but impressively developed outpost of civilization—the Etruscan culture, dating from some time between the tenth and seventh centuries BCE. Etruscan territory eventually included the small city of Rome. The Romans broke away from the Etruscans in the sixth century BCE and later glorified their origins in the myth of Romulus and Remus, twin sons of the war god Mars.

Rome's growth from a minor enclave to the most powerful empire in the history of western civilization, and its transition from republic to imperial dictatorship, is the story of two millennia of warfare, power, wealth, and treachery—all centered in one city. Numerous overlapping causes are put forth to explain the empire's collapse, but its heart—the city of Rome itself—remains as a permanent reminder of the glory of ancient Rome.

The Roman Empire's Eastern offshoot, the Byzantine Empire, lasted until 1453.

Key Players

Alexander the Great *356–323 BCE*	Julius Caesar *100–44 BCE*
Never defeated in battle, Alexander conquered the entire Persian empire in just three years, guiding his troops from atop his black horse Bucephalus. He extended Greek rule as far as the Hydaspes River in India. After 12 years of campaigning, Alexander died of fever at 33, and his empire was divided among his generals. He founded many cities, including Alexandria, in Egypt.	Caesar grasped power during a time of great tumult for the Roman Republic. He conquered large parts of Gaul and invaded Britain twice, also fighting a civil war. Having proclaimed himself dictator for life, he was assassinated in 44 BCE, leading to a power struggle that his adopted son Octavian (later Augustus) won, transforming the republic into an empire.

Great Civilizations of Ancient America

Early humans most likely arrived in the Americas via a Bering Strait land bridge that once connected far northeastern Asia to what is now Alaska. In search of food and warmth, they migrated southward, populating two continents and creating flourishing pre-Columbian civilizations in Mesoamerica (the mid-latitudes) and South America.

The Olmecs

The earliest-known civilization in the Americas was that of the Olmecs, who lived in the tropical lowlands around the Gulf of Mexico from around 1200–400 BCE. The Olmecs developed both a writing and a numerical system. Their complex political organization was based on a class system that included a priesthood. The Olmecs produced a wealth of stonework, ranging from small jade axe-heads to colossal statues of their gods. One of the main Olmec centers was at La Venta.

The Mayans

At its height, the Mayan empire spread from the Yucatan Peninsula and southern Mexico through northern Central America, including modern-day Guatemala, Belize, El Salvador, and parts of Honduras. Although the Mayan culture existed in various forms circa 1800–1000 BCE, the Classic period lasted from about 300 to 900 CE. During this time, the Mayans produced works of both artistic and intellectual magnificence. Great stepped-pyramid temples, dedicated to the Mayan gods, at Palenque, Tikal, and Copan are testaments to Mayan architectural and organizational skills. The Mayans had a sophisticated system of hieroglyphic writing and were also expert mathematicians, incorporating the concept of zero and building on the Olmec tradition of calculating in

In Fact...

Animals were very important to Mesoamerican civilizations.

- The jaguar was a symbol of power and strength, and feline motifs can be found on many artifacts. The Mayans thought the jaguar was a link between the living and the dead, while elite Aztec warriors were known as Jaguar knights.

- Quetzalcoatl, the Aztec creator god, is represented as a plumed serpent.

- Sacrifices of small animals such as chickens were often used in religious rituals, and human sacrifice was practiced by the Aztecs and Incas.

units of 20. The Mayan's 365-day solar calendar is evidence enough of their astute astronomical observations.

Religion was very important to Mayan culture. Ceremonial life was associated with the cycles of nature and the planets, and the priests used a separate 260-day calendar to schedule many of their rituals. Human sacrifice was part of the culture and, as period artwork shows, was carried out by a priest cutting open a person's chest and removing the still-beating heart. The Mayans worshipped many different gods, but the Maize God was one of the most important. For unknown reasons, the great Mayan centers went into decline in the ninth century and were abandoned shortly afterward.

Machu Picchu, some 8,000 feet (2,400 m) high in the Peruvian Andes, is the best-preserved ancient South American site. Its original Incan use still puzzles historians and anthropologists.

The Aztecs and the Incas

In the sixteenth century, the Americas were home to two mighty civilizations. Originally from the North, the Aztec tribe founded their capital city, Tenochtitlán, on a swampy island in Lake Texcoco (near modern-day Mexico City) in 1325 CE. A century later, the Incas embarked on a campaign of conquest farther down the Pacific Coast.

Both civilizations practiced ritual sacrifice, and the Aztecs believed that the gods, in particular the Sun God Huitzilopochtli, required regular offerings of blood to ensure the continuation of the world. On one occasion, 20,000 people were sacrificed over a four-day period to celebrate the consecration of a new temple.

When the Spanish conquistador Hernando Cortés arrived on the shores of Mexico in 1519, many Aztecs believed him to be a returning god, and he was welcomed by the emperor Montezuma. Cortés, however, put the emperor under arrest and he was subsequently killed by Spanish troops. Within two years of the Spanish landing, the Aztec empire had disintegrated.

The short-lived Incan empire, covering most of western South America, developed in the early 1400s on the ruins of earlier cultures, including the mysterious Chavin people. The Incas' gold-sheathed architecture and solid gold statuary and ornaments were more than a temptation for the Spanish conquistadors, who enslaved the native people and plundered the empire's treasure. The last Incan stronghold fell in 1572.

Ancient Trade Routes: The Road to Riches

Cinnamon sprinkled on a latte, the pure silk in a blouse . . . It's hard to imagine early navigators taking many months to travel thousands of miles and risking attack by pirates to acquire such indulgences. But that is the history of trade in the ancient world.

Prehistoric peoples traded things they had for things they desired. Along with agriculture came the development of marketplaces. Imperial rulers fostered trade as a means of increasing tax revenues and spreading their culture. The invention of wheeled carts made it possible to travel greater distances in search of luxuries, and people began to follow in the literal tracks of others, developing the first great trade routes.

The Silk Road

The name "Silk Road" actually applies to several different routes that took traders from China to Central Asia, Northern India, Parthia in Mesopotamia, and the Roman empire. Some 4,000 miles (6,440 km) long, it passed through the vast mountain ranges, forests, and deserts between China and the West.

Caravans from the West carried gold and other valuable metals as well as precious stones and glass to trade for Chinese silk, porcelain, jade, and bronze items. These valuable goods were exchanged and bartered along the way, changing hands many times before reaching their final destination. Ideas and beliefs also spread from region to region, notably Buddhism, which spread from India into China. Marco Polo followed the Silk Road to China and later thrilled Europe with his accounts.

The Spice Route

Spices have been traded for thousands of years. Ancient Egyptian hieroglyphs tell of the trade in spices, which were so valuable that they were used in place of money and were seen as the greatest of gifts. The Queen of Sheba once presented King Solomon

Key Player

Chang Ch'ien
157–87 BCE

During the Han dynasty China was troubled by raiding tribes. In 138 BCE Chang Ch'ien, commander of the imperial guards, volunteered to go in search of new alliances. Captured and held for 10 years, he eventually escaped to journey as far as Bactria, in modern-day Afghanistan, passing through Ferghana (Turkistan) on the way. His journey lasted 13 years, and he returned to China with a wealth of knowledge. To many, he is the father of the Silk Road.

with "twenty talents of gold and spices of very great store."

For many centuries, Arabs controlled the trade between the East and the Mediterranean, monopolizing trade by refusing to reveal their sources and exaggerating the difficulty of obtaining their aromatic goods. The earliest sea spice route was probably from the East Indies across the Indian Ocean, and then either north to the Persian Gulf or across the Arabian Sea to the Red Sea. From these destinations, spices went to Babylon and on to Europe.

The Trans-Saharan Route

Gold attracted the attention of explorers and traders throughout history. Before the discovery of the New World in the fifteenth century, roughly two-thirds of the gold circulating in the Mediterranean came from West Africa. Trade between Africa and the Mediterranean was initiated by the Berber peoples of the desert, who crossed the Sahara with their camel trains. The Greek historian Herodotus (c. 485–425 BCE) mentions the trans-Saharan trade routes in his writings.

Before the Muslim conquest of North Africa in the late seventh century, trans-Saharan trade was sporadic. The expansion of Islam throughout the world increased the demand for gold, and the Arabs turned increasingly to West Africa, trading salt and other goods for the precious metal.

Ancient trading routes included the Silk Road, the spice route over land and sea, and the trans-Saharan route.

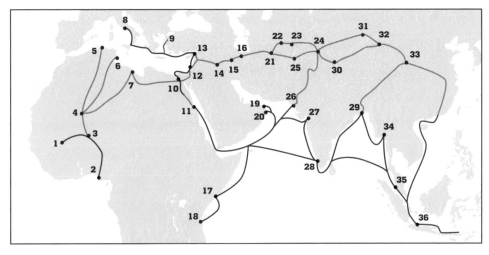

1 Mali	**7** Tripoli	**13** Antioch	**19** Muscat	**25** Bactra	**31** Tupan
2 Niger River	**8** Rome	**14** Baghdad	**20** Sur	**26** Barbaricon	**32** Dunhuang
3 Timbuktu	**9** Constantinople	**15** Hamadan	**21** Merv	**27** Barigaza	**33** Lanzhou
4 Oulata	**10** Alexandria	**16** Rey	**22** Bukhara	**28** Muzirio	**34** Rangoon
5 Algiers	**11** Berenike	**17** Malindi	**23** Samarkand	**29** Calcutta	**35** Malacca
6 Tunis	**12** Tyre	**18** Mombasa	**24** Kashgar	**30** Hotan	**36** Java

The Renaissance: A Rebirth in Europe

Renaissance means "rebirth." But as applied to what happened in Europe beginning in the fourteenth century, the Renaissance was more a "rediscovery" of ancient Greek and Roman culture and thought that spurred a period of incredible richness in the arts, new directions in philosophy and religion, and the beginnings of modern science.

The Renaissance is one of very few historical periods that named itself, appropriate for an age characterized by self-awareness. There are no specific dates for the start of the Renaissance, a time of transition between the Middle Ages and the modern age when European scholars rediscovered the works of classical writers such as Plato, Aristotle, and Ptolemy in their quest for self-improvement and read the ancient texts in classical Latin or Greek.

They also turned to the Arab world, acquiring works by Muslim scientists and philosophers such as Persian physician Avicenna and the Spanish Muslim Averroes, who integrated Islamic beliefs with the classical philosophies of Aristotle and Plato.

Key Player

Niccolò Machiavelli
1469–1527

A Florentine diplomat, historian, and political philosopher, Machiavelli's most famous work is *Il Principe* (The Prince). He wrote that a ruler should always act in the best interests of the state, even if that means using force or deceit, giving rise to the term Machiavellian.

A Change of Philosophy

One of the most significant advances in the sciences was the development of a new attitude toward the acquisition of knowledge itself. The scientific method sought to understand the world through empirical observation and experiment and to provide mechanistic explanations. Considerable progress was made in such fields as astronomy, physics, and anatomy, but science soon came into conflict with the Roman Catholic Church.

When Copernicus, on the basis of his observations, proposed that the Sun, and not the Earth, was the point about which the planets revolved, the Church banned his book. Galileo, who demonstrated that the planets are held in their orbits by physical laws and not by angels, spent the last eight years of his life under house arrest. Such ideas were eventually accepted by the scientific community, nonetheless, largely through the power of the recently invented printing press.

A New Religion?

Although many artistic works of the Renaissance were dedicated to the glory of God, the approach to religion changes, with more emphasis given to life on Earth and less to the hereafter. A new humanistic approach, in which "the genius of man . . . the unique and extraordinary ability of the human mind" (Giannozzo Manetti, fifteenth-century Florentine politician and scholar) carried more weight than divine revelation, was also influential and laid the groundwork for the Enlightenment—the eighteenth-century movement that advocated reason as the ultimate authority.

The Cradle of the Renaissance

The exceptional political makeup of fourteenth-century Italy contributed to the cultural flowering that marked the Renaissance. At the time, Italy did not exist as a single political entity but was made up of several self-governing regions, including wealthy city states such as Venice, Genoa, Pisa, Florence, and Milan.

Citizens from these great centers enjoyed more intellectual and political freedom than those of other European countries, and original thought was encouraged rather than feared. The cities were also great trading centers, and traveling merchants brought new ideas from around the world, stimulating discussion and debate.

Florence is generally considered the birthplace of Renaissance art, and the patronage of the wealthy Medici family may have been a decisive factor. The Medicis commissioned many works of art to celebrate their wealth and importance.

Global Explorations by Land and Sea

Today, we tend to throw around the word "global" casually: global trade, the global economy, and global communication. It's hard for us to imagine a time when people in one part of the world had no concept of people existing elsewhere. But humans are born travelers, with a yen to explore the unknown.

Into the East

Marco Polo (1254–1324) came from a Venetian family of merchants and explorers. In the thirteenth century, Genghis Khan had established the vast Mongol empire, bringing peace to the region and allowing trade between the Far East and Europe. Marco Polo's father Niccolò and uncle Maffeo were among the first Europeans to take advantage of the new trade opportunities. In 1260, they set off from Venice to travel the Silk Road to China, where they were befriended by Kublai Khan, the Mongol emperor.

The Polo brothers made a second journey in 1271, taking 17-year-old Marco. On the three-and-a-half year journey, they passed through the Hindu Kush and crossed the Gobi desert before finally reaching Xanadu, the summer palace of Kublai Khan. Marco's capacity for colorful storytelling endeared him to the emperor, and young

Voyages of rediscovery by Marco Polo, Columbus, and Magellan served to establish contact between the disparate civilizations of the world.

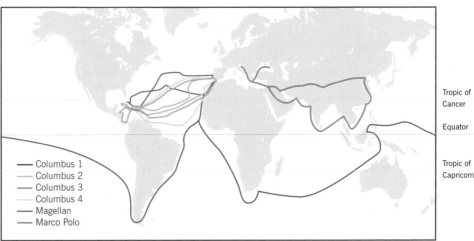

Tropic of Cancer

Equator

Tropic of Capricorn

— Columbus 1
— Columbus 2
— Columbus 3
— Columbus 4
— Magellan
— Marco Polo

Polo spent the next 17 years in China in his service, traveling throughout the empire. Returning to Venice, he wrote *Il Milione*, a popular and controversial account of his experiences.

The New World

Christopher Columbus (c. 1451–1506) was born in Genoa in Italy. As a seafaring trader based in Lisbon, he nurtured the idea of sailing west to China. Like most Europeans at the time, Columbus knew the world was round, though he badly miscalculated the distance and didn't anticipate that a "New World" lay between Europe and the fabled Far East.

Financed by the Spanish Crown, Columbus set off on the first of his four voyages across the Atlantic on August 3, 1492. On October 12, Columbus and his crew landed on an island he named San Salvador. He also explored the northern coasts of Cuba and Hispaniola, leaving behind some of his crew to found the settlement of La Navidad in present-day Haiti.

On his second voyage (1493–1496), Columbus explored more islands including Dominica, Guadaloupe, Antigua, and Jamaica; founded additional settlements in Hispaniola; and explored the southern coast of Cuba, turning back before he realized that it was an island. On his third voyage (1498–1500), Columbus reached mainland South America for the first time and also explored the island of Trinidad. On his final voyage (1502–1504), Columbus visited Central America.

Columbus died believing he had reached Asia. The sea route remained undiscovered until Magellan's travels, though Columbus's voyages began the Spanish colonization of the New World.

The Whole Way Round

Portuguese-born Ferdinand Magellan (1480–1521) was employed by the Spanish Crown to find a westward route to the Spice Islands (now the Moluccas). Portuguese adventurers already knew a route via Africa, but a treaty forbade the Spanish to use it.

In 1519, Magellan set sail from Spain with a fleet of five ships and a crew of 260 men. A mutiny and a shipwreck did not prevent Magellan seeking the elusive strait to Asia, and on November 28, 1520, the fleet's three remaining ships reached the Pacific, via the strait now named after Magellan.

Magellan was killed the following year during a tribal war on the island of Mactan in the Philippines—unknown to the West until Magellan's voyage. Of the original fleet of five, only the *Victoria* returned to Spain. Just 18 men survived to conclude the first voyage around the world.

IN THE KNOW

Despite a meticulously kept log, on their return to Spain the crew of Magellan's ship *Victoria* found that their records were off by a day. Their discovery established the need for an International Date Line. This line, with some variations, is the 180° line of longitude. To the east of this line, the date is always one day ahead of the date to the west.

Three Great Modern Revolutions

For most of history, wars were fought soldier-to-soldier. Despite occasional peasant and slave uprisings, it wasn't until the American Revolution that ordinary people rose up against a powerful state and won their freedom. A few years later, the French Revolution demonstrated that, like all warfare, "people's wars" have unintended consequences.

The French Revolution

In late eighteenth-century France, the cost of continuing unrest and three wars had brought the country to the verge of bankruptcy, taxation had increased, and a succession of bad harvests had caused famine. But these severe problems didn't faze King Louis XVI and his wife, Marie Antoinette. In 1789, the lack of democratic reform prompted even more unrest among the lower and middle classes, culminating in the storming of the Bastille prison on July 14 in an effort to steal the gunpowder and firearms stored there. The King and Marie Antoinette tried to flee but were captured. In 1793, the royals were guillotined, the monarchy was abolished, and France became a republic.

Extremists gradually seized control, and even a hint of counter-revolutionary behavior brought instant retribution. During a two-year "Reign of Terror," nearly 18,000 people were executed and thousands imprisoned. A new legislature, the *Directoire*, was set up to govern, and it lasted until Napoleon Bonaparte took power in 1799.

The Russian Revolution

Russia in the early twentieth century was ruled by unpopular Tsar Nicholas II. Social and economic conditions were wretched, and protests against bread shortages broke out in St. Petersburg in March 1917. The tsar dispatched his troops to restore order, but many soldiers mutinied. Civil authority soon collapsed, and the tsar abdicated. Nicholas, his wife, and children were murdered three months later.

A moderate provisional government assumed power but was challenged by the Soviets, who launched a second revolution in 1917 that led to the formation of the communist Soviet Union.

IN THE KNOW

Although earlier versions had existed, the guillotine will always be inextricably linked to its use during the French Revolution. It takes its name from Dr. Joseph-Ignace Guillotin, who proposed this grisly device as being more humane than existing methods of execution.

Key Players

M. Robespierre	Vladimir Lenin	Mao Zedong
1758–1794	*1870–1924*	*1893–1976*
Maximilien Robespierre was a member of the so-called Committee of Public Safety during the French Revolution. Although still surrounded by controversy, he is widely held to be responsible for much of the slaughter that ensued; however, Robespierre—like the victims of his policies—met the guillotine in July 1794, and his "Reign of Terror" came to an end.	The return of Vladimir Ilyich Lenin to Russia from exile in Switzerland in April 1917 accelerated the downfall of the provisional government that had replaced Tsar Nicholas II. Lenin's call for "all power to the Soviets" helped to rally support for his Bolshevik Party. Following the revolution, he became the leader of Russia, and then in 1922 of the Soviet Union.	By fall 1934, nationalist troops had cornered the Communists, who were forced to retreat. Under the leadership of Mao, some 100,000 people began the 8,000-mile (12,500-km) "Long March" to Yunan in Shaanxi Province. The route passed through treacherous terrain and only about 20,000 survived, but the journey cemented Mao's authority as a great leader.

The Chinese Revolution

In the early 1920s, the KMT (Chinese Nationalist Party) formed an alliance with the Communist Party (CCP) to end the rule of warlords in the North. However, beset by differences, the alliance collapsed, and in 1927 hundreds of Communists were executed, forcing the survivors to flee to the countryside.

During the Sino-Japanese war (1937–1945) the KMT and Communists reluctantly joined forces, but civil war between the two parties broke out again in 1946. By 1949 the Communists had won. Their leader Mao Zedong proclaimed the People's Republic of China with Beijing as its capital, and mainland China became a Communist nation.

The Seven "New" Wonders of the World

Choosing alternative lists of the Seven Wonders is a fun pursuit. Now it seems that an international poll taken in 2007 has yielded a list that may take hold. The Swiss-based New 7 Wonders Foundation tallied more than 100 million electronic votes, but the contest results remain controversial: Some countries mobilized people to vote repeatedly.

Chichén Itzá

Chichén Itzá is a temple city of the Mayan civilization, located on the Yucatan peninsula in Mexico. Around 987 CE, the Toltec king Quetzalcoatl from central Mexico made it his capital. The large step-pyramid of Kukulcan, with its ornate sculptures of plumed serpents, is one of the most impressive structures on the site, while a deep well reminds visitors of the price paid to appease the gods—it was used for human sacrifice.

Machu Picchu

The splendid Incan city of Machu Picchu (Old Mountain) lies 7,710 feet (2,350 m) above sea level, deep in the Amazonian forest above the Urubamba Valley in Peru. It was built around 1440 CE for the Incan Emperor Pachacútec Yupanqui but abandoned less than a century later, probably due to a smallpox outbreak. It remained a "lost city" until rediscovered in 1911 by U.S. archaeologist Hiram Bingham. Whatever its purpose, Machu Picchu is an extraordinary legacy of the Incan civilization.

Christ the Redeemer Statue

The *Christ the Redeemer* statue overlooking Rio de Janeiro's harbor is the city's iconic image. Atop Corcovado Mountain, which juts up from Brazil's Tijuca Forest National Park, the 130-foot (40-m) tall white statue of Christ towers above the city with arms spread wide in benediction. It took nine years to sculpt and place the statue, which opened to the public on October 12, 1931.

Colosseum

The Colosseum is an elliptical amphitheater in the center of Rome. Its construction began in 72 CE under the orders of Vespasian, and it was the largest stadium ever built in the Roman Empire. Many gladiatorial contests and other public spectacles were staged in front of capacity crowds of 50,000. The last recorded gladiatorial contest took place in 404 CE, but hunts were held until 523.

Petra

The city of Petra is located in the valley of Wadi 'Araba in Jordan, about 50 miles (80 km) south of the Dead Sea. It is approached via a narrow gorge and remained hidden to the Western world until Swiss explorer Johann Ludwig Burckhardt visited it in 1812. Described as "a rose-red city half as old as time," Petra is enclosed by rose-colored mountains, into which are carved many amazing buildings.

The Great Wall of China

The Great Wall built was built by the Ming dynasty to defend against invading Mongol tribes to China's north. At its peak, over 1,000,000 men guarded it. Work on the Ming Wall (the most famous wall of an older defense system) ended in the seventeenth century. Crossing mountains and deserts, it is said to have once run for 4,163 miles (6,700 km).

Taj Mahal

Built in Agra, India, by Mughal Emperor Shah Jahan as a mausoleum for his favorite wife, the Taj Mahal blended both Hindu and Muslim architectural styles. It took some 20,000 laborers 18 years (1630–1648 CE) to finish the white marble structure.

Conversation Starter Compare the new Seven Wonders with the ancient originals chosen some 2,500 years ago: Egypt's Great Pyramid at Giza (the only survivor) and Lighthouse at Alexandria; Greece's statue of Zeus on Mount Olympus and the Colossus of Rhodes; Turkey's Temple at Artemis; Persia's Mausoleum of Halicarnassus; and the Hanging Gardens of Babylon.

Around 50,000 years ago, humans set out from Africa to discover the globe and to populate it. All over the world a familiar pattern played itself out, as civilizations and empires came and went. But can you remember who, where, when, and why?

Out of Africa: A Guide to Human Migration

1 Where are the oldest modern human skulls to be found?

2 When is it thought that the first modern humans reached the Americas?

    a) *7,000 years ago*
    b) *17,000 years ago*
    c) *70,000 years ago*
    d) *700,000 years ago*

The First Civilizations: Three Giant Leaps

1 What is the earliest-known civilization?

2 What was the name of the pharaoh who united all of Egypt?

3 What were the names of the two great cities of the Indus civilization?

Great Empires of the Ancient World

1 Alexander the Great was not Greek. Where was he from?

2 Three great victories, one in 490 BCE and two in 480 BCE, secured Greek independence in the face of a Persian invasion. Where were they?

3 Who are the mythical founders of Rome?

Great Civilizations of Ancient America

1 Which is the earliest-known civilization of the ancient Americas?

    a) *the Aztecs*   b) *the Incas*
    c) *the Mayans*   d) *the Olmecs*

2 What form does Quetzalcoatl, the Aztec creator god, take?

3 In which mountain range will you find the ancient city Machu Picchu?

Ancient Trade Routes: The Road to Riches

1 How long was the Silk Road?

    a) *1,000 miles (1,610 km)*
    b) *2,000 miles (3,220 km)*
    c) *3,000 miles (4,830 km)*
    d) *4,000 miles (6,440 km)*

② Name the man who is sometimes known as the "father of the Silk Road."

③ Demand for which commodity was the driving force behind the establishment of the trans-Saharan trade route?

The Renaissance: A Rebirth in Europe

① Where is considered the birthplace of Renaissance art?

② Name the wealthy family whose patronage of the arts may have helped bring about the renaissance.

③ What is the title, in English, of Niccolò Machiavelli's most famous work?

    a) *The Princess*   b) *The Prince*
    c) *The Queen*   d) *The King*

④ What observation—controversial at the time—did the astronomer Copernicus make?

Global Explorations by Land and Sea

① How old was Marco Polo when his father and uncle took him across Asia?

    a) *7*   b) *12*
    c) *17*   d) *22*

② True or False: Ferdinand Magellan was the first man to go around the globe.

③ Name the only ship to survive of the five that originally set out on Magellan's voyage.

④ At what line of longitude, with some exceptions, is the International Date Line?

Three Great Modern Revolutions

① Who was the king at the start of the French Revolution?

    a) *Louis XIV*   b) *Louis XV*
    c) *Louis XVI*   d) *Louis XVII*

② In which city did the protest riots that triggered the Russian revolution in 1917 break out?

    a) *Ekaterinburg*   b) *Moscow*
    c) *St. Petersburg*   d) *Volgograd*

③ With which party did the Chinese Communist party fight a civil war?

The Seven "New" Wonders of the World

① In which South American city is the statue of *Christ the Redeemer*?

    a) *Buenos Aries*   b) *Montevideo*
    c) *Rio de Janeiro*   d) *São Paulo*

② Name the city that Swiss explorer Johann Ludwig Burckhardt called "a rose-red city half as old as time."

③ In which country is Chichén Itzá?

Chapter Five

Invention and Discovery

The course of human history is marked by amazing

inventions and evolving technologies. From the birth

of agriculture and the civilizations that followed,

history has been one long march of progress—

despite taking the occasional step backward.

This chapter tells the story of innovations from the

ancient (writing, mathematics) to the futuristic

(the International Space Station, nuclear power),

concisely reviewing their impact on the world

of today and tomorrow.

Agriculture: The Endless Quest for Food

Agriculture probably arose from the gathering part of hunting and gathering. Prehistoric humans most likely observed that edible plants and berries reappeared at certain places and times. Seasonally, humans would return to these sites for "intensive gathering," gradually learning to increase harvests by domesticating native plants.

No one knows precisely when or where farming began, though organized land cultivation was under way in the Fertile Crescent 6,000–7,000 years ago. It appears that different groups of people "invented" agriculture independently. Much that we know of early farming comes from archaeological studies of prehistoric villages, but this record is thin. Yet it has been found that once people could grow food, they began to develop tools and techniques for processing and storage. Domesticating animals for food, transport, and other uses probably predated farming.

The March of Technology

Written records give a better picture of farming in classical Greece and Rome. Roman farmers used plows, diggers, cutters, scythes, rakes, shovels, spiked harrows, and axes. They composted animal, human, and plant waste for fertilizer and rotated crops to increase productivity. The Middle Ages saw the introduction of the wheeled plow and open-field farming. The Chinese invented the horse collar, enabling horses to do heavier pulling. Early windmills facilitated grinding of grain. Irrigation and drainage were improved. The Industrial Revolution brought new means of powering farm machinery; a steam-driven tractor appeared in 1862, and the first gas tractor in 1892.

The most bitterly debated technological advance of the last century was the use of chemical pesticides, beginning with DDT. Using chemicals to eliminate pests and diseases seemed to promise an end to farming's biggest problem. But it was soon observed

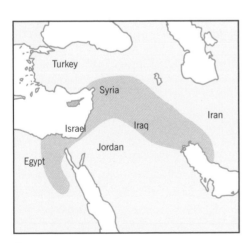

The Fertile Crescent was the area of the Middle East where agriculture first began. It covers parts of what we now know as Iran, Iraq, Israel, Syria, Jordan, Egypt, and Turkey.

that certain insects developed resistance, requiring stronger, more frequent applications. Noted biologist Rachel Carson warned of the effects of pesticides on humans and wildlife in her influential 1962 book *Silent Spring*. DDT has been banned in some countries but is still used in many parts of the world today.

The Green Revolution

In 1944, a joint project of the Rockefeller Foundation and the government of Mexico showed that agricultural production could be increased by simultaneously introducing new food plants and modern farming methods. Using a high-yield variety of dwarf spring wheat, the project had amazing results. In only 10 years, Mexico went from importing half of its wheat to total self-sufficiency.

The Mexican approach, translated to other areas of the world, has been mostly successful; agriculture now supplies enough food to meet global needs. But this Green Revolution also brings social and environmental problems. Food distribution among the rich and the poor is still inequitable.

Key Player

Norman Borlaug
b. 1914

Born in Iowa, Borlaug was one of the lead scientists on the Mexico project and developed the strain of high-yield dwarf spring wheat that sparked the Green Revolution. He was awarded the Nobel Peace Prize in 1970, though later resistance to high-yield agriculture on the part of financial backers made it difficult to fund new projects in Africa, which Borlaug had undertaken with President Jimmy Carter.

Environmental damage caused by intensive farming methods and continued use of pesticides and organic and inorganic fertilizers can have destructive consequences for land, water, and air. The question today is how long agriculture, and the environment as a whole, can continue to sustain growing populations.

New Old Ideas

In the United States, Europe, and other parts of the world, efforts to return to more traditional agricultural practices are gaining strength in wealthier countries, where consumers can afford organic products. Organic farming requires more labor and is less productive but avoids harmful pesticides, artificial fertilizers, food engineering (gene modification), and land use that depletes the soil.

Purchasing locally grown foods in season is another method to decrease the impact of intense, or industrial, agriculture. Buying from local farms, supporters say, reduces the enormous energy requirements of intensive farming and global transportation of foodstuffs, and is found to work equally well in wealthy and poor regions.

The Written Word and the Printed Page

The written word was crucial to the development of civilization. The capacity to create a repository of knowledge has assured the progress of humankind as generation after generation builds on the foundations laid down by its predecessors.

The earliest printed book was the *Diamond Sutra* produced in China in 868 CE, although printing had started long before that time. The earliest writing was etched into clay tablets with a chisel or stylus (a sharpened writing instrument) or into stone, wood, or bone. Paper first appeared as papyrus, made by the Egyptians from the stems of the eponymous grasslike plant, then later as untanned animal skins the Greeks called parchment, and finally as the paper we know today, invented in China in about 10 CE.

The Gutenberg Press revolutionized printing, first in Europe and then in the wider world.

Gutenberg and Caxton

In 1450, Johannes Gutenberg invented the printing press, with moveable type. The Gutenberg press made printing much cheaper and more accessible. William Caxton (c. 1422–1492), the first English printer and a translator and importer of books into England, was close to Margaret, the duchess of Burgundy, sister of the English king Edward IV. She became one of his most important patrons and encouraged his translation of *The Recuyell of the Histories of Troye* from French into English. In the early 1470s, Caxton spent time in Cologne learning the art of

Writing

The ancient Egyptians are believed to have invented one of the first organized systems of writing c. 3400 BCE. They wrote on papyrus (a mat of reed fibers) using a reed as a pen. Later, the end of the reed was made into a primitive nib by splitting it to channel the ink.

Parchment

Parchment, a fine leather "paper," was introduced in 2500 BCE and was easier to write on with quill pens made from long feathers.

The pencil

The first graphite pencils were made in England's Lake District in 1564. Conrad Gesner, a Swiss-German naturalist, thought about creating a wooden holder, but it was not until 1705 that the French chemist Nicolas Conte developed the process used to make today's pencils.

printing. He traveled to Bruges in 1472, where he and Colard Mansion, a Flemish calligrapher, set up a press. In 1476, Caxton returned to London and established the first printing press in England. Caxton's own translation of *The Recuyell of the Histories of Troye* was the first book printed in English, and he printed more than a hundred books in all, including Chaucer's famous *Canterbury Tales*.

The Newspaper

The first English-language daily newspaper, *The Daily Courant*, appeared in London in 1702. The next big development in printing came in 1886 when Ottmar Mergenthaler invented the linotype composing machine, followed by the invention of silkscreen printing by Samuel Simon in 1907. Silk fabric was originally used as a printing screen in this process, in which an impermeable stencil transfers words onto the screen. Since the 1940s, polyester has superseded silk as the screen.

IN THE KNOW

The production of modern books, including the one you're reading now, relies almost entirely on computer technology. Written with word-processing software, books are edited, designed, and illustrated with the aid of a variety of specialized software programs. They're then sent to a "repro house," which prepares digital files and color references that are finally sent to a printer.

Modern Printing

Today's most common commercial printing processes are lithography and offset lithography, both based on the fact that oil and water don't mix. Invented in Bohemia in 1796, lithography involves chemically etching an image onto a metal or plastic plate, then coating areas to be printed in an oil-based substance and other areas with water-based material; oily ink is repelled by the water. In offset lithography, the inked image is first transferred to a rubber blanket, then printed.

Today's newspapers and many large-circulation magazines are printed by high-speed web offset presses onto huge continuous rolls of paper run over a series of cylinders.

Used for small projects, digital printing doesn't require any plates; inks are transferred directly to paper. Colors are applied in one step, not the multiple runs required by offset printing.

The fountain pen	The typewriter	The word processor
Lewis Waterman produced the first practical fountain pen in 1884, although there had been prototype pens in use since two or three decades before.	The first typewriters were produced around the same time as the fountain pen, and they gradually changed the way writers worked, allowing for the revision of work through a primitive form of cutting and pasting.	It was the invention of the word processor in the late 1970s and then the appearance of the now ubiquitous Microsoft Word software in 1983 that transformed writing into electronic form.

Mathematics: One Language for All

Human beings have been tallying things up for ages, from the number of animals in a herd counted on the fingertips of prehistoric people to the billions of computations mastered in nanoseconds by high-speed computers today.

For as long as humanity can remember, numbers have been a second language—a universal one spoken by people in every part of the world. Mathematics, a word derived from the Greek *mathema*, meaning learning, study, or science, relies on the principles of logic to reach conclusions and devise systems. Math is part of all our lives, whether we're following a cake recipe or pondering the perfect ratios of a right triangle.

Nothing New

Mathematical phenomena have fascinated people throughout the ages. A major development came around 3000 BCE, when Egyptians developed the very decimal system that made the value of pi so difficult to pin down. Around 2100 BCE, the Babylonians put a system in place that used the number 60 as a base. We use it today to divide time: 60 seconds to a minute and 60 minutes to the hour.

The Greek philosopher Pythagoras came along around 550 BCE to define a right triangle—that is, the sum of the squares of the two sides must be the same as the square of the hypotenuse.

Pythagoras thought that whole numbers, such as minus 4 or plus 2, were the be-all to understanding how both math and the world worked. But a century and a half later the Greeks would find that some numbers—the so-called irrational ones—could not be expressed as a ratio of two whole numbers.

Euclid, a towering figure in mathematics and author of *The Elements*, arrived on the scene around 300 BCE to devise geometry, a system defining how different figures and shapes relate to one another in space.

Pi, Number with No End

About a hundred years later, another Greek, named Archimedes, discovered a constant without end. He formed 96 different sides into the approximate shape of a circle and compared the circumference to the diameter.

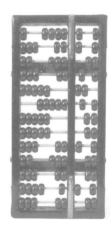

An abacus is an age-old counting device in which beads are moved on rods held by a frame.

Thus came the number known as pi—a source of fascination because a circle's circumference is always the same as the length of the circle's diameter time pi.

The pi number, though, is never exact. It's around 3.14159, and it keeps going and going to the right of the decimal point into infinity. Modern computers have stretched pi out for a quadrillion digits to confirm something else about pi: The numeral patterns on the right side of the decimal point never repeat themselves.

A Bead on Decimals

Advances in mathematics were hardly confined to Greece. In the first century BCE, the Chinese devised a decimal system of their own. They used sticks, or counting rods, and beads arrayed on a frame device called an abacus. By moving the beads on the abacus, one could quickly count in decimal divisions such as ones, tens, hundreds, thousands and so on.

Around 825 BCE, the Arabs popularized our modern numerical system of zero through nine and advanced the fields of algebra, in which letters stand for unknown

Key Player

Leonardo Fibonacci
c. 1170–c. 1250

Leonardo Fibonacci of Pisa, Italy, was called the greatest mathematician of the Middle Ages. His *Liber Abaci* introduced the Arabic number system to Europe around 1202. In his famous sequence (0, 1, 1, 2, 3, 5, 8 and so on), the two previous numbers add up to the next one. Above 2, dividing any number in the series by its predecessor (as in 8 ÷ 5) invariably yields something around 1.6, the "golden ratio" found throughout nature.

numbers in equations. They also gave us trigonometry, the study of right triangles and how the measures of their sides and angles relate.

Later, in France in 1637, René Descartes put forth the notion that math was an ideal model for the process of reasoning. And by the 1660s, Sir Isaac Newton had invented calculus, a way to figure the rates at which different quantities change. Gottfried Wilhelm Liebniz, a German philosopher and mathematician, contributed mightily to the development of calculus a decade later.

Something New

By the 1960s, educators, especially in the United States, were veering away from drilling multiplication tables into students and encouraging them instead to embrace the broad concepts of such thinkers as Euclid and Descartes. This so-called new math has bred a modern generation of mathematicians adept at complex tasks—among them, using actuarial tables to design insurance policies and programming computers to make them work as efficiently as possible for vastly different kinds of projects.

The Fight for Life: A History of Medicine

Today's array of medicines can be bewildering, but the modern understanding of the body and what ails it is surprisingly newfound. With the exception of discoveries such as the circulation of the blood by William Harvey in the seventeenth century, medicine did not really have much of a scientific footing until about 150 years ago.

In the nineteenth century, many believed the cause of major diseases was "miasma" or "bad air." The standard treatment, therefore, was to burn huge bonfires to cleanse the air. However, social reformers began to campaign for piped water, drains, and proper sewage disposal—changes that eventually made a big contribution toward cutting the death toll from cholera and many other infectious diseases.

The Study of Disease

English physician John Snow (1813–1858) first suggested that contaminated water, rather than bad air, caused cholera. An investigation he carried out in London traced one outbreak to a contaminated water pump. Snow was also a believer in the germ theory of disease put forward by French chemist Louis Pasteur (1822–1895) and German scientist Robert Koch (1843–1910).

The twentieth century saw further advances in biochemistry, microbiology, and the understanding of disease. Antibiotics, antidepressants, statins, and myriad other new drugs were introduced to treat diseases once thought untreatable, including infection, mental illness, cancer, and heart disease. Growing interest in the environmental and genetic factors that cause disease fuels efforts at preventing them for as long as possible in an aging population.

1628	1666	1736	1775	1785	1796	1816	1874
William Harvey writes about the circulation of the blood.		First appendectomy is performed by Claudius Amyand in France.		William Withering introduces digitalis for the treatment of heart disease.		René Laennec invents the stethoscope.	
	Thomas Sydenham writes on the treatment of fevers.		Percival Pott suggests that environmental factors may cause cancer.		Edward Jenner introduces the smallpox vaccination.		Louis Pasteur instruments sh placed in boili to sterilize the

Key Players

Alexander Fleming
1881–1955

Born in Scotland, Fleming spent all his medical career at St. Mary's Hospital in London, except for his service in the Royal Army Medical Corps during World War I. Here he saw many fatal cases of wound infection, which prompted him to search for a non-toxic antibiotic. It was in 1928 that he discovered penicillin, although it was not until the 1940s that it began to be used widely.

Joseph Lister
1827–1912

Lister attended the first ever surgical operation carried out under general anesthetic in 1846, when the toll from post-surgical infection was still great. Lister introduced antiseptic procedures in 1867. His work led to a dramatic decrease in the rate of post-surgical sepsis and encouraged surgeons to attempt more adventurous operations, such as abdominal surgery.

Christiaan Barnard
1922–2001

In 1967, Christiaan Barnard made history by transplanting the heart of a 17-year-old girl killed in a car accident into 59-year-old Louis Washkansky. At first it appeared successful, but Washkansky died 18 days later. Other operations followed, but patients' bodies rejected the transplants. The program was abandoned until more effective drugs were discovered in 1974.

1897	1910	1921	1944	1951	1953	1978	1981
Ronald Ross discovers the malaria parasite.		Banting and Best isolate insulin for the treatment of diabetes.		Richard Lawler performs the first kidney transplant.		The first test-tube baby is born in England.	
	Paul Ehrlich announces the discovery of a treatment for syphilis.		Alfred Blalock performs the first "blue baby" operation.		John Gibbon performs first successful open heart surgery using heart-lung machine.		AIDS is first recognized as a new disease.

The Periodic Table: Order out of Chaos

The Periodic Table is a system of organizing the chemical elements according to their atomic structure. It was devised by a mid-nineteenth century Russian chemist and inventor and is the most enduring of the several classification schemes for the elements put forward in a time of invention and discovery.

Dmitri Ivanovich Mendeleev (1834–1907) presented his ideas to the Russian Chemical Society in 1869, introducing the gentlemen to the "periodic table" that arranged the elements, the basic substances of the universe, according to their atomic weights.

The table is an arrangement of rows and columns that reveals the "periodicity" among the elements, the tendency of similar properties (metallic nature, reactivity, and so on) to occur at regular intervals.

Along the rows, the atomic weight increases incrementally, while the columns contain elements that possess similar properties. The groups are separated by a mid-section consisting of transition elements containing elements like iron, titanium, and cobalt, characterized by having pigmented compounds and magnetic properties.

IN THE KNOW

The Periodic Table ends with uranium, which has an atomic number of 92. But a number of synthetic elements with higher atomic numbers have been created using nuclear reactions in nuclear reactors or particle accelerators. These are known as transuranium elements, and they include plutonium.

Gaps in the Jigsaw

Like all great scientific efforts, the Periodic Table allowed its inventor to make predictions, suggest experiments, and answer questions. Mendeleev also identified "gaps" within his table, which corresponded to elements not yet discovered. When these elements were later identified, they proved to have the properties that Mendeleev had predicted, confirming his table's accuracy.

Groups

The International Union of Pure and Applied Chemistry numbers the groups of elements from 1–18 (1 for the alkali metals, 18 for the inert gases). Each of these groups displays similar properties; for example, the alkali metals react with water to give an alkaline solution, but the reactions become increasingly vigorous as you move down the group's column.

In Fact...

The Periodic Table is generally divided into 18 groups of elements of similar properties, while the lathanide and actinide metals are incredibly similar to one another.

GROUP 1
1 Hydrogen (H)
3 Lithium (Li)
11 Sodium (Na)
19 Potassium (K)
37 Rubidium (Rb)
55 Cesium (Cs)
87 Francium (Fr)

GROUP 2
4 Beryllium (Be)
12 Magnesium (Mg)
20 Calcium (Ca)
38 Strontium (Sr)
56 Barium (Ba)
88 Radium (Ra)

GROUP 3
21 Scandium (Sc)
39 Yttrium (Y)
57 Lanthanum (La)
89 Actinium (Ac)

GROUP 4
22 Titanium (Ti)
40 Zirconium (Zr)
72 Hafnium (Hf)
104 Rutherfordium (Rf)

GROUP 5
23 Vanadium (V)
41 Niobium (Nb)
73 Tantalum (Ta)
105 Dubnium (Db)

GROUP 6
24 Chromium (Cr)
42 Molybdenum (Mo)
74 Tungsten (W)
106 Seaborgium (Sg)

GROUP 7
25 Manganese (Mn)
43 Technetium (Tc)
75 Rhenium (Re)
107 Bohrium (Bh)

GROUP 8
26 Iron (Fe)
44 Ruthenium (Ru)
76 Osmium (Os)
108 Hassium (Hs)

GROUP 9
27 Cobalt (Co)
45 Rhodium (Rh)
77 Iridium (Ir)
109 Meitnerium (Mt)

GROUP 10
28 Nickel (Ni)
46 Palladium (Pd)
78 Platinum (Pt)
110 Darmstadtium (Ds)

GROUP 11
29 Copper (Cu)
47 Silver (Ag)
79 Gold (Au)
111 Roentgenium (Rg)

GROUP 12
30 Zinc (Zn)
48 Cadmium (Cd)
80 Mercury (Hg)

GROUP 13
5 Boron (B)
13 Aluminum (Al)
31 Gallium (Ga)
49 Indium (In)
81 Thallium (Tl)

GROUP 14
6 Carbon (C)
14 Silicon (Si)
32 Germanium (Ge)
50 Tin (Sn)
82 Lead (Pb)

GROUP 15
7 Nitrogen (N)
15 Phosphorus (P)
33 Arsenic (As)

51 Antimony (Sb)
83 Bismuth (Bi)

GROUP 16
8 Oxygen (O)
16 Sulfur (S)
34 Selenium (Se)
52 Tellurium (Te)
84 Polonium (Po)

GROUP 17
9 Fluorine (F)
17 Chlorine (Cl)
35 Bromine (Br)
53 Iodine (I)
85 Astatine (At)

GROUP 18
2 Helium (He)
10 Neon (Ne)
18 Argon (Ar)
36 Krypton (Kr)
54 Xenon (Xe)
86 Radon (Rn)

LATHANIDE METALS
58 Cerium (Ce)
59 Praseodymium (Pr)
60 Neodymium (Nd)

61 Promethium (Pm)
62 Samarium (Sm)
63 Europium (Eu)
64 Gadolinium (Gd)
65 Terbium (Tb)
66 Dysprosium (Dy)
67 Holmium (Ho)
68 Erbium (Er)
69 Thulium (Tm)
70 Ytterbium (Yb)
71 Lutetium (Lu)

ACTINIDE METALS
90 Thorium (Th)
91 Protactinium (Pa)
92 Uranium (U)
93 Neptunium (Np)
94 Plutonium (Pu)
95 Americium (Am)
96 Curium (Cm)
97 Berkeelium (Bk)
98 Californium (Cf)
99 Einsteinium (Es)
100 Fermium (Fm)
101 Mendelevium (Md)
102 Nobelium (No)
103 Lawrencium (Lr)

H																	He
Li	Be											B	C	N	O	F	Ne
Na	Mg											Al	Si	P	S	Cl	Ar
K	Ca	Sc	Ti	V	Cr	Mn	Fe	Co	Ni	Cu	Zn	Ga	Ge	As	Se	Br	Kr
Rb	Sr	Y	Zr	Nb	Mo	Tc	Ru	Rh	Pd	Ag	Cd	In	Sn	Sb	Te	I .	Xe
Cs	Ba	*	Hf	Ta	W	Re	Os	Ir	Pt	Au	Hg	Tl	Pb	Bi	Po	At	Rn
Fr	Ra		Rf	Db	Sg	Bh	Hs	Mt	Ds	Rg							

	La	Ce	Pr	Nd	Pm	Sm	Eu	Gd	Tb	Dy	Ho	Er	Tm	Yb	Lu
*	Ac	Th	Pa	U	Np	Pu	Am	Cm	Bk	Cf	Es	Fm	Md	No	Lr

Great Inventors: Da Vinci, Nobel, Edison

The great inventions of human history also need their great inventors. Often, these men and women are so capable of innovative thought that they don't make just one contribution to the world, but many. Here are three of the greatest.

The Renaissance Man

Born in 1452, Leonardo da Vinci was an all-around genius and is often cited as the very model of the "Renaissance Man." Born near Florence, he developed an insatiable curiosity and was active as an artist, scientist, inventor, musician, and writer.

His most famous paintings are the *Mona Lisa* and *The Last Supper*. Apart from these, he left relatively few works of art behind, but he is remembered for his many sketchbooks and notebooks.

These books included his designs for a great variety of contraptions, from a helicopter (da Vinci had a lifelong fascination with flight), to a solar-powered device and even a calculator.

Da Vinci on the Mind
"Iron rusts from disuse; stagnant water loses its purity and in cold weather becomes frozen; even so does inaction sap the vigor of the mind."

He also made accurate anatomical drawings, most famously *Vetruvian Man*, whose limbs spread wide within a circle. He was revered as a teacher, and his physical beauty and charisma were noted by his biographer Giorgio Vasari.

Nobel's Explosive Invention

One of the great chemical industrialists, Alfred Nobel was born in Stockholm, Sweden, in 1833 and was educated in St. Petersburg, Russia.

He trained as a chemical engineer, became interested in the powerful liquid explosive nitroglycerin, and began to experiment with it. Tragically, Nobel's younger brother Emil and several other people were killed in an explosion after an experiment went wrong in 1864. Nobel's work with nitroglycerin was banned in Stockholm (where he had relocated the previous year), but he continued his inquiries on a barge in Lake Malaren.

He then found a way to make nitroglycerin into a paste that could be shaped into rods and inserted into drilling holes for blasting rocks. Nobel patented this material as "dynamite" in 1867, along with a detonator that could be ignited by way of a fuse.

The invention of dynamite greatly reduced the cost of blasting rock, drilling tunnels, digging canals, and carrying out other kinds of construction work, thereby making a huge contribution to the Industrial Revolution.

The manufacture of dynamite in numerous countries made Nobel a rich man. He also was involved with the development of synthetic rubber and artificial silk, and by the time of his death in 1896 he held 355 patents.

Edison's Flash of Brilliance

Lightbulbs are cheap; when one breaks, plunging the room into darkness, we just screw in another. Yet this invention of Edison's changed human society forever. Before the invention of the lightbulb, candles and gas lamps were the source of illumination. Electricity offered the possibility of an alternative lighting device, and Edison jumped at the chance. He announced his invention of the electric lightbulb in 1879, and by the end of the century, millions of people were lighting their homes with electric lighting.

Thomas Alva Edison (1847–1931) was an amazingly prolific inventor. Dubbed the Wizard of Menlo Park after the site of his research lab in New Jersey, he first found fame with the phonograph, an early device for playing recorded sound.

Nobel on Peace
"I intend to leave after my death a large fund for the promotion of the peace idea, but I am skeptical as to its results."

He virtually introduced electricity to the world, inventing the first electric light and power system, the first true motion-picture camera, and a wealth of other everyday wonders. It is for his lightbulb, however, that Edison is best remembered.

Edison's lightbulb had a simple structure: Two metal contacts in the base connect to an electric circuit. These are attached, inside the bulb, to two stiff wires that are attached to the filament. The wires and filament sit in a glass bulb filled with an inert gas like argon. When the light is switched on, an electric current flows through the filament and makes it glow. The basic electric incandescent bulb has hardly changed since Edison's day and time.

By the time of his death in 1931, Thomas Edison owned more than a thousand patents in the United States and in many other countries as well.

Edison on Invention:
"If I find 10,000 ways something won't work, I haven't failed. I am not discouraged, because every wrong attempt discarded is another step forward."

Conversation Starter The potential for his explosive discoveries to be used for evil ends troubled Alfred Nobel a great deal, and he bequeathed funds to found an award for activities in the pursuit of peace. The Nobel Prize is also awarded for achievements in the realms of physics, chemistry, physiology or medicine, and literature.

The Industrial Revolution: No Going Back

Like all revolutions, the change from 7,000 years of agriculture-based societies to modern industrial economies happened quickly—the blink of an eye in historical terms. In the beginning, few people of the eighteenth century foresaw that improving some mechanical technology in England would soon turn the world on its head.

The seeds of the Industrial Revolution, initially limited to Britain, go back to a series of technical innovations in textile manufacturing—culminating with James Watts's 1765 application of steam power milling cotton. From the mid-1700s onward, Western culture was dominated by new methods of production and a new philosophy of mass consumption. In fact, industrialization altered the world to its core.

What Industry Needed

To yield more goods than traditional, small-scale manufacturing, industry needed new technologies and energy sources, which science and engineering began to supply in abundance. Making large quantities of goods required standardized machinery and parts.

Centralizing work in factories speeded production, and faster transportation—steam ships and steam-driven railways—cut the time to receive raw materials and then distribute goods to distant markets. Industry took in huge amounts of money, and governments welcomed the goals of industrialists and their contribution to what Scottish economist Adam Smith called "the wealth of nations."

All these requirements came together in England first, then in France, Belgium, Germany, and North America. By 1859, U.S. investment in industry totaled almost a billion dollars. American companies were beginning to mass-produce and export rubber goods, clothing, shoes, guns, farm machinery, and Isaac Singer's new sewing machines.

Conversation Starter Luddites were roving bands of English weavers who aimed to destroy the textile machinery displacing them. The movement, named after a probably mythical rebel named Ned Ludd, began in 1811. Today, "Luddite" describes a person opposed to technological advances.

Though Russia was slow to industrialize, their loss in the Crimean War spurred Tsar Nicholas I to adopt modernization and to free the land-bound Russian peasants, creating laborers for new factories.

The Human Impact

In the last half of the 1700s, Europe saw major population growth, and more people needed jobs than farming and home-based manufacturing could provide. This workforce, including women and children, moved to urban centers where factories were concentrated. The work was hard: 14 hours a day, six days a week, for low wages. Living and working in dismal industrial cities put enormous stress on poor and working-class families.

It was a different story for the growing middle class. People with higher-paying jobs prospered, developing an ethic that valued work above all else and attributed poverty to laziness and decadence (This was Scrooge's attitude in Charles Dickens's *A Christmas Carol*.) In democratic America, wealth made it possible to buy (or marry) one's way into high society.

Labor reforms, starting with laws protecting women and children, came slowly, but strong labor unions began to emerge near the end of the nineteenth century. Thanks in large part to middle-class women and to social critics like Dickens, health and sanitation improvements were undertaken in the latter 1800s, and free education was extended to the children of laborers.

The transition from agriculture to industry is still underway, most notably in China, India, and developing countries worldwide. More to the point, experience teaches that once industrialization occurs, there's no going back.

Coal was at the heart of the Industrial Revolution, powering everything from factories to steamships.

Communication: From Telegrams to E-mail

Today, e-mail allows instant communication with anyone, anywhere—a miraculous alternative to letters and phone calls. It's also one of the crowning achievements in telegraphy (the electronic communication of written messages over a distance) and a hallmark of the Information Technology Revolution that began in the 1980s.

Telegraphy has a long history, starting with the use of smoke signals, beacons and semaphore—a flag language that allowed messages to be relayed between towers about 20 miles (32 km) apart.

The Electric Telegraph

Developments in electromagnetism led to the invention of the electric telegraph by William Cooke and Charles Wheatstone in Great Britain. A different version was presented by the American physicist (and portrait painter) Samuel Morse who, together with his assistant Alfred Vail, invented the Morse code—a system of short and long electrical pulses representing letters. A message in words was translated into a string of dots and dashes, sent down a cable, and translated back into words at the other end. The result was a telegram—also known as a cablegram, cable, or wire. Morse sent a famous telegram from the Capitol in Washington to Vail in Baltimore on May 24, 1844, reading "What hath God wrought?"

The newfangled telegraph spread rapidly throughout North America over the next 20 years. By 1853, telegraph wires stretched the length of the United Kingdom. Transatlantic cables were laid successfully in 1858, and England and India were connected in 1870, with Australia linked in 1872. A telegraph line across the Pacific made telegraphy global by 1902.

The last years of the twentieth century saw telegraph services closing down all around the world as they gave way to facsimile (fax) technology in the mid-1970s and then the Internet and e-mail in the late 1980s–early 1990s. Today the old-fashioned telegram still exists, but only as a novelty.

Conversation Starter The World Wide Web came into use in 1989. The growth of the Internet has been so rapid that there are now around a billion users of the Web—that is, around one person in six of the world's population.

The Telephone

Alexander Graham Bell, a Scot who immigrated to Canada and did scientific research in Ontario and the United States, had always been interested in speech; his mother was deaf, as was his wife.

Bell wanted to invent an instrument that would turn sound vibrations into electrical impulses and back again. On March 10, 1876, he was experimenting with a transmitter in one room of his Boston laboratory as his co-worker Thomas Watson worked on the receiver next door. When Bell called out, "Mr. Watson, come here, I want to see you," and Watson heard him, Bell's request became the first words ever transmitted by telephone.

The first telephones lacked a dial and had a separate mouthpiece and earpiece. Users had to ring a switchboard operator and ask for the call to be connected. The job of switchboard operator became a respectable career for many young women who had few other options at the time.

The First Cell Phones

The first mobile phone handsets, introduced in the 1980s, were the size of bricks. They beamed calls to antennae on nearby phone towers linked to ordinary phone lines. Each provided calls to one "cell"—an area of reception—and were therefore called cell phones. Cheaper, tinier computer chips led to the digital mobile phones of today.

Of course, today you can do much more with a mobile phone than just make calls. These diminutive multitaskers can take pictures; play music, movies, and videos; and give you access to the Internet and e-mail—and that's just for starters.

IN THE KNOW

Satellites were essential to the Information Technology Revolution. Used for a huge range of purposes, they make possible everything from television and telephone phone networks to global positioning systems and military communications. In the half century since the Russians launched the satellite *Sputnik* (1957), communication has truly gone global.

The Internet

What is known as the Internet started as a network of research computers set up by the U.S. Advanced Research Projects Agency in 1963. Improvements in data transfer in the 1980s led to the Internet of today.

A vast global network, the Internet connects thousands of local networks together through so-called backbone systems plugged into smaller networks that are, in turn, attached to individual computers.

The Internet is the superhighway on which the Information Technology Revolution speeds. The computer-based information systems developed over the past three decades, along with their software applications and computer hardware, have transformed the way we live our lives and, quite possibly, even the way we think.

The Moving Image and the Silver Screen

Modern Hollywood blockbusters are crammed so full of the latest computer technology that it's easy to forget just how recent cinema is as an art form. Incredibly, in little over a century, the world of the moving picture has changed from a novelty to a multi-million-dollar film industry that spans the globe.

The moving images on a cinema screen are made possible by a phenomenon known as the persistence of vision. This is easy to demonstrate: Look at an object, then look at a blank page; now notice that the image of the object persists for a short time. If a series of images is displayed at the right rate (modern film runs at 24 frames per second), the eye will see them as continuous.

The Earliest "Movies"

Motion pictures were launched when the Belgian physicist Joseph Plateau introduced a spindle viewer called the Fantascope, or Magic Wheel, in 1832; it was the first device that showed pictures that appeared to move. Various types of motion picture technologies were later developed, most notably the "series photography" of British-born American Eadweard Muybridge.

Special glasses (one lens red, the other green) enabled audiences to view three dimensional, or 3-D, movies.

First Cinemas

The first-ever public demonstration of cinema in the United States was in 1891, when members of the Federation of Women's Clubs

1894	1895	1902	1906	1907	1908	1914	1921
Fred Ott's *Sneeze*. The first close-up film, and first ever to be copyrighted.		*Le Voyage dans la Lune*, the first special-effects and sci-fi film, made by Georges Méliès.		"Broncho Billy" stars in the first silent western.		The first color film *The World, The Flesh and The Devil* appears.	
	The first motion picture seen by a paying audience in New York City.		*The Story of the Kelly Gang*, the first feature-length film, opens in Melbourne.		*Dr Jekyll and Mr Hyde*, the first horror film, premieres.		D. W. Griffith's *Dream Street* becomes the fi[...] film to use sou[...]

were shown a short film from the kinetoscope invented by Thomas Edison.

Then came Cinématographe, a combined movie camera and projector developed in France in 1895 by brothers August and Louis Lumière. The device made it possible for film to be seen by a large audience. By the turn of the century, movies were popular attractions in amusement arcades and vaudeville theaters. Filmmakers also began to shift toward a more narrative style, filming different scenes and editing them into order—a technique still used in modern cinema.

Movies Take Off

The first kinetoscope parlor—called a nickelodeon—("nickel" for the price of admission, "odeon" from the Greek "theater") opened in Pittsburgh in 1905. Films also began to be projected on screens, and director Edwin S. Porter's *The Great Train Robbery* (1903) was the first box-office hit.

With the spread of cinemas, Hollywood became home to a fledgling film industry. In 1913, the director D. W. Griffiths began to introduce new techniques, breaking scenes into multiple shots and using camera angles that added an extra dimension to film. After many failed attempts, synchronized sound arrived in the early 1920s. Around this time, figures like Walt Disney, the pioneer of animation, made their mark.

The 1930s and '40s were the "Golden Age of Hollywood." Audiences chose from a rich array of films, many of which became classics. The year 1939 alone gave the world *Gone With the Wind, The Wizard of Oz, Stagecoach, Wuthering Heights,* and *It's a Wonderful Life.*

Today, computer-generated imagery (CGI) and digitization transform the moving images on the silver screen in a way that is, if nothing else, astonishing.

IN THE KNOW

The producer of a film—the person with overall responsibility for the project—starts with only a story idea. This is written up as a "treatment," a 30–40 page description of the story. A screenwriter then turns the story into a screenplay with dialogue and stage directions. With the screenplay complete, the producer pitches it to potential financial backers.

1928	1941	1944	1960	1972	1975	1977	1995
Dali and Luis Bunuel shock audiences with surrealism.		*Double Indemnity* becomes an atmospheric "film noir" classic.		*The Poseidon Adventure* starts a trend in disaster movies.		The *Star Wars* trilogy introduces computer-generated effects.	
	Citizen Kane introduces low-angle shots, overlapping sound, and complex flashbacks.		Hitchcock's *Psycho* becomes famous for its shower scene and score.		Spielberg's *Jaws* is the first film to take in over U.S.$100 million.		*Toy Story* becomes the first all computer-generated film.

Radio and Television Bring the World Home

Harnessing the electromagnetic waves in the atmosphere, physicists figured out how to translate them into sound and pictures and send both on long-distance journeys to receivers. Our experience of the world has never been the same since.

Before radio, communication over long distances required wires. In the late 1800s, the only two modes of long-distance discourse, the telegraph and the telephone, tethered people to those wires on both ends. Radio signals, though, could travel in air.

A Princeton professor named Joseph Henry and a British physicist named Michael Faraday experimented independently in the 1830s with electromagnets, leading both to put forward a theory known as induction. The idea was that current running through one wire could produce current in another wire, even though the two wires were not connected.

Soon, other scientists were establishing that electromagnetic waves indeed traveled through space, and at the speed of light. Developments came quickly.

Catching the Waves

In 1887, Heinrich Hertz, a German physicist, sent and detected these waves. By 1891, Nikola Tesla, an Austro-Hungarian, invented a coil that functioned as a high-frequency transformer. Four years later, using the Morse code, a system of dots and dashes that represented the letters of the alphabet, the Italian inventor Guglielmo Marconi was sending messages through the air that were picked up by receivers more than a mile away. Only six years later, in 1901, he would send the signals from England to Canada.

In quick succession came a device called the vacuum tube, which detected and amplified the radio waves and a wave generator that actually broadcast music and the human voice. The credit

Key Player

Philo T. Farnsworth
1906–1971

Though John Logie Baird, Vladimir Zworykin, and many other inventors had a hand in the development of television, American Philo Farnsworth was the first to create a true working television. He introduced his invention to the news media on September 1, 1928, with the televising of a movie.

for the tube generally goes to an American electrical engineer named Lee De Forest and for the generator to a Canadian physicist named Reginald Fessenden.

Called "the wireless," radio served a vital role in keeping communications going between ships at sea and from ship to shore. When the S.S. *Republic* smashed into another ship in the Atlantic, a radio call went out that brought help to the scene and saved most of the imperiled passengers.

On November 2, 1920, listeners in Pittsburgh, Pennsylvania, could hear the results of the U.S. presidential election over the air on a station called KDKA. Generally considered the birthplace of professional broadcasting, it grew out of the efforts of a tinkerer and Westinghouse engineer named Frank Conrad. Radio broadcasts in Europe also began in the early 1920s.

By 1930, millions upon millions of radios had been sold around the world, and a mass medium had arrived. It brought the world into households in ways never before imagined—from the Metropolitan Opera House and the gifts of Enrico Caruso to the classic comedy of George Burns and Gracie Allen; from the rooftops of London under siege during the blitzkriegs of World War II to the fireside chats of President Franklin

Delano Roosevelt that united an anxious nation and stiffened its resolve though the Great Depression and the war.

TV Makes Its Debut

Radio's so-called Golden Age of Broadcasting lasted until the early 1950s. Then came television, which used transmitters to translate light from electromagnetic waves into pictures. Many of the great American radio shows—*The Lone Ranger*, *Our Miss Brooks*, and *Superman* among them—found new venues in the visual medium. Burns and Allen and other international radio stars like Bob Hope and Jack Benny made successful transitions to television. Radio's format changed largely to recorded music, and, in the 1990s, talk radio.

The exploration of space advanced broadcast technology even further. Starting in the 1960s, cable television operators bounced video signals off satellites in order to connect many remote locales into unified networks. Satellite transmission also made it possible to provide these areas with more channels and better transmission quality than could be provided by over-the-air broadcasts.

More recently, satellites began to be used to feed the broadcasts from space directly into the home without the intermediate cable connection.

IN THE KNOW

A broadcast on October 30, 1938, proved the power of radio. With his *The War of the Worlds*, actor Orson Welles simulated a live news report of a Martian invasion of New Jersey. Thinking it real, people panicked and crammed highways trying to escape. Many checked into hospitals to be treated for shock.

Splitting the Atom: The New Atomic Age

Splitting the atom changed the world, unleashing vast amounts of nuclear energy pent up within an atom's core. This energy can be used both as a potentially valuable power source or to produce devastating explosions that have the capacity to destroy all life.

The foundations of work in nuclear fission were laid by Enrico Fermi, Lise Meitner, and Otto Frisch. The world was on the brink of World War II and, believing German scientists to be working on the atom bomb in secret, Fermi, Leo Szilard, and Albert Einstein warned President Franklin D. Roosevelt that the United States must develop its own nuclear bomb.

In June 1942, the United States put the Army Corps of Engineers (USACE) in charge of the top-secret bomb-building effort, the Manhattan Project. Meanwhile, Fermi and fellow researchers at the University of Chicago were trying to achieve the first controlled nuclear reaction. They succeeded on December 2, 1942 (under the abandoned west stands of the university's stadium, no less), paving the way for further research in the USACE's new laboratory in Oak Ridge, Tennessee.

Key Player

Enrico Fermi
1901–1954

Fermi showed great ability from an early age, starting out in research in X-rays. By the age of 26 he became a professor of physics in Rome, having already published over 30 papers. His groundbreaking work on splitting the atom earned him a Nobel Prize.

Chain Reaction

The key to the chain reaction is a fuel source that is readily "fissionable," or able to be split. Only two elements are suitable for this: uranium-235 and plutonium-239 (although the latter wasn't available at the time).

The Oak Ridge scientists faced the challenge of getting enough "enriched" uranium-235 to sustain the chain reaction. Once the team had found a solution, it had the raw material it needed.

Theoretical physicist J. Robert Oppenheimer headed the team of scientists who labored for two and a half years from 1943 to build the first atomic weapons. Their laboratories were located in remote Los Alamos, New Mexico.

The United States spent over $2 billion on the Manhattan Project. Yet at the end of the war, it was revealed that Germany had, in fact, made little progress in its own nuclear research.

Peaceful Uses

Since its militarily inspired invention, the splitting of the atom has not only created nuclear bombs but also provided nuclear energy to make electricity. Nuclear power stations are sometimes considered "clean" energy sources. Because they don't produce greenhouse gases they could help alleviate global warming. Concerns persist, however, over their safety because of disasters, including that of Chernobyl, in the USSR, in 1986. The impact of storing nuclear waste is also a matter of controversy.

The First Atom Bombs

The first fission bomb, or A-bomb, was nicknamed "The Gadget" and was detonated in the New Mexico desert on July 16, 1945. The white-hot blaze turned orange as it cooled, and the characteristic radioactive mushroom cloud extended as high as 30,000 feet (9,150 m). The intense heat turned the desert sand below to glass.

The atom bomb has been used only twice in war. To end World War II, the U.S. Air Force plane *Enola Gay* dropped an A-bomb, nicknamed "Little Boy," on Hiroshima, Japan, on August 6, 1945, at 8:15 A.M. By 8:16 A.M. it had killed some 75,000 people and injured another 69,000.

The mushroom cloud is an icon of doom. The Nuclear Nonproliferation Treaty of 1968, signed by 189 countries as of 2008, aims to limit the spread of nuclear weapons.

Everything for half a mile around had been instantly vaporized. The blast zone itself measured three miles (5 km) in diameter.

Three days later, the plutonium bomb "Fat Man" leveled the city of Nagasaki in a fraction of a second, killing almost 40,000 people and injuring 25,000 more. Japan surrendered the following day, the power of the atomic bomb having spoken.

Numerous tests have been conducted as well, and a growing number of countries, including the United Kingdom, France, Russia, China, North Korea, India, and Pakistan, have the capacity to create a nuclear explosion.

The International Space Station

The International Space Station is an extraordinary work in progress. Unlike the competitive "space race" of the Cold War years, the construction and manning of the station exemplifies international cooperation in both science and politics—a window on the universe and a glimpse of what humans can achieve by working in concert.

The International Space Station (ISS) orbits the Earth nearly 16 times per day at a speed of just over 17,000 mph (27,350 kph) and is visible from the Earth with the naked eye. Construction began in 1998 by the space agencies of the United States, Russia, Japan, Canada, and the European Space Agency to replace previous space station programs, such as Russia's Mir 2. Work on the ISS is expected to be completed in 2016 at a cost of about $130 billion (U.S.).

A Diverse Crew

ISS provides its international crew, currently comprising three members, with more than 15,000 cubic feet of work and living space. It has been visited by astronauts from 15 different countries and by five "space tourists"—each of whom has paid $25 million (U.S.) for the privilege. Powered by solar panels, it has been supplied and serviced by the Russian *Soyuz* and *Progress* spacecrafts and by U.S. space shuttles. In April 2008, Europe's new *Jules Verne* cargo ship made its maiden voyage to the ISS and delivered tons of needed supplies.

In Fact...

The first human in space was Russian cosmonaut Yuri Gagarin on April 12, 1961. American astronaut Alan Shepard followed less than a month later. In 1962, John Glenn was the first American to orbit Earth, a distinction that surely helped elect the Ohioan to the U.S. Senate in 1973.

During the "space race," Soviet achievements included first woman (Valentina Tereshkova, 1963), first multi-person crew, and first space walk. Americans took first in space docking, lunar orbit, and putting men on the moon.

The first non-American, non-Soviet in space was Vladimir Remek, a Czechoslovakian, in 1978. The first American female, Sally Ride, flew in 1983, and Guion Bluford, Jr., the first African American, the same year.

In 2003, China's first manned flight carried taikonaut Yang Liwei aloft. Mike Melvill, a South African, piloted the first privately financed manned flight in 2004.

A Station of Many Modules

The space station is built from a number of pressurized aluminum modules. Additional research labs from Japan and Europe will be added to expand the station's experimental capabilities. The goal of research conducted on the ISS is to develop the technology needed for human-based space and planetary exploration and even, one day perhaps, colonization. Other expected benefits include new therapies for disease, better ways of producing materials, and a greater understanding of the universe from a vantage point outside the Earth's atmosphere.

Among the many modules that make up the space station are the following:

• The Russian Zarya and Zvezda modules with living quarters and life support.

• The U.S. Unity Connecting Module, which provides various docking ports.

• The Destiny Laboratory, built by the United States, which provides general laboratory facilities for scientific research.

• The Quest Airlock, built by the United States, which is a doorway that makes ISS-based spacewalks possible.

• The Canadarm2, built by Canada, which is a new-generation robotic arm that serves as the ISS's space crane.

• The Pirs docking compartment, built by Russia, which adds additional spacewalking and docking capabilities.

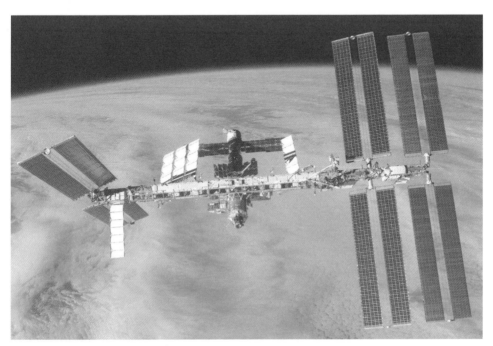

From humankind's first steps in organized agriculture, the pace of progress has been astounding, punctuated by great inventions and peopled by great inventors. But can you remember who invented what, and when?

Agriculture: The Endless Quest for Food

1 What is the name for the area in which organized agriculture first arose?

2 In which year was the first steam-driven tractor launched?

   a) *1862*   b) *1872*
   c) *1882*   d) *1892*

3 In 1944 a joint project between the Rockefeller Foundation and the government of which country improved agricultural yields significantly?

   a) *Malawi*   b) *Mali*
   c) *Mexico*   d) *Morocco*

The Written Word and the Printed Page

1 The earliest known book was printed in 868 CE. What is it known as?

2 Who invented the printing press with moveable type?

3 When was the first practical fountain pen introduced by Lewis Waterman?

   a) *1864*   b) *1874*
   c) *1884*   d) *1894*

Mathematics: One Language for All

1 True or False: The number pi never repeats itself.

2 Whom is the sequence that starts: 0, 1, 1, 2, 3, 5, 8. . . known after?

The Fight for Life: A History of Medicine

1 In what year did William Harvey write about the circulation of the blood?

   a) *1428*   b) *1528*
   c) *1628*   d) *1728*

2 Who introduced the smallpox vaccine in 1796?

The Periodic Table: Order out of Chaos

1 Who invented the concept of the Periodic Table as it is now known?

2 True or False: The atomic weight of elements increases as you move from left to right and top to bottom.

3 Which is the first element in the Periodic Table?

Great Inventors: Da Vinci, Nobel, Edison

1 What is the name of Da Vinci's famous drawing of a man with limbs outstretched within a circle?

2 What was Alfred Nobel's most famous invention?

The Industrial Revolution: No Going Back

1 What was the name given to the bands of English weavers intent on destroying the machinery that was replacing them?

2 Name the tsar who industrialized Russia.

Communication: From Telegrams to E-mail

1 What is the name for the visual system of communication that uses flag signals?

2 What was the first sentence spoken via the telephone?

The Moving Image and the Silver Screen

1 How fast does modern film run, in terms of frames per second?

2 True or False: The first color film predates the first film with sound.

Radio and Television Bring the World Home

1 In which year did a radio broadcast of *The War of the Worlds* panic American citizens?

2 In which decade did satellites begin to play a role in broadcasting?

   a) *1960s*   b) *1970s*
   c) *1980s*   d) *1990s*

Splitting the Atom: The New Atomic Age

1 What was the name of the U.S. project to develop a nuclear weapon during World War II?

2 In which U.S. state was the first ever nuclear device exploded?

The International Space Station

1 Who was the first person in space?

2 In which year did Valentina Tereshkova become the first woman in space?

   a) *1961*   b) *1962*
   c) *1963*   d) *1964*

3 True or False: The ISS is visible from Earth with the naked eye.

Chapter Six

Conflicts of the Modern Age

The history of the world is marked by conflict, and this chapter is the story of the wars that have shaped the modern age—from the restoration of the Union in the American Civil War to the European conflicts that became world wars in the first half of the twentieth century . . . from the Cold War standoff between East and West to today's ongoing conflict in the Middle East, Afghanistan, and the Balkans.

Warring States: The American Civil War

The United States had been in existence for just over 70 years when the issues of slavery and states' rights tore it apart, pitting family against family and friend against friend in the four-year-long Civil War. More than 600,000 men died—about a quarter of the fighting forces—in the struggle to decide whether the Union would survive.

Divisions between the largely industrialized northern states and the agricultural South had been simmering for some time. Slavery had been abolished in the North, but large plantations in the South were dependent on slave labor.

Debate about slavery was at the forefront of U.S. politics, and in 1860 the Democratic Party split and nominated two candidates for president. Republican candidate Abraham Lincoln wasn't an abolitionist but did oppose the extension of slavery into the western territories. While Lincoln didn't win the popular vote, he defeated his rivals by gaining the most electoral college votes.

Before Lincoln took office, six states (South Carolina, Mississippi, Florida, Alabama, Georgia, and Louisiana) voted to leave the Union. In February 1861, representatives of the six, plus Texas, met to form

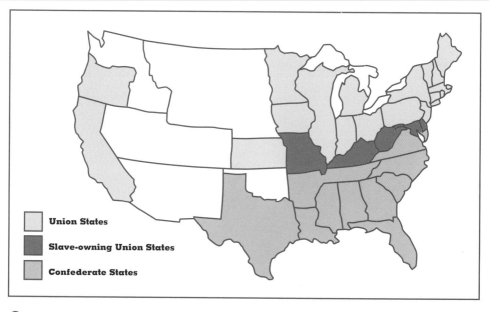

Union States

Slave-owning Union States

Confederate States

the Confederate States of America, with Jefferson Davis as President—but Lincoln refused to recognize the Confederacy.

The First Shots

On April 12, 1861, Confederate forces fired on Unionists at Fort Sumter in South Carolina, starting the Civil War. Four more southern states announced their secession, and Richmond, Virginia, became the Confederate capital. In total, 23 states remained in the Union, including five border, or slave-owning, states (West Virginia, Kentucky, Missouri, Maryland, and Delaware).

The Union quickly moved to impose a naval blockade to weaken the Confederate economy. Confederate soldiers, however, won the first major battle of the war at Bull Run, Virginia, just 30 miles from Washington, D.C.

The war was fought on two main fronts: in the East as the Confederates tried to move northward, and in the West as Union forces pushed through Kentucky and Tennessee, capturing key cities and cutting Confederate supply lines. Buoyed by early successes, General Robert E. Lee led the

Key Player

Abraham Lincoln
1809–1865

The 16th president of the United States and the first Republican to hold the office, Lincoln guided the country through the painful years of the Civil War and helped to ensure the preservation of the Union. Lincoln introduced a number of anti-slavery measures, including the Emancipation Proclamation of 1863. Re-elected in 1864, he was assassinated the following year by a Confederate sympathizer.

Confederates into the North for the first time, crossing the Potomac River into Maryland. On September 17, 1862, the Battle of Antietam, near Sharpsburg, Maryland, resulted in the heaviest loss of life by American troops in a single day—over 21,000 dead. Neither side won, but Lee's men were forced to retreat.

The Turning Point

The Confederates enjoyed successes at the battles of Fredericksburg (1862) and Chancellorsville (1863) before finally meeting defeat at the Battle of Gettysburg, Pennsylvania, in July 1863, the turning point of the war.

The next year, Ulysses S. Grant was made commander of the Union troops. He ordered Major-General William T. Sherman to torch Atlanta and march through Georgia to the sea in the most destructive campaign against civilians of the war. Gradually, the whole of the South came under Union control, and Lee finally surrendered his troops on April 9, 1865. Though President Lincoln was assassinated eight days later, the Union was restored, and slavery ended at last.

World War I: Death on a Grand Scale

Many military historians now regard World War I as "a tragic and unnecessary conflict" in the words of one, John Keegan. That the nations of Europe chose all-out warfare rather than diplomacy to settle old scores and jealousies remains baffling. That millions died and millions more were wounded, displaced, and disillusioned is cold, hard fact.

On June 28, 1914, in the Bosnian capital of Sarajevo, a Serb nationalist shot Archduke Ferdinand, the heir to the Austro-Hungarian Empire. Austria retaliated by declaring war on Serbia a month later. Within weeks, all the major countries in Europe were at war, and the conflict spread to their colonies. The two opposing sides became known as the Central Powers (Germany, Austria, Hungary, and Italy) and the Allies (France, Russia, and Great Britain, and later, the United States).

A Bloody Stalemate

The Germans advanced through neutral Belgium into northern France, pushing back British forces at the Battle of Mons on August 23, 1914. The German army advanced to within 43 miles (70 km) of Paris, but at the first Battle of Marne (September 6–12), the Allies forced the Germans to retreat to north of the Aisne River in northwestern France. The German initiative had been lost, and major battles came to be fought in an area called the Western Front.

Both sides dug lines of fortified trenches stretching 400 miles (650 km) from the Belgian coast to the French-Swiss border. Between the trenches lay the figurative "no man's land," the scene of many bloody battles—among them the first Battle of Ypres (autumn 1914); the second Battle of Ypres (May 1915); the Battle of Verdun (February–December 1916); the Battle of the Somme (summer–autumn 1916); and the third battle of Ypres (summer–autumn 1917), which ended with the British taking Passchendaele Ridge on November 6.

Conversation Starter On May 7, 1915, the British liner *Lusitania* was sunk by a German submarine, killing 1,198 people, 128 of them American. The attack helped persuade the United States that entry into the war was inevitable, and it joined the Allies in 1917.

Breaking the Impasse

The Battle of Cambrai (November–December 1917) signaled a turning point in the war, though neither side emerged victorious. For the first time, the Allies used tanks en masse along with artillery and air power, successfully forcing the German lines back 5 miles in six hours at the cost of 4,000 casualties. This new tactic proved that tanks could overcome otherwise impregnable trench defenses.

An Unsatisfactory Conclusion

In the spring of 1918, Germany launched its last major offensive on the Western Front. The Germans were initially successful, forcing the Allied lines back to within shelling distance of Paris. The Allies responded with a series of forceful counteroffensives, leading exhausted German troops to start surrendering in large numbers in November 1918.

The Austro-Hungarian Empire's fall, combined with the widespread hunger and uprisings in Germany, forced the abdication of Kaiser Wilhelm, and the nation's new government signed an armistice at 11:00 A.M. on November 11, 1918. The terms ending the war were severe for the Germans and are widely regarded as having sowed the seeds for World War II, which would start only 20 years later following the rise of the Nazi Party.

IN THE KNOW

The horrors of World War I were exemplified by the Battle of the Somme, which began on July 1, 1916. British and French artillery shelled German lines for over a week, and the Allied infantry expected little resistance when it went "over the top." However, the Germans had deep dugouts, and on the first day of the battle, Allied forces suffered over 40,000 casualties, with nearly 20,000 dead or missing. Casualties from both sides totaled over a million during the 4 1/2- month campaign.

Trench warfare in World War I meant long periods in filthy conditions, with bursts of deadly action in "no man's land" when soldiers "went over the top" to advance against the enemy.

The Spanish Civil War: A Bloody Preview

Following the Russian Revolution, communism was held out as the great hope of ordinary people living under harsh regimes. But to the established powers, communism seemed the worst of threats. In mid-1930s Spain, the ideologies of left and right clashed violently; the resulting civil war foreshadowed the worldwide conflict to come.

In the early 1930s, Spain was undergoing rapid political change. The monarchy had been replaced by a new republican government, and Spain had entered a period known as the Second Republic. Composed of a coalition of left-wing and center politicians, the elected government was essentially socialist. Its introduction of a number of controversial reforms, including land redistribution and reform of the Church and army, generated strong opposition from the country's former ruling elite.

The Trigger

In February 1936, the left-wing Popular Front won the general election, and the political situation deteriorated rapidly. Rising tensions and the assassination of right-wing opposition leader José Calvo Sotelo culminated in an attempted military coup beginning in Spanish Morocco on July 17, 1936. The coup initially failed, but it signaled the start of the Spanish Civil War.

Despite the Non-Intervention Agreement of August 1936—designed to prevent the conflict spreading into Europe—the Spanish Civil War was marked by foreign

In Fact...

Who supported whom in the Spanish Civil War?

The Republicans (Republicanos)

- the Spanish regions of Catalan and Basque, which wanted independence

- the Soviet Union, Mexico, and the "International Brigades"

- workers and communists

The Nationalists (Nationales)

- The Spanish cities of Seville and Cadiz

- Italy, Germany, and Portugal

- high-ranking army and naval officers, the Catholic Church, and landowners interference. The Soviet Union recruited volunteers and sent money and arms to the Republicans, or Loyalists, while the right-wing Nationalists received military support from the fascists in Italy and Nazi Germany.

The International Brigades

International observers saw the war as a fascist attack on a democratic government. It attracted thousands of young people from other parts of the world, eager to fight for democracy. Many of these were recruited through the communist parties of Italy, France, and other countries (Paris was the primary recruitment center for international volunteers). Although the majority of volunteers were communists, they also came from socialist, liberal, and anarchist backgrounds.

In all, more than 30,000 volunteers from more than 50 different countries fought on the Republican side in units that came to be known as the International Brigades. This mission proved to be costly: In the end, more than 10,000 of these idealistic youths lost their lives in the struggle between 1936 and 1939.

Key Player

Francisco Franco
1892–1975

Franco was a successful officer in the Spanish army, and in 1926 he became the youngest general in the country. He was a member of the group that participated in the coup against the democratically elected government in 1936. He headed the rebel forces during the civil war, leading them to victory in 1939. Spain became a totalitarian state. Franco governed the Falange party until his death.

A Nationalist Victory

The Nationalists, under the leadership of General Francisco Franco, inched their way to victory despite fierce Republican resistance. After several failed attempts, Franco took the capital, Madrid, and resistance collapsed. On April 1, 1939, the Republicans surrendered and Franco became leader of all Spain, setting up a dictatorship that lasted until his death in 1975.

The Aftermath

The Spanish Civil War is notorious for the barbarous killings that took place. In many ways, the atrocities committed by both sides of the conflict can be seen as a portent to those that followed in World War II.

On part of the Nationalists, examples of these brutalities included the bombing of Madrid and Guernica, primarily by German planes, and mass executions of schoolteachers, anti-Church sympathizers, and civilians. On the other side, the Republicans murdered members of the Church, the nobility, rich landowners, and industrialists. Over 1,000,000 people were killed, and thousands more fled into exile.

World War II: The World at War

World War I left much unresolved in Europe. Harsh, economically devastating postwar treatment of Germany led directly to the rise of Hitler and the Nazis, setting the stage for World War II. In effect, both wars and the years between were one war in three acts.

The Treaty of Versailles signed by the Allies and Germany in 1919 deprived Germany of its overseas possessions, forced the country to pay huge reparations, and restricted its army. Europe was hit by economic depression in the late 1920s, further weakening national pride and contributing to the rise of the Nazism that had brought Hitler to power. The National Socialist German Workers (Nazi) Party promised Germans they would rebuild the economy, create jobs, and restore national self-esteem.

The Rise of Hitler

In 1933, Austrian-born Adolf Hitler (1889–1945) became Chancellor of Germany and then, on the death of President Hindenburg the following year, its Führer (leader). Almost immediately, he began planning for the expansion of Germany. He reoccupied the Rhineland in 1936 and forced the unification of Austria with Germany in 1938. The Allies did little to halt his belligerence, adopting a policy known as appeasement. But then, when Germany invaded Poland on September 1, 1939, Britain and France declared war.

Axis Victories

German forces enjoyed success in the early years of the war, and blitzkrieg (lightning war) tactics quickly defeated Poland, Belgium, Holland, Denmark, Norway, and France. By June 1940, Britain alone remained unoccupied, and German forces were encouraged by the entry of Italy into the war under the fascist leader Benito Mussolini.

The war spread to North Africa, and the following year saw the Axis Powers conquer Yugoslavia, Albania, and Greece and gain the assistance of Romania, Hungary, and Bulgaria. On June 22, 1941, the Germans

IN THE KNOW

Before the start of the war, Hitler spoke of the "annihilation of the Jewish race in Europe." Although hundreds of thousands of Jews were killed in the war's early years, mass extermination did not begin until 1942 when leading Nazis met to address the "Final Solution to the Jewish Question." They set up massive camps, in which millions of Jews were gassed—more than 2,000,000 were killed in Auschwitz alone.

invaded the Soviet Union, besieging Leningrad, capturing Kiev, and marching to within 15 miles (24 km) of Moscow before the harsh Russian winter and a Red Army counteroffensive stopped their progress.

In December 1941, the Japanese attack on Pearl Harbor turned the conflict into a truly global one. Within a few months, Japan had control of Southeast Asia and was threatening India and Australia.

The Allies Strike Back

Allied forces began to gain the upper hand in 1942. The Americans won important sea battles in the Pacific against the Japanese, and General Bernard Montgomery led British forces to victory at El Alamein in Egypt. On the Eastern Front, the German Sixth Army surrendered to the Soviets in February 1943, after months of fierce fighting amid the ruins of Stalingrad.

A year later, on June 6, 1944, Allied forces under U.S. General Dwight D. Eisenhower landed on the beaches of Normandy. August saw the liberation of Paris, and within a month almost the whole of France was free. By April 1945, the Allies were taking control of Germany, and Hitler committed suicide in his bunker in Berlin.

On May 8, the war in Europe came to its formal end, much to the Allies' rejoicing. The Japanese surrendered in August, and the world was at peace at last. The deadly conflict resulted in approximately 15,000,000 military deaths. Among the 40,000,000 dead were 6,000,000 European Jews, 20,000,000 Russians, 4,500,000 Poles, and 2,000,000 Japanese.

In Fact...

The war in the Pacific was punctuated by three key events:

- On the morning of December 7, 1941, Japan made an unprovoked attack on the American fleet at Pearl Harbor, Hawaii. Over 400 Japanese aircraft destroyed two battleships, one mine layer, two destroyers, and 188 aircraft. The United States immediately declared war on Japan.

- Over-extension on the part of the Japanese and the increasing power of the U.S. Navy turned the tide in mid-1942. After rebuffing a Japanese invasion force bound for New Guinea at the Battle of the Coral Sea, the Navy won a decisive victory on June 4, 1942, at the Battle of Midway. The August 31 Battle of Milne Bay, in New Guinea, was the first land defeat of the Japanese, and it came at the hands of Australian troops.

- On the morning of August 6, 1945, the U.S. Air Force dropped the world's first atomic bomb on the Japanese city of Hiroshima. The bomb, nicknamed "Little Boy," killed up to 80,000 Japanese civilians. Three days later a second bomb—"Fat Man"—killed 35,000–40,000 in Nagasaki. Many more died later from radiation poisoning. On August 14, the Japanese surrendered unconditionally to the Allied forces.

The Cold War: A Four-Decade Standoff

The term Cold War hardly does justice to the 40-year period when the whole world lived under constant threat. Two antagonists—both superpowers and both armed to the teeth—seemed poised to ignite global nuclear war. No one was more surprised than the Soviet Union and the United States when their bitter standoff suddenly, quietly ended.

Although the Soviet Union and the Americans were allies in the war against Nazi Germany, they were ideologically distant. Tensions between the two superpowers emerged near the end of World War II and in the immediate postwar period. As early as March 1946, Britain's wartime prime minister Winston Churchill warned that "an iron curtain has descended across the continent."

NATO vs. the Warsaw Pact

The North Atlantic Treaty Organization (NATO) was established in 1949 by Western European countries, Canada, and the United States to protect themselves against communist aggression. NATO members (now numbering 26) are obliged to help one another in the event of an attack by an enemy state. When West Germany joined NATO in 1955, the Soviet Union established its own alliance, the Warsaw Pact. This consisted of the communist states of Central and Eastern Europe and allowed the Soviets to send troops into Eastern European countries. It was dissolved in 1991.

IN THE KNOW

After the end of World War II, Berlin was split into four zones, each controlled by an Allied power. As Cold War tensions grew, Germany split in two, and so did Berlin. Attracted by freedom and prosperity, more than 3,000,000 people fled to the West via West Berlin. In 1961 the East German government built the Berlin Wall to prevent the exodus. In 1989, the Wall was dismantled, a first step toward the German reunification of 1990.

Cold War Hot Spots

There was never any direct military action between U.S. and Soviet forces, but the two sides fought a number of proxy wars around the world for four long decades. To contain Soviet influence, the United States often supported unsavory dictatorships and forged uneasy alliances in its desire to stop the spread of communism. The Soviets gave ideological and military support to new communist satellite nations and, in the 1980s, occupied Afghanistan to stem the tide of Islamic extremism into the USSR.

The Cold War became a massive arms race, each side stockpiling enough nuclear weapons to destroy life on the entire planet many times over. The potential for mutual assured destruction (MAD) deterred any military action, though some crises did threaten to escalate into major conflicts: the Berlin Blockade (1948–1949), when the Soviets cut off land routes to West Berlin; the Korean War (1950–1953); the Vietnam War (1959–1975); and the Soviet–Afghan War (1979–1989). In each war, one superpower sponsored a military campaign against the other.

The closest the Soviets and the United States came to outright war was the Cuban Missile Crisis of 1962. For two weeks, the world held its breath as U.S. and Soviet leaders engaged in threats and counterthreats over the secret installation of Russian ballistic missiles in Cuba. The crisis ended in compromise. Recent evidence indicates that the supposedly unarmed missiles may have been equipped with nuclear warheads.

The Brandenburg Gate was an icon of the division of Berlin by the Berlin Wall, which ran just to its west. In 1989, when the wall came tumbling down, the Brandenburg Gate reopened and West German Chancellor Helmut Kohl became the first to walk through.

Victory without War

Relations between the two superpowers improved in the 1980s with the election of Mikhail Gorbachev as president of the Soviet Union. Gorbachev pursued a policy of *perestroika* (remodeling) and *glasnost* (openness).

The rise of the Solidarity trade union movement in Poland, plus increasing discontent in the satellite nations of Eastern Europe, led to the fall of several governments in 1989. (The events were symbolized by the tearing down of the Berlin Wall by West and East Germans alike.) The USSR chose not to intervene, and in December 1991 the Soviet Union became the Russian Federation. The Cold War had come to an end.

Conversation Starter Since 1947, the cover of every issue of the journal *Bulletin of the Atomic Scientists* has included an image of a clock depicting how close humankind is to midnight, or "catastrophic destruction." You can view the clock at www.thebulletin.org.

The Vietnam War: A Futile Intervention

The convolutions of the Vietnam War owed much to the Cold War strategies of European and U.S. powers. Everyone agreed that the small, rural southeast Asian country should be a bulwark against communist expansion—everyone except the North Vietnamese. As U.S. military involvement grew and the war widened, so did protest at home.

During World War II a national resistance group, the Viet Minh under the communist leadership of Ho Chi Minh, began to seek Vietnamese independence from France. After the Japanese surrender, the Viet Minh took power.

In September 1945, Ho Chi Minh declared independence. Allied forces then agreed that China and Great Britain should occupy Vietnam and that the French should assume control. But the French became embroiled in the First Indochina War, which lasted until the Viet Minh won a decisive victory at Dien Bien Phu in 1954.

A Growing Divide

The 1954 Geneva Conference made a provision to divide Vietnam north/south along the 17th parallel. The split was supposed to last only until elections in 1956. The Viet Minh under Ho Chi Minh controlled North Vietnam, while the southern State of Vietnam was under Emperor Bao Da. The following year, a new Republic of Vietnam under President Ngo Dinh Diem was declared. The United States welcomed the establishment of such a strongly anti-communist state in the area, but Diem's rule was corrupt, and thousands died during his time in power. Opposition to Diem grew, and in 1959 the North Vietnamese Central Committee in Hanoi issued a secret resolution authorizing an armed struggle.

The next year, communists in the south established the National Front for the Liberation of South Vietnam (NLF). In response, the number of U.S. "military

In Fact...

Fear of the "domino effect"

shaped much American foreign policy in the mid-twentieth century. The American government believed that if one country were to become communist, it would cause others to follow. To instill concern in the public mind, the domino analogy was used: If one upright domino in a row falls, it topples all the others. This domino effect, or "theory," was used to justify American intervention in more than one conflict during the Cold War.

Key Players

Ho Chi Minh	Ngo Dinh Diem	Lyndon B. Johnson
1890–1969	*1901–1963*	*1908–1973*
The leader of the Viet Minh independence movement and founder of the Democratic Republic of Vietnam (North Vietnam) in 1945, Ho Chi Minh was president from 1946 to 1969. The capital, Saigon, was renamed Ho Chi Minh City in his honor.	Ngo Dinh Diem was the first president of South Vietnam. A staunch nationalist, he imposed harsh and repressive anti-communist and anti-Buddhist measures. In 1963, Diem was overthrown in a coup and executed.	Johnson became U.S. president following the assassination of John F. Kennedy in 1963. He also authorized the escalation of American involvement in Vietnam. In 1964, he was elected in his own right, winning by a huge margin.

advisers" in the south was increased in 1964. An attack on U.S. Navy vessels in the Gulf of Tonkin gave President Johnson the excuse to use force. The American ground war began in March 1965, involving more than 500,000 U.S. military personnel at its height.

To prevent surprise jungle attacks, the Americans employed defoliants (most famously, Agent Orange) to destroy large forested areas. The effects of defoliants are said to include cancers and birth defects, and it is estimated that there have since been more than 4,000,000 casualties.

The Tet Offensive and Beyond

In January 1968, the Viet Minh attacked over a hundred cities in the "Tet offensive." Although the attack eventually failed militarily, the North won a political victory.

The U.S. anti-war movement gathered strength, and the U.S. gradually withdrew its troops. Then, in 1973, the Paris Peace Accords formally ended U.S. involvement. On April 30, 1975, the South Vietnamese capital of Saigon fell to the North Vietnamese, and the Socialist Republic of Vietnam came into being on July 2, 1976.

Arab–Israeli Conflicts: Fight for a Homeland

The 1948 international recognition of Israel, formerly Palestine, as a Jewish state was an act of goodwill. Yet it set off a violent conflict between Israelis, displaced Palestinians, and quickly drew in the neighboring Arab countries. Every effort at peaceful resolution has proved ephemeral, and the powder keg fuse is still lit.

In the early twentieth century, the Jewish people were spread throughout the world; anti-Semitic persecution was rife, and a movement for a permanent Jewish homeland in Palestine gained momentum.

In the Balfour Declaration of 1917, the British government pledged support. After World War I, Palestine became a British-run territory and Jewish immigration increased. Tensions between Arabs and Jews surfaced immediately, and there were many clashes up to the start of World War II.

The First Clashes

During World War II, millions of Jews fell victim to the Nazis' "Final Solution." Their plight touched the hearts of many, and at the end of the war, Britain turned to the United Nations for help. While the Jews accepted the plan for separate Arab and Jewish states, Palestinian Arabs rejected it.

Arab and Israeli paramilitary forces clashed violently, but the state of Israel came into existence in 1948. Forces from Egypt, Syria, Lebanon, Iraq, and Jordan attacked the new country, but after a brief war Israel had gained more territory than before.

The Suez Crisis

War broke out again in 1956, in response to Egypt's nationalization of the Suez Canal. Israel, aided by France and Britain, invaded the Sinai Peninsula and gained control of

A current map of the Middle East

the Gaza Strip, but pressure from the United States and the United Nations (U.N.) forced a cease-fire. Under U.N. terms, Israel withdrew from Egyptian territory, and Egypt demilitarized the Sinai and permitted free navigation of the Suez Canal. The fledgling United Nations established and monitored a buffer zone on the Sinai Peninsula, the first time it had taken such action.

The Six-Day War

In 1967, war erupted again when tension between Israel and Syria caused Egypt to expel U.N. peacekeepers from the peninsula and close the Straits of Tiran to Israeli shipping. Some 100,000 Egyptian soldiers massed on the border, and Egypt's president, Gamal Abdel Nasser, called on Arab states to unite against the state of Israel, then less than two decades old.

Fearing an imminent invasion, Israel launched a massive air strike and succeeded in destroying over 300 Egyptian planes. This surprise attack gave Israel the edge, and the so-called Six-Day War gave the country control of the Sinai Peninsula, the Gaza Strip, the West Bank, eastern Jerusalem, and the Golan Heights.

Key Player

Yasser Arafat
1929–2004

Yasser Arafat was the chairman of the Palestine Liberation Organization and president of the Palestinian National Authority until his death in 2004. A controversial figure, he fought continuously for the establishment of a Palestinian homeland and was regarded as a heroic freedom fighter by his people. In 1994, he shared the Nobel Peace Prize with Israel's Yitzhak Rabin and Shimon Peres.

The Yom Kippur War

On October 6, 1973, the Jewish holiday of Yom Kippur, Egyptian and Syrian forces launched a surprise attack on Israel but were beaten back by the Israeli army. America, fearful of Soviet intervention, pressured the United Nations into brokering a cease-fire, which came into effect on October 26.

A Lasting Peace?

In 1978, U.S. President Jimmy Carter oversaw talks between Egypt and Israel. The resultant Camp David Accords led to the signing of the 1979 Israel–Egypt Peace Treaty and the first recognition of Israel by an Arab state.

The Palestinian people remained without a homeland, and in 1987 they rose up against Israeli occupation. From then on, a great deal of world opinion has pressured Israel to find a solution.

In 1993, the Oslo Peace Accords granted the Palestinian Authority limited self-rule; in return, Palestinians recognized Israel's right to exist. Peace efforts have since been less successful, and the Arab-Israeli conflict continues with no end in sight.

War in Afghanistan: The Soviet Quagmire

Afghanistan became the hotbed of Islamic fundamentalism the world sees today only after the 1979 Russian invasion. With Western financing, young Muslims were recruited, trained, and armed in the 1980s to combat occupying Soviet forces. These fighters, called the Mujahideen, turned Afghanistan into a humiliating failure for the Russians.

In the 1970s, the rise of Islamist states in Iran and Pakistan concerned the Soviet Union. Nervous about the potential spread of Islamic extremism into some of the southern Soviet republics with large Muslim populations, the USSR decided to use Afghanistan as a buffer zone.

In 1979, a hard-pressed communist regime in the Afghan capital of Kabul requested Soviet assistance to fight an insurgency and, as with U.S. involvement in Vietnam 15 years before, initial military assistance quickly became a full-scale deployment.

The American Response

At this time, American politics was still dominated by a fear of spreading communism, and President Carter denounced the invasion as "the most serious threat to peace since the Second World War."

As well as imposing a trade embargo against the USSR, America also supported the insurgency through the Central Intelligence Agency, which gave covert assistance to the anti-communist Mujahideen.

A pattern very similar to what the Americans had faced in Vietnam emerged as the Soviet troops became bogged down in a war that had no apparent end. Eventually, in the face of rising casualties and after a decade of conflict, Soviet forces withdrew in 1989.

The Taliban Ascendancy

Within two years, the Taliban—one of the most conservative insurgent groups—had taken control of Kabul and executed Mohammad Najibullah, the former president of Afghanistan. Though the stability was initially welcomed by the Afghan people, rule under the strict Taliban soon proved to be repressive in the extreme.

Among the many things prohibited by the Taliban were television, movies, dancing, music, kite-flying, computers, and the display of photographs; they also destroyed priceless artwork. Life for women was particularly harsh, and with few exceptions, women were not permitted to work or to receive an education after the age of eight. Women were also forced to wear the burqa, (a heavy dress that covers the whole body), and they could no longer travel without being accompanied by a close male relative.

Kabul, the capital of Afghanistan, is situated in a narrow valley in the east of the country. The city was the main base of the Soviet forces during their invasion, but after their withdrawal it subsequently fell to and became divided among the militias in 1992. In 1996, it was captured by the Taliban, who held control until 2001.

Men and women who violated the laws were beaten by the religious police; those accused of more serious offenses faced public execution. Human rights abuses and the lack of elections denied the Taliban official recognition from all but three countries.

A Spreading Ideology

As radical Islam spread around the world, attacks on Western targets increased, culminating in the deadly assaults on the World Trade Center in New York and the Pentagon in Washington on September 11, 2001. Suspicion immediately fell upon Osama bin Laden and al-Qaeda, an organization that had its roots in the anti-Soviet insurgency. The U.S. government believed that bin Laden was directing operations from within the sanctuary of Afghanistan and demanded

that the Taliban government turn him over. Negotiations broke down, however, and on October 7, 2001, the United States launched what it called Operation Enduring Freedom to remove the Taliban from power and hunt down bin Laden. The American war effort was supported by a coalition that included the UK, France, Germany, Australia, and a smattering of troops from other nations.

Anti-Taliban forces in Afghanistan, the Northern Alliance, fought on the side of the United States, and within a relatively short time had gained control of a number of provinces. On November 12, the Taliban moved from Kabul and by early December had retreated to the mountains along the Afghanistan–Pakistan border. From its mountain hideaways, the Taliban regrouped and continues to attract new recruits.

Conversation Starter The United States rained "Shock and Awe" on Baghdad, Iraq, in March 2003. Was the attack "preemptive," defined in military usage as based on incontrovertible evidence of imminent attack? Or was it "preventive," based on possible future threats?

War in the Balkans: Europe's Hot Spot

A look at the map of old Yugoslavia shows the hodgepodge of states that were first tossed together after World War I and managed to stay together only under strong, centralized communist rule. Today, Yugoslavia is just a memory, yet the region—beset with ethnic and religious resentments—remains the most volatile part of Europe.

The Socialist Federal Republic of Yugoslavia was formed at the end of World War II. It consisted of six republics—Bosnia-Herzegovina, Croatia, Macedonia, Montenegro, Serbia, and Slovenia. The federation comprised an uneasy mix of religious, cultural, and historical consolidations under communist dictatorship of Josip Broz Tito. And tensions grew apace after Tito's death in 1980.

The Fall of a Federation

The growing burden of debt and unequal economic and social development fueled ethnic and religious tensions. When 1991 elections in Slovenia and Croatia gave power to nationalist parties, both moved toward secession from the federation.

Slovenia's battle for independence against federal Yugoslav troops lasted just 10 days and did not involve huge loss of life. In Croatia, however, the Serbs committed many atrocities, including the large-scale massacre of captured Croatian soldiers and civilians. The Vance Peace Plan of 1992 ended the fighting and created United Nations–controlled zones in territory claimed by the rebel Serbs as the Republic of Serbian Krajina. In 1995, Croatia successfully reclaimed most of this territory, resulting in the exodus of 200,000 Serbs.

In 1992, Bosnia declared independence, which led to an outbreak of violence between the Muslim and Serb peoples of the region. Bosnian Serbs wished to remain within the

In Fact...

Modern Balkan conflicts fall into two periods:

- The conflicts that erupted during the breakup of the Socialist Republic of Yugoslavia: the war in Slovenia (1991); the Croatian War of Independence (1991–1995); and the Bosnian War (1992–1995).

- The conflicts in Albanian-populated regions: the Kosovo War (1996–1999); the Southern Serbia conflict (2000–2001); and the Macedonia conflict (2001).

federation and received backing from the Yugoslav People's Army and Serbia. A separate conflict took place within central Bosnia, where the predominantly Muslim army was fighting Bosnian Croats who wished to be part of a greater Croatia.

The Bosnian conflict was by far the bloodiest in the Balkans, and large numbers of the Muslim population became victims of the genocide policy known as ethnic cleansing. International peacekeepers proved ineffective, and by 1993, Bosnian Serbs controlled about 70 percent of Bosnia.

A Brief Pause

American pressure to end the war in Bosnia led to the Dayton Agreement in November 1995, which created two self-governing entities in Bosnia—the Bosnian Serb Republic and the Muslim (Bosnjak)-Croat Federation. During the late 1980s, the province of Kosovo in Serbia lost many of its autonomous powers under the presidency of Slobodan Milosevic, and life for the Albanian people there became increasingly repressive.

In 1996, the Kosovo Liberation Army (KLA) was established to fight for an independent Kosovo and began a series of attacks on the Serb and Yugoslav security forces.

Yugoslavia was once made up of seven states that since 1991 have broken apart and re-formed with new boundaries—and a firm hold on old animosities as well.

The Serbian response was brutal, and full-scale war broke out in 1999.

In March 1999, NATO forces carried out their first-ever attack on a European country, bombing military facilities and other strategic targets in Kosovo and Serbia. Approximately 800,000 of the 1,500,000 Albanians in Kosovo were forced to leave by Serb forces. In June 1999, the United Nations took over the administration of Kosovo, and many Serbs left the province. Those who remained were subjected to retaliatory violence.

Flash Points

Ethnic violence surfaced yet again in the Southern Serbia and Macedonia conflicts of 2001, both involving clashes between Albanian militants and the state security forces, though neither caused large loss of life. In both cases, peace agreements ended the conflicts, but the situation remained fragile afterward.

In 2003, the Federal Republic of Yugoslavia became the union of Serbia and Montenegro, and Yugoslavia disappeared from the European map. Three years later, Montenegro declared its independence. In February 2008, Kosovo declared its independence from Serbia as well.

The span of human civilization has been marked by a great many wars. This chapter has touched upon only some of the key ones that have shaped the modern age. But can you remember the names of the generals or the dates of the battles?

Warring States: The American Civil War

1 In which year did the American Civil War start?

a) *1851*   b) *1861*
c) *1871*   d) *1881*

2 Which six states voted to leave the Union initially?

World War I: Death on a Grand Scale

1 On what date was Archduke Ferdinand shot by a Serb Nationalist, triggering World War I?

a) *June 28, 1914*   b) *July 28, 1914*
c) *June 28, 1915*   d) *July 28, 1915*

2 At which battle did Allied forces use tanks en masse for the first time?

The Spanish Civil War: A Bloody Preview

1 Name the incumbent political party at the start of the Spanish Civil War.

2 Which European capital city was the main recruitment center for the International Brigades?

3 For how long did General Franco's dictatorship last?

a) *16 years*   b) *26 years*
c) *36 years*   d) *46 years*

World War II: The World at War

1 What is the name of the treaty signed at the end of World War I, which many see as sowing the seeds for World War II?

2 In which year did Hitler become Chancellor of Germany?

a) *1929*   b) *1933*
c) *1937*   d) *1941*

3 True or False: The atomic bomb dropped on Hiroshima was nicknamed "Fat Man."

The Cold War: A Four-Decade Standoff

1 Who coined the term "iron curtain" in relation to the division of Europe?

2 What was the name of the Soviet alliance equivalent to NATO?

3 In which year did the Berlin Wall fall?

　a) *1989*　　　b) *1990*
　c) *1991*　　　d) *1992*

4 What does the term *perestroika*—used by Gorbachev in relation to the changes made to the Soviet structure—actually mean?

　a) *Redirection*　　b) *Recovery*
　c) *Regrowth*　　　d) *Remodeling*

5 Where will you find the most famous image of a "doomsday clock" illustrating just how close the world stands to catastrophic destruction?

The Vietnam War: A Futile Intervention

1 With which nation did the Viet Minh fight the First Indochina War?

2 What was the name of the Vietnamese capital before it was renamed Ho Chi Minh City?

Arab–Israeli Conflicts: Fight for a Homeland

1 The Six-Day War was fought between which two nations?

　a) *Israel and Egypt*
　b) *Israel and Jordan*
　c) *Israel and Lebanon*
　d) *Israel and Syria*

2 What was the name of the talks between Israel and Egypt in 1978?

3 True or False: Yasser Arafat was awarded the Nobel Peace Prize.

War in Afghanistan: The Soviet Quagmire

1 Which American president denounced the Soviet involvement in Afghanistan as "the most serious threat to peace since the Second World War"?

2 In which year did the Soviet forces withdraw?

3 What was the name of the Afghan alliance that fought on the side of the U.S. and Western troops to oust the Taliban?

　a) *The Northern Alliance*
　b) *The Eastern Alliance*
　c) *The Southern Alliance*
　d) *The Western Alliance*

War in the Balkans: Europe's Hot Spot

1 Name the seven republics that once made up the Socialist Federal Republic of Yugoslavia.

2 Name the president of the Federal Republic of Yugoslavia, under whom the province of Kosovo lost most of its autonomy.

Chapter Seven

The Structure of Society

Monarchies and feudalism were among the earliest forms of government, and systems granting a modicum of power to the people arose in thirteenth-century England with the Magna Carta. Some 500 years later, democracy caught fire and spread; however, it is far from the only form of governance. This chapter reviews the various systems of government and the economic systems underpinning them.

Forms of Government: Democracies

The idea of democracy arose in ancient Greece with some of the great thinkers, and the notion that the people—not kings or lords or tyrants—can run their own affairs has been put into practice in the modern world. How did it come about? Read on.

Some of the earliest writings dealing with society and politics were those of the Greek philosophers Socrates (470–399 BCE), Plato (428–348 BCE), and Plato's student of 20 years, Aristotle (384–322 BCE). Indeed, it was in the ancient Greek city of Athens that the seeds of democracy first fell on fertile ground. The very word means "power to the people"—Greek *demos* (people) and *kratos* (power).

Plato and Aristotle

Plato's *The Republic* moves from grappling with questions of justice to the concept of an ideal state. Plato wrote of governments, describing the "truly just and good . . . [correspond] to our ideal

society where the best rule." He expressed disdain for four types of societies: timarchy, the military aristocracy of Sparta; oligarchy, government by the few; democracy, or rule by many; and tyranny, with total political power vested in one person.

Democracy, Plato said, "is a charming form of government, full of variety and disorder and dispensing a sort of equality to equals and unequals alike." But he also held that "democracy passes into despotism."

Aristotle, after studying and comparing more than 150 constitutions, wrote in *The Politics* his theories of the ideal constitution and form of government. He wrote that "all [political] associations are instituted for the purpose of attaining some virtue." Aristotle believed the archetypal government to be one in which "laws should be sovereign on every issue," suggesting that virtuous rulers were bound by laws and could institute a system of checks to ensure governance with a measure of self-discipline.

The Greek assembly, where citizens voted by raising their hands, was one of the first forms of democratic government. Yet the term "citizen" excluded women, slaves, and immigrants. The Romans also held elections, but votes of the wealthy counted for more than those of ordinary citizens.

Voting is the lifeblood of democracies. The growing use of electronic voting machines over paper ballots has raised alarm because the machines are more easily rigged.

Modern Democracies

The foundations of modern democracy were laid in the thirteenth century with the Magna Carta (Great Charter) of 1215. This charter became the basis for English common law, which gradually invested more power in the people. The first British parliament was elected in 1265.

In the 1700s, the roots laid down in England grew into a spreading tree. American colonists developed Republicanism, a government system in which the people choose representatives to make policy decisions on their behalf—a "liberal democracy." From ancient Greece, this had been seen as preferable to "direct democracy," wherein the people themselves decide policy matters through voting, risking what is called "the tyranny of the majority"—political decisions so far above the interest of a minority that they can be the equivalent of despotism.

After the colonists overthrew British rule in 1781, the U.S. Constitution was ratified in 1789. It was soon followed by the Bill of Rights, based on the Bill of Rights declared by the English Parliament in 1689.

Democracy spread through Europe after the 1789–1799 revolution in France, the first of many socialist democracies to rise on the Continent.

Conversation Starter In 2005, the United Nations formed the U.N. Democracy Fund to spur the development and progression of democratic ideals without supporting a particular form of democracy. The first funds went to the Palestinian Territories in 2006.

Three More Forms of National Government

Political science generally categorizes the main forms of modern government as democracy, communism, socialism, and fascism. But there is no perfect example of any type of government, because national governments must respond and adapt to shifting social and economic situations and external pressures.

Communism

Communism is an ancient concept: Land is owned by the community, and all people receive according to their needs. In fact, Karl Marx held that ancient hunter-gatherer cultures were essentially communistic.

In the eighteenth century, modern democracies (page 161) arose largely in response to Enlightenment philosophy. Communism is primarily a twentieth-century development, reacting to the effects of the Industrial Revolution economy on workers and the weakening of old imperial powers. The first communist government was the Soviet Union, formed soon after the 1917 Russian Revolution. The new state drew on Marxist principles, as interpreted by Vladimir Lenin and other theorists. The Russian system reached its height of power during the Cold War, under the oppressive rule of Joseph Stalin.

Today's communist nations are for the most part single-party states, in which one party generally controls all functions of government; however, as with any form of government, there is a wide spectrum of different types of governance.

In many cases modern communism has evolved; however, the original ideal of a classless state with no private ownership has worked for small groups—certain monastic orders, for example, in which everyone works as they're able, benefits are equally distributed, and no member is excluded.

Red Square, Moscow, was for many years the icon of Communism with the buildings of the Kremlin as a backdrop and Lenin's Mausoleum at its heart.

Socialism

Modern democratic socialism takes many forms, from central control of a limited range of activities, such as universal education, to the nationalization of all industry and public services. One of socialism's earliest advocates, the Welsh industrial reformer Robert Owen, proposed non-competitive industrial environments, but Owenite communities established in early nineteenth-century Britain and the United States ultimately failed.

Socialist philosophy was altered by the publication of the *Communist Manifesto* in 1848, which abandoned utopian dreams in favor of "scientific socialism." Other nineteenth-century thinkers pushed for a compromise position—a non-communist form of reformist government within a capitalistic framework, often called "social democracy." Countries including England, France, Germany, Sweden, Australia, and New Zealand have successfully integrated socialist programs such as national health insurance and retirement plans with democratic governance.

Key Player

Sir Thomas More
1477-1535

In 1516, More's book *Utopia* told of a strange, wonderful place where everything is ruled by reason. A clear contrast with the politics of greed and power grabs, *Utopia* gave a new word to the language and profoundly influenced the later formulation of communist and socialist theories. A lawyer, More became England's lord chancellor under King Henry VIII, but as a devout Catholic, he refused to support Henry's claim to be head of the Church of England. More was tried on trumped-up charges of treason and was beheaded.

Fascism

Strictly speaking, fascism was limited to Italy under the post–World War I dictatorship of Benito Mussolini. But it is also applied to mid-twentieth-century Germany, Spain, Japan, Argentina, and a few other locations.

Fascism is based on absolute state power enforced by threatened and real violence. (Mussolini originated the word, taking it from the Latin fasces—a Roman emblem of penal authority consisting of a bundle of birch rods and an ax.) The state is usually personified by a charismatic, authoritarian leader with military connections: Hitler in Germany, Francisco Franco in Spain, Juan Peron in Argentina, and Japan's Emperor Hirohito. Highly emotional propaganda encourages blind devotion to state and leader. Germany's Nazi party added rabid genocidal racism to the mix, leading to the mass murder of millions of Jews and other "undesirables." In Europe, the sole fascist survivor of World War II was Franco's Spain, which remained publicly neutral in the war.

The Rise and Fall of European Communism

Russia and its neighbors went through turbulent times from Lenin's Bolshevik Revolution in 1917 to the dissolution of the Soviet Union in 1991. As significant, Russia and its communist allies stood in stark opposition to the capitalist democracies of the West.

In 1848, Karl Marx and Friedrich Engels wrote *The Communist Manifesto*, a work that advocated ridding society of private property and launching a revolution in the pursuit of a society without class divisions.

The manifesto greatly influenced the Russian revolutionary Vladimir Lenin (1870–1924) and his Bolshevik ("majoritarian") followers long before their revolution of 1917. Marx and Engels developed a theory of communism; Lenin put it to work.

The Rise of Stalin

Lenin's death brought to power the man associated most closely with communism's ills. Joseph Stalin's political and ethnic purges and his relentless pursuit of the pol-

icies of industrialization and collectivization left millions dead and radically changed what had become the Union of Soviet Socialist Republics (USSR). His greatest test came with the 1941 German invasion of Russia: Despite heavy casualties, his armies turned back the German tide at Stalingrad in 1942–1943. Stalin captured Berlin in 1945.

After World War II, the USSR, France, Great Britain, and the United States determined that Germany should be divided and temporarily occupied. At the Yalta Conference, Stalin gave U.S. president Franklin D. Roosevelt and British prime minister Winston Churchill his word that the Soviets would not seek to dominate Eastern Europe. Yet the USSR soon exerted its influence

1848	1917	1918	1922	1924	1941	1945	1949	1953	1954
Karl Marx publishes *The Communist Manifesto*.		British, American, and French troops fight alongside tsarist forces.		Lenin dies and Stalin begins to accumulate complete power.		The Yalta Conference is held at the end of World War II.		Stalin dies.	
	The February and October revolutions take place in Russia.		The USSR is established with Stalin and Lenin at the helm.		Germany invades Russia.		The USSR becomes a nuclear power.		The Warsaw Pact is signed.

and dropped, in Churchill's words, an "iron curtain" across Europe.

As a counterweight to the recently formed North Atlantic Treaty Organization (NATO), the USSR and eight Eastern European nations created the Warsaw Pact in 1955. Still, those forced to live under Soviet rule had other ideas. While uprisings in the 1950s in Hungary and other countries were crushed, by the end of the decade, some 3,000,000 Eastern Europeans had fled the USSR through Berlin. The Soviets reacted by erecting the Berlin Wall in 1961.

The Fall

With his 1980 Solidarity Movement in Poland, Lech Walesa founded the first non-communist labor

Key Player

Mikhail Gorbachev
b. 1931

In 1985, Gorbachev began his process of *glasnost*, encouraging people to become more open. This was coupled with *perestroika*, a process of restructuring intended to transform the nation's economy in just 500 days. By 1989, Gorbachev spoke of a policy of non-intervention with leaders of the Warsaw Pact nations, and Soviet troops began to withdraw from these states.

union in the Soviet Union. Meanwhile, dissatisfaction with Soviet policy spread like a virus. In 1985, USSR head of state Mikhail Gorbachev instituted several reforms, and the die for change was cast.

In 1989, Poland overthrew Soviet rule. The same year, the Hungarian communist party disbanded and re-formed as socialists, and East Germany and Czechoslovakia followed suit. On November 9, 1989, the Berlin Wall—for decades the symbol of the world's divisions—was torn down to great rejoicing.

The mighty USSR ended not with a bang but a whimper. In 1993, it was replaced by the Russian Federation, and a representative democracy spread in its wake across much of Eurasia.

he Hungarian evolution is ut down.		The Cuban Missile Crisis raises tensions.		The Strategic Arms Limitation Treaty (SALT I) is signed.		Gorbachev comes to power and begins reforms.		Germany is reunified.	
956	**1961**	**1962**	**1968**	**1971**	**1979**	**1985**	**1989**	**1990**	**1991**
	The Berlin Wall is built.		Reforms in Czechoslovakia are stopped by a Soviet invasion.		SALT II is signed.		The Berlin Wall falls.		The Soviet Union becomes the Russian Federation.

The World as One: The United Nations

Ask a group of people what the job of the United Nations is and whether it does its job well, and the answers you'll receive will vary as widely as the nations themselves—only to be expected when so many member nations (currently numbering 154) attempt to make policy together and serve their own interests at the same time.

The United Nations (U.N.) was created to replace the unsuccessful League of Nations—an organization that was founded in the wake of World War I yet failed to prevent the outbreak of World War II.

U.S. president Franklin Delano Roosevelt used the term "United Nations" in 1942 when speaking of the 26 nations uniting to fight against the Axis powers during World War II. The United Nations was chartered shortly after that war, in October 1945.

Signing the Charter

As the first country to be attacked by an Axis power (Japan), China was afforded the honor of being the first signatory to the new U.N. charter. Forty-nine other nations also signed as original members, with Poland becoming the fifty-first shortly thereafter.

The charter of the United Nations stipulates that the organization work toward establishing and supporting peaceful international relations, with nations collaborating to solve international problems such as failing economies, starvation, and genocide.

Respect for human rights and basic freedoms are also concerns of the United Nations. Among its agencies are the World Health Organization (WHO), the U.N. Educational, Scientific, and Cultural Organization (UNESCO), and the U.N. Children's Fund (UNICEF). Though headquartered in New York City, the United Nations maintains offices in Vienna, Geneva, and other major cities.

Inside the United Nations

The General Assembly, which meets each year in New York, is one of six bodies governing the United Nations. The assembly consists of all member sovereign nations. The other bodies are the Security Council of five permanent and 10 elected members, the Economic and Social Council, the Trusteeship Council, the International Court of Justice, and the Secretariat, of which the Secretary General is the head.

The permanent members of the Security Council (China, France, the Russian Federation, the United Kingdom, and the United States) are considered the "policemen" of the organization. This powerful group is charged with making many of the United Nation's most difficult decisions and operates with the intention of providing effective resolutions to international conflicts.

Peacekeeping and Law

Part of the organization's mission is to keep the peace and protect civilians. Soldiers in blue helmets are often the United Nation's most visible presence around the world. In 1988, U.N. peacekeeping forces as a whole received the Nobel Peace Prize.

The role of the U.N.'s International Court of Justice (IJC), based in The Hague, Netherlands, is twofold: In accordance with international law, it settles trade or other disputes submitted by member nations, and it issues advice on issues referred to it by U.N. agencies. Starting in the 1990s, the court held International Criminal Tribunals in the wake of wars in Rwanda and the former Yugoslavia. In 2002, the U.N. General Assembly initiated the formation of a related court, the International Criminal Court (ICC), charged with trying the most serious crimes against international law.

The U.N. Headquarters, on Manhattan's East Side, was designed by an international team of architects and was completed in 1953. A major renovation is scheduled for completion in 2015.

In Fact...

Millennium Development Goals
embody the focus of the United Nations on various issues throughout the world. The stated aims of these goals are to . . .

- Eradicate poverty and hunger.
- Achieve universal primary education.
- Promote gender equality and empower women.
- Reduce child mortality.
- Improve maternal health.
- Combat HIV/AIDS, malaria, and other diseases.
- Ensure environmental sustainability.
- Create a global partnership for development.

These goals set by the United Nations are scheduled to be achieved by the year 2015. The progress toward each goal can be monitored on the U.N. website—www.un.org.

World Population: A Visual Guide

As civilization took hold some 5,000 years ago, so did systems of agriculture, allowing more and more people to be supported on the same amount of land. World population has continued to grow ever since, passing a billion in the early 1800s and currently standing at around 6.8 billion.

The United States, unlike many Western nations, is still growing in population, and this growth has largely been fueled by immigration. The inscription at the foot of the Statue of Liberty underlines this influx, reading: "Give me your tired, your poor; Your huddled masses yearning to breathe free..."

Greenland, home to just under 60,000, has the lowest population density of any country, according to a 2004 U.N. report.

IN THE KNOW

Trying to account for every person in every country throughout the world is a daunting task but a vital one. Census-takers counting sample populations must always consider the various elements that can affect a particular population's growth— among them, infant mortality, birth rates, disease, and migration.

South America boasts a population fast approaching 400 million, and almost half of these people live in Brazil, the world's fifth most populous nation.

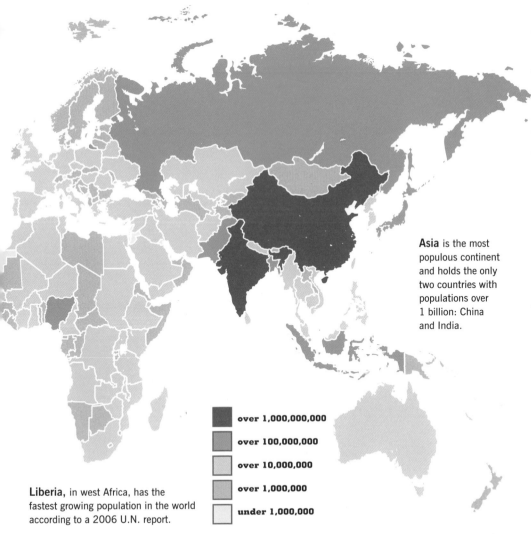

Conversation Starter Many questions are asked about the world's capacity to cope with a human population whose growth accelerates with every passing year. Does the planet have sufficient resources to sustain such numbers? What impact will pollution, land development, and agricultural engineering have on the Earth's capacity to provide for ever-growing numbers of people?

Asia is the most populous continent and holds the only two countries with populations over 1 billion: China and India.

Liberia, in west Africa, has the fastest growing population in the world according to a 2006 U.N. report.

over 1,000,000,000
over 100,000,000
over 10,000,000
over 1,000,000
under 1,000,000

Centers of Power: Capitals of the World

A capital city is where the heart of a nation's power lies, but capitals are often far more than just the center of political life. They're usually the cultural and economic centers as well, and their histories can reflect the growth of their nations as a whole.

As new nations were either split or were born anew from other nations over the last few centuries, new capital cities came into being as a matter of course. By definition, a political capital is the seat of government of a nation or state. Other cities are financial or cultural "capitals," two being Shanghai and New York City.

Creating a Capital

Capital cities are sometimes designed and developed from scratch as the seat of the national government. Among the examples are Washington, D.C., in the United States; Canberra in Australia; Islamabad in Pakistan; Abuja in Nigeria; and Naypyidaw in Burma (Myanmar).

Some cities founded as capitals lost that distinction over time. An example is St. Petersburg, built by Tsar Peter the Great in 1703 as capital of the Russian Empire. The capital was moved to Moscow after the 1917 Bolshevik Revolution.

Washington and Ottawa, capitals of the United States and Canada, respectively, are among North America's most cosmopolitan cities.

Buenos Aires, the capital of Argentina, is so culturally sophisticated it is often referred to as "the Paris of South America."

IN THE KNOW

In the 1950s, Brazil decided to move its capital from Rio de Janeiro to the interior of the country. Built from scratch, the new capital city of Brasilia was largely intended to help populate the interior and create jobs when the massive project was undertaken—a reason for its nickname Capital da Esperança (City of Hope).

Shifting Capitals

In times of peril or war, some countries have had to move their governments from the capital cities; for example, Berlin was the capital of Prussia, which became Germany in 1871. After Germany split in the wake of World War II, the West German capital was moved to Bonn. Berlin again became the capital in the 1990s, after the USSR fell.

European capitals such as London, Amsterdam, and Madrid were great seats of power in the seventeenth-century colonization period.

Singapore is a world capital but happens to be a city-state—not the capital of a whole country.

Canberra was built as Australia's capital in 1913 in a new territory formed between the rival cities of Sydney and Melbourne.

Abuja was designed and planned as the new capital of Nigeria in the 1980s. It replaced Lagos as the capital in 1991.

Iconic Leaders
of the Modern World

Some born leaders rouse people so powerfully that their leadership transcends borders. Tied to a great cause, whether for good or bad, they are able to unite followers in the pursuit of their goals. Here are profiles of three great leaders who fit the bill.

Nelson Mandela

South African Rolihlahla Mandela (b. 1918), the son of a chieftain, was dubbed "Nelson" by a teacher. He became eager to practice law in a land where apartheid (segregation) was set in stone by the ruling Afrikaaners of Dutch descent. After earning a law degree in Johannesburg, Mandela opened a law office in 1952 and grew more active in a black liberation group, the African National Congress (ANC).

Rivonia Trial, Pretoria Supreme Court, April 20, 1964 "I [Mandela] have fought against white domination, and . . . against black domination. I have cherished the ideal of a democratic and free society in which all persons will live together in harmony and with equal opportunities. It is an ideal which I hope to live for and achieve. But, if needs be, it is an ideal for which I am prepared to die."

After police massacred blacks in Sharpeville township in 1960, Mandela tried to sabotage the ruling regime. Two years later, he was sentenced to five years in prison. In 1963, he was sentenced to life after a second trial found him guilty of treason for incendiary activities on the part of the ANC.

Mandela was hospitalized for tuberculosis in 1988, and South African blacks and the international community alike campaigned for his release from prison. President F. W. de Klerk freed Mandela, who then went on to head the ANC.

In 1993, Mandela and de Klerk were awarded the Nobel Peace Prize after working in concert to end apartheid and bring democracy to all South Africans. The next year, Mandela was elected as South Africa's first black president and entered the pantheon of great world leaders.

Conversation Starter Does a great leader always have to be good? *Time* magazine awards the annual title of "Person of the Year" not to the person who does the most good, but the person who makes the biggest difference to the world, good or bad.

Pope John Paul II

Karel Wojtyla was born in Wadowice, near Krakow, Poland, in 1920. He was ordained a priest at age 26, and by the time he was 43, he had become an archbishop. He joined the College of Cardinals in 1967. Eleven years later, this relatively unknown cardinal was elected the 264th pope. Not only was John Paul II from a communist nation, but he also became the first non-Italian pope in four and a half centuries.

John Paul II's 26-year service as pope of the Roman Catholic Church, the third longest, saw him travel to more countries (129) than any other pope. He was a man of many "firsts": the first pope to be greeted in the White House (1979); the first to visit a synagogue (in Rome in 1986); the first to visit a mosque (in Syria in 2001).

In 1981, a Turk named Mehmet Ali Agca tried to assassinate John Paul II as he was being driven through St. Peter's Square. The pope survived and by 2000 had worked to gain the pardon of the man convicted of attempted murder. Ali Agca was then returned to Turkey.

John Paul II's work with communist countries led them to gradually allow their citizens more religious freedom. Some historians say such work helped to break the hold of the USSR on the Warsaw Pact nations. Pope John Paul II lives on as a symbol of hope and peace the world over.

"The greatness of work is inside man." From the poem *I. Material*, written before Karel Wojtyla became pope in 1979.

Vladimir Ilyich Lenin

Vladimir Ilyich Lenin was born into a well-educated, democracy-minded family in 1870 in Simbirsk, Russia. It was the 1887 hanging of his older brother for involvement in a threat against the life of Tsar Alexander III that set young Vladimir on the revolutionary path. He earned a law degree but was more interested in spreading Marxist propaganda than law. In 1895, he was arrested and exiled to Siberia.

Lenin returned to Russia in 1900, and years of travel and radical politics followed. He considered World War I to be an imperialist war fought by the working classes against their own interests. He felt that they should instead be engaging in civil war against the ruling class.

"Freedom in a capitalist society always remains about the same as it was in ancient Greek republics: Freedom for slave owners."

In 1916, he retreated to Switzerland and wrote *Imperialism, the Highest Stage of Capitalism*. The next year, the February Revolution in Russia toppled Tsar Nicholas II, and Lenin returned to his homeland. Greeted as a hero, he inspired the October, or Bolshevik, Revolution that would establish Russia as a Marxist, or communist, state in 1917.

Though Lenin died in office and governed for only six years, his impact was such that his body still lies in state at the Kremlin's Red Square. His revolution altered the political landscape not only of Russia but also of much of the globe.

The Father of Modern Economics

Adam Smith, a Scot who lived from 1723 to 1790 and who studied moral philosophy at the University of Glasgow, was a creative thinker as well as an economist. While many others had written on the subject of economic theory before Smith, he is widely credited with the invention of economics as a subject for academic study.

The Wealth of Nations

The modern free economies of the world owe a debt of gratitude to Adam Smith. The theories he expounded in his 1776 work *An Inquiry into the Nature and Causes of the Wealth of Nations*, written at the dawn of the Industrial Revolution, laid down the foundation for free enterprise.

Smith believed that self-interest is inherent to human nature. In a nutshell, Smith's combination of philosophy and economics supported free trade and competitive markets. He claimed the best interests of the majority would be served if the free market were given free rein, and he held that the role of government in the economy should be to ensure robust competition.

The Invisible Hand

Applying philosophy to the competitive nature of markets is considered one of Smith's greatest accomplishments. Smith believed that competition would encourage businesses to strive for more wealth. In his theory, seeking maximum profit becomes the guiding factor for business, and this so-called invisible hand results in more good being done for more people.

The publication of Smith's magnum opus philosophizing on the wealth of nations is seen as the catapult that launched the discipline of economics. To this day, Smith's economic philosophy continues to be used by free-market capitalists in arguments against government regulation of trade.

Conversation Starter A great deal of economic debate surrounds what are known as "public goods"—goods and services that wouldn't exist if it were left to market forces. Such public goods as street lighting, the armed forces, and emergency services like policing and firefighting are funded through taxation. Just how much tax should be levied to pay for such public goods?

Key Players

| Karl Marx | John Maynard Keynes | Milton Friedman |
| *1818–1883* | *1883–1946* | *1912–2006* |

Karl Marx, born in the Kingdom of Prussia, was a reforming philosopher and political economist who did not agree that competition led to economic progress. His books *The Communist Manifesto* (1848) and *Das Kapital* (1867) provided the bedrock of economic and political theory for the subsequent rise of communism.

The General Theory of Employment, Interest, and Money (1936) by Keynes, an Englishman, was published during the Great Depression and advocated increased spending by governments to alleviate the damaging effects of "boom and bust" economics. The book ushered in a new era of political and economic thought.

The Quantity Theory of Money by American Milton Friedman (1956), along with the economic problems of the 1970s, went a long way toward bringing the Keynesian era to a close—most dramatically in the freeing up of the British and American economies under Margaret Thatcher and Ronald Reagan in the 1980s.

Politics and Economics

While the study of economics has led to innumerable advances, the nature of economic change means there is no "one size fits all" solution to the economic challenges faced by countries the world over. International trade agreements were forged in the early 1990s, and "global trade" has become a byword of the twenty-first century.

Economics is inextricably tied up with politics, and politicians ancient and modern have always campaigned on economic issues such as taxes, jobs, and employee benefits. Indeed, until around a hundred years after economics became a discrete discipline thanks to Adam Smith, this area of study was most commonly termed "political economy."

World GDP: A Visual Guide

Broadly speaking, a nation's **Gross Domestic Product (GDP)** is a measure of its wealth. Debate continues regarding the right way to measure wealth, or even whether wealth should be measured as opposed to some other indicator of well-being. Nevertheless, GDP remains a useful, if flawed, yardstick of a nation's economic status.

Billions of U.S. Dollars

- 2,000+
- 1,000–2,000
- 500–1,000
- 200–500
- 100–200
- 50–100
- 20–50
- 10–20
- 5–10
- 0–5

IN THE KNOW

In 2007, the GDP of the United States was by far the largest in the world, around three times greater than that of Japan, the world's second largest economy. However, Japan boasts a higher Human Development Index value for the quality of life; it ranks eighth in the world compared to the United States, which is placed twelfth.

Conversation Starter Along with the various measures of a country's economic output are others that measure quality of life. One such measure is the Human Development Index, taking stock of life expectancy, literacy, education, and standards of living. Whether such a measure is a more useful indicator of a nation's "wealth" than GDP is a question that is hotly debated.

Buy, Buy, Buy: The World of Stock Markets

Stock markets and financial exchanges have been around for a long time, but it wasn't until the twentieth century that these exchanges took on true economic significance. The level of globalization of the stock markets has increased massively in the past few decades, even if playing the market can be a hair-raising roller-coaster ride.

What's a Stock?

A stock represents a share in a business, and a person who owns such a share is known as a shareholder. Each stock costs a certain amount, and some yield a regular financial dividend. There are public and private companies, and there is public and private stock. A public company trades openly on the stock market, while privately held stock is traded only among other owners of the stock.

Buying and Selling

If a person decides a company is a worthy investment, buying stock is a way to share in that company's success. A successful company returns more to investors than they put in. An unsuccessful company may fail to pay anything at all.

This means the value of the stock rises and falls according to the returns an investor may expect. Such fluctuation in price opens the way to another form of investment in which a person may purchase stocks not just because of a good dividend, but also because

the stock is apt to rise in value; that will mean a profit if an investor chooses to sell at the right time. Stock markets regulate the selling and buying of stocks, and the market prices reflect the demand and supply of a particular stock.

Speculating on rising stock prices adds volatility to the stock markets, mainly because buyers and sellers make rash decisions. This "market sentiment" has played an important role in the many "bubbles" and "crashes" in history.

The History of Stock Markets

An early example of an equities market existed in the second century BCE in Rome, but it wasn't until after the medieval era that many European countries established markets. In the 1700s, the French market "bubbled" when Scottish economist John Law established a successful bank in Paris

Black Tuesday sees stocks crash in the United States and the beginning of the Great Depression in 1929.

The New York Stock Exchange 1896–2006

The Largest Securities Trading Floor in the world is claimed by UBS, a Swiss bank, in Stamford, Connecticut. It is home to about 1,400 staff who process roughly $1 trillion (U.S.) transactions a day.

and then purchased the ailing Mississippi Company, a Louisiana trade outfit. In what came to be known as the Mississippi Scheme, Law promoted Louisiana as a land with mountains full of silver and gold. Speculators rushed to buy shares. Some who sold early made huge fortunes, but most speculators were ruined when share values collapsed in October 1720.

It wasn't until 1792 that the United States entered into trading, and the New York Stock Exchange was established in the same year.

In 1944, John Maynard Keynes, a British economist, was instrumental in establishing a global, post–World War II financial system, setting the stage for the World Bank Group, an international financial institution that grants financial and technical assistance to developing countries around the world.

IN THE KNOW

The stock markets in developing countries are known as "emerging markets." Although such markets were once not considered worthy of serious investments, massive increases in the level of globalization have seen an influx of funds into such countries. With fast growth they promise the greatest returns, but also the highest risks.

Stocks crash in the wake of 9/11.

The "dot com boom" of the 1990s sees huge levels of speculative investment into Internet companies.

The oil crisis of 1973 causes stocks to dip sharply and inhibits the markets over the next decade.

From the different ways in which society is governed to the great names who have shaped the world as it is today, this chapter has looked at just how the world really works. But can you remember what has shaped the world as we know it?

Forms of Government: Democracies

1 In which Greek city did Socrates, Plato, and Aristotle reside?

2 What was the title of Jean-Jacques Rousseau's defining work?

3 In which year was the U.S. Constitution ratified?

a) *1759* b) *1769*
c) *1779* d) *1789*

Three More Forms of National Government

1 In which European country was the first communist government formed?

a) *Bulgaria* b) *Romania*
c) *Russia* d) *Yugoslavia*

2 What was the title of Thomas More's most famous work?

The Rise and Fall of European Communism

1 In which year were the February and October revolutions in Russia?

2 What was the name given to the communist followers of Lenin?

3 What was the name of the Polish non-communist labor movement founded by Lech Walesa?

4 Over what period of time did Soviet premier Mikhail Gorbachev set out to reform his nation?

a) *5 months* b) *1 year*
c) *500 days* d) *5 years*

The World as One: The United Nations

1 In which city will you find the U.N. headquarters?

a) *Brussels* b) *London*
c) *New York* d) *Paris*

2 Which country was the first to sign the U.N. charter?

3 What does the acronym UNESCO stand for?

4 By what date are the United Nations' Millennium Goals intended to be achieved?

World Population: A Visual Guide

1 During which century did the world's population pass 1 billion?

a) *1500s*　　b) *1600s*
c) *1700s*　　d) *1800s*

2 Which of the following figures is closest to the world's current population?

a) *6.8 billion*　　b) *8.2 billion*
c) *9.4 billion*　　d) *12.1 billion*

Centers of Power: Capitals of the World

1 Which Russian tsar built St. Petersburg, which for a time was the capital of Russia?

2 Brasilia has been the capital of Brazil since the 1950s, but which city was previously the capital?

3 Which city is the longest-serving capital in the world?

a) *Brussels*　　b) *London*
c) *New York*　　d) *Paris*

Iconic Leaders of the Modern World

1 What is the name of the party that was led by Nelson Mandela?

2 Which leader was born Karel Wojtyla?

3 In which academic subject did Vladimir Lenin take his degree?

The Father of Modern Economics

1 Name the man who is widely viewed as "the father of economics."

2 What was the title of the work that he published in 1776?

3 Which American economist is credited, at least in part, with bringing the Keynesian era to a close?

World GDP: A Visual Guide

1 What does the acronym GDP stand for?

2 Which country has the largest GDP in the world?

Buy, Buy, Buy: The World of Stock Markets

1 In which year did stocks crash on Black Tuesday, marking the beginning of the Great Depression?

a) *1928*　　b) *1929*
c) *1930*　　d) *1931*

2 What name was given to the period of stock market growth driven by Internet companies?

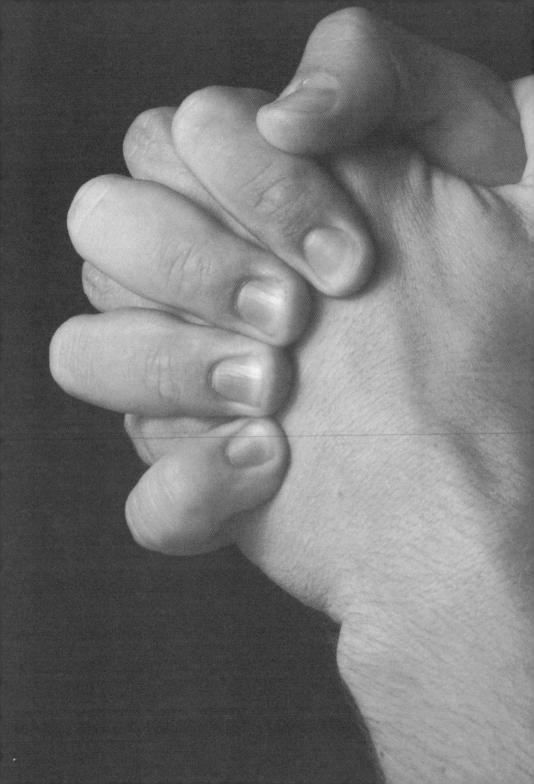

Chapter Eight

Religion and Thought

In every historical period and culture, humans have inevitably sought answers to life's eternal questions. While previous chapters in this book have looked at the practical realms of life, this one focuses on the service and worship of a supreme being or the supernatural. In their many forms, religions are the bedrock of the faithful, and sometimes of civilizations. Then there are those people whose thinking alone gave us insights into the meaning of life and the workings of society—philosophers from ancient times to the present day.

The Religions of the World

The map of world religions reflects the political and social history of humankind. Eternal quests for meaning, along with conquests, migration, trade, and evangelistic fervor have helped to shape the beliefs of nations and peoples alike.

Every human society has had some form of religious belief or practice. In simplest terms, religion is the belief that the world is inspired and directed by a superhuman power of some type.

Christianity, with some 2.1 billion followers, is the largest of the world's religions. Though it originally began in the Middle East, Christianity is no longer the dominant faith there. It is, however, the predominant religion in much of Europe and in North and South America.

Like some other religions, Christianity is divided into a number of different churches: In Russia, Orthodox Christianity is the leading religion. In South America, most Christians are Roman Catholics, and the same holds true in southern Europe. Protestantism is more prevalent in both northern Europe and North America.

With more than 1.5 billion adherents, Islam is the world's second most popular faith. Following the faith are most people of the Middle East and North Africa, a significant number in South and Southeast Asia, and long-standing minorities in the Balkans

The United States is unusual for a developed nation in that a greater than usual proportion of its population holds religious beliefs, most commonly Protestant Christianity.

South America is predominantly a Catholic Christian continent. This is a legacy of the Spanish and Portugese Conquistadors, who brought the continent under colonial rule.

and eastern Europe. An influx of immigrants from former European colonies has seen the number of Muslims in Western Europe rise in recent decades.

Hinduism, the world's third largest religion, is prevalent in India, though large populations of Sikhs and Muslims can also be found on the Indian subcontinent. Although Buddhism originated in India, the countries with the largest Buddhist populations are now China, Japan, and Southeast Asian states such as Vietnam and Thailand. Buddhism also has many followers in the Western world.

A notable exception to the dominance of Islam throughout the Middle East is Israel. Large populations of Jews are also found across Europe and North America, the latter home to more than 40 percent of the world's Jews. In fact, New York City has the second largest population of Jews of any city in the world, after Tel Aviv.

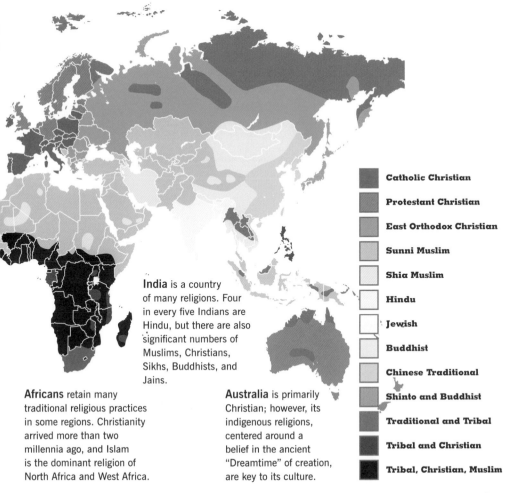

India is a country of many religions. Four in every five Indians are Hindu, but there are also significant numbers of Muslims, Christians, Sikhs, Buddhists, and Jains.

Africans retain many traditional religious practices in some regions. Christianity arrived more than two millennia ago, and Islam is the dominant religion of North Africa and West Africa.

Australia is primarily Christian; however, its indigenous religions, centered around a belief in the ancient "Dreamtime" of creation, are key to its culture.

Catholic Christian

Protestant Christian

East Orthodox Christian

Sunni Muslim

Shia Muslim

Hindu

Jewish

Buddhist

Chinese Traditional

Shinto and Buddhist

Traditional and Tribal

Tribal and Christian

Tribal, Christian, Muslim

Judaism and the Children of Abraham

Judaism is the oldest of the three largest "Abrahamic religions" of Judaism, Christianity, and Islam. Jewish tradition began in the Middle East around 1800 BCE with the Covenant between God and Abraham, in which Jews believe God promised "to make Abraham a father of a great many nations" (Genesis 17:1–8) and "to give Abraham's descendants all the land from the river of Egypt to the Euphrates" (Genesis 15:18–21).

Abraham is considered to be the patriarch of Judaism, and its followers—sometimes still called the Children of Abraham—believe he left his homeland (in what is now Iraq) to settle in Canaan (Israel), God's "Promised Land." Abraham's son Isaac and grandson Jacob are also important figures in Judaism. Jacob's descendants, the Hebrews, were forced into slavery in Egypt. They were freed when God bestowed the 10 plagues upon Egypt, whereupon Moses led the Hebrews out of Egypt in a journey known as the Exodus.

The practice of Judaism revolves around the study and observance of the Torah, the Jewish holy book. The Torah, which means law, contains 613 commandments from God. It is read in its entirety each Jewish calendar year in a synagogue, the Jewish house of worship.

The Branches of Judaism

In the 1800s, Judaism divided into three main branches: Orthodox, Conservative, and Reform. The Orthodox adopted the most strict observance of the laws, including those set down in Leviticus that delineate which foods can be consumed and how they must be prepared in order to "keep kosher." The Orthodox also strictly follow the commandment in the Torah to observe the Sabbath, a 24–25-hour period of rest, reflection, and separation ("havdalah") from the secular concerns of daily life. The Sabbath starts just before sundown on Fridays.

The Conservative movement, in contrast, holds that Judaism has a built-in flexibility that allows more room for religious practice. This approach, say Conservatives, provides succeeding generations with the opportunity to find ways to continue to relate to the faith in a world that changes in ways that cannot be foreseen—that is, changes that cannot be foretold in the written and oral Judaic traditions.

Reform Congregations

Enter the Reform movement, sparked by Jews who questioned the traditional teachings on how the sacred texts came to be. Many Reform Jews hold that the so-called "oral law," or Talmud, was created by humans and not, as the Orthodox would say, given to Moses by God.

Reform congregations hold that a principled, moral, and ethical life can be lived as a Jewish person even if one does not strictly carry out the well-defined ceremonial rituals enumerated in the Torah.

The Festival of Hanukkah

Hanukkah is an eight-day festival that takes place in midwinter and celebrates the rededication of the Temple of Jerusalem in the second century BCE. The Jewish people had lost control of the Temple to the Syrians, but a revolt led by Judah the Macabee regained control. Judah and his followers ritually cleansed the Temple but had only enough sacramental oil to keep the menorah (a candle that represents eternal light) burning for one day; however, the oil burned miraculously for eight days, until more oil had been prepared.

The Wailing Wall—the most sacred site for Jews in Jerusalem—is the only remaining part of the second Temple, which was destroyed by the Romans in 70 CE.

The Menorah

The menorah plays a very important role in Hanukkah. Every evening a family member lights one of the eight candles with the shammash (meaning servant) candle, which stands at the center of the menorah. Gifts are exchanged during the festival, and it is meant to be a happy time for everyone.

In Fact...

Passover celebrates the escape of the Jewish people from slavery under the Pharaohs of Egypt—and matzoh, or unleavened bread, has its origins in the story. On the run in the desert, the Jews had no time to wait for their bread to rise, so they made do with a flat cracker. Matzoh became a staple of the ritual meal, or seder, that marks the holiday. Matzoh is also eaten throughout the year and is an essential ingredient in some Jewish recipes.

The seder plate is an important part of the eight-day Passover festival, which commemorates the release of the Jewish people from slavery in Egypt. A Jewish family will gather together for a special ritual meal, the seder. At the center of the meal is the seder plate on which are placed symbolic foods.

Christianity:
The Path of Christ

The Christian religion is based on the life and teachings of Jesus Christ. According to Christian theology, Christ is the Messiah, or Savior, who was sent by God to offer salvation to humankind. Christians believe that Christ's coming was the fulfillment of messianic prophecies outlined in the Old Testament of the Bible.

Christianity developed out of the Judaic tradition. The Christian Bible is composed of two parts: the Old Testament, primarily based upon the Torah, the Jewish holy book, and the New Testament, which details the teachings of Jesus and his apostles.

The Life of Christ

The New Testament tells little about the early life of Jesus, but it does say that he was born in Bethlehem in Judea (southern Israel) and was brought up in Galilee. Although Jesus was born to Mary and her husband Joseph, Christian doctrine holds that He was the Son of God, conceived by the Holy Spirit and born of the Virgin Mary.

The New Testament has much more to say about the later life of Jesus Christ. Love, compassion, and repentance are considered to be the key themes of Jesus' teachings, which were often given in the form of parables—stories with a moral principle.

Christianity's defining events are the crucifixion of Christ, which took place outside Jerusalem, and His resurrection. The essential Christian belief is that Christ died on the cross to atone for the sins of the world and to offer humankind eternal salvation.

The Catholic Church

The Catholic Church began in Jerusalem shortly after Christ's crucifixion. By the middle of the first century CE, the Church

Christ is born.		The Edict of Milan proclaims the toleration of Christianity in the Roman Empire.		Christianity becomes the official religion of the Roman Empire.		A series of crusades are launched to claim the Holy Lands of the Middle East for Christianity.
4 BCE	**33 CE**	**313**	**325**	**380**	**1054**	**1095-1272**
	Christ is crucified.		The Council of Nicea declares a universal Christian doctrine: the Nicene Creed.		The Great Schism divides the Church along the lines of East and West, or Orthodox and Latin.	

was based in Rome. Roman emperors persecuted early Catholics because of their rejection to the Roman moral code.

The oppression of Christians subsided in 312 CE, when Roman Emperor Constantine I converted to Christianity after having a vision of an inscription engraved in the cross on which Christ was crucified: "By this sign, you will conquer."

After Christianity became a sanctioned religion in Rome, the influence of the Catholic Church increased. By the end of the fourth century, it became the official religion of the Roman Empire, establishing what is now known as Roman Catholicism.

When the Roman seat of power moved to Constantinople (now Istanbul), the Eastern churches were brought under state control and the popes gained more power. The Great Schism of 1054 divided Catholicism into the Roman Catholic Church and the Eastern Orthodox Church, which was based in Constantinople.

With the sixteenth century came the Protestant Reformation, when Catholics who questioned papal authority broke from the Church.

IN THE KNOW

The German university professor and Augustine monk Martin Luther began the Protestant movement. His writings, or theses, were seen as an attack on Catholicism and the pope, and he was excommunicated in 1521. The protestations of his legions of supporters gave rise to the general name "protestant" for new denominations such as Lutheran, Anglican, Methodist, Baptist, and Presbyterian.

1517	1534	1611	1620	1729	1830
	The Church of England is declared as no longer being under the authority of the Pope.		The Pilgrim Fathers set sail for North America.		The Church of Latter Day Saints (Mormonism) is established.
Martin Luther nails his 95 Theses to the door of Wittenberg Castle Church, which become a key element in the Protestant Reformation.		The King James Bible is published.		The rise of Methodism begins under John Wesley.	

Islam and the Prophet Muhammad

With more than 1 billion followers, Islam is the second largest religion in the world after Christianity. The word Islam means submission (to the will of God), and believers are known as Muslims. Like Christianity and Judaism, Islam is a monotheistic religion, with Muslims regarding Allah as the one true deity.

Islam accepts as its foundations the traditions of the two other so-called religions of the book, Judaism and Christianity. At the same time, it regards Abraham, Moses, and Jesus as messengers of Allah.

The Qur'an teaches that the prophet Muhammad was the God Allah's final messenger. In the seventh century CE, he received divine revelations to correct changes that had veered from God's true teachings through the ages.

The Life of Muhammad

Muhammad was born in about 570 CE in the city of Mecca, on the west coast of Arabia. At the age of 40, Muhammad received the first of his visions from God. These convinced him that he had been chosen as a prophet of God, and he began preaching the word of Islam to the people of Mecca. Hos-

tility from the authorities caused Muhammad and his followers to leave the city in 622 for Medina, in a migration known as the Hijra.

Once settled, Muhammad took religious and political control and in 629 led 10,000 men in the conquest of Mecca. The religion of the Arabian Peninsula was replaced by the worship of the one God, Allah.

IN THE KNOW

In Islam, there is no distinction between social and religious life, and all aspects of both are governed by Sharia law. Sharia law comes from a combination of sources including the Qur'an, the Hadith (the sayings and conduct of Muhammad), and fatwas (rulings determined by Islamic scholars). The issue of whether Sharia law should be implemented in secular Islamic societies is at the heart of civil debate in many Muslim countries.

The Qur'an

The Qur'an (also spelled Koran, and meaning "recitation") is the sacred text of Islam. The book is considered the literal word of God. According to Islamic belief, the word was revealed to the Prophet Muhammad, by the archangel Gabriel over a 22-year time period. It is the duty of every believer of Islam to read and understand the Qur'an in the original Arabic.

In Fact...

The Five Pillars The Five Pillars (the testimony of faith, prayer, alms giving, fasting, and pilgrimage) form the framework of a holy Islamic life.

- The testimony of faith (Shahadah) concerns bearing witness with two phrases: "There is no true god but Allah" and "Muhammad is the Messenger of God." These must be recited with conviction at prayer time and by those wishing to convert to Islam. The fundamental tenet of Islam, Shahadah affirms monotheism and rejects the existence of any deity other than Allah.

- Salah, or Salat, is the requirement for Muslims to pray five times a day (sunrise, noon, afternoon, sunset, and evening). A muezzin, or crier, traditionally summons worshippers from the tower or minaret of a mosque. Ritual prayer, a private matter, may be performed anywhere, and worshippers face in the direction of Mecca when praying.

- Because all things belong to God alone, wealth accumulated on Earth is considered to be held in trust by individuals. Muslims who can afford it give the needy a percentage of their wealth. Giving alms (zakat) is a way of purifying one's worldly possessions. Indeed, the original meaning of zakat is "purification." It is considered a religious obligation rather than a voluntarily paid tax.

- Fasting (sawm) is a means of ritual self-purification and spiritual growth. During the holy month of Ramadan, the ninth month of the year, Muslims abstain from food and drink (as well as sexual relations) from dawn to dusk. Believers are encouraged to repent their sins, think of the needy, and express gratitude toward God during Ramadan.

- The annual pilgrimage (hajj) takes place in the twelfth month (Dhu al-Hijjah) of the Muslim calendar. Every year, over 2,000,000 pilgrims from all around the world travel to the holy city of Mecca to observe a sequence of ritual acts. These include seven circlings of the Ka'aba—a granite cube covered by a gold-embroidered silk curtain, the most sacred site in Islam; touching the Black Stone set in the Ka'aba's eastern corner; running seven times between Mount Safa and Mount Marway; and symbolically stoning three pillars at Mina, where Ishmael banished the temptations of Satan. The Qur'an commands every able Muslim to undertake the haji at least once in a lifetime.

The crescent and star was the symbol of Turkey's Ottoman Empire (1299–1922 CE) and later came to be considered an emblem for Islam in general.

Hinduism: The Eternal Law

With around a billion believers, Hinduism has the third largest following of any religion and is one of the oldest. Unlike many other religions, the beliefs of Hinduism cannot be attributed to any one book or founder or teacher, nor is there a single doctrine.

The philosophy of Hinduism can be traced all the way back to the Vedic civilization, which flourished in the Indus Valley (located around the Indus River, now in modern-day Pakistan) some 3,000 years ago. By around 900 BCE, the Vedic period had produced a body of sacred texts known as the four vedas, believed to have been revealed to humans from an eternal source. These scriptures laid down the foundations of Hinduism.

Central to Hindu philosophy is the belief that one universal eternal truth—created by Brahman, the Supreme One—is present in all things. Unlike followers of other major religions, Hindus believe that it is possible to achieve union with the Supreme One while still on Earth, since the Supreme One and a believer's soul (known as *atman*) are one and the same. To Hindus, the various gods of the Hindu pantheon are but reflections of Brahman in one form or another, and they merely assume different identities to meet the various challenges and crises in the world of gods and mortals.

The Circle of Life

Hindus believe existence is a cycle of birth, death, and rebirth, or *samsura*. The form in which the soul is reincarnated depends upon how the previous life was lived. This is expressed in the law of karma, the law of cause and effect; all experience is linked to past actions in this or other lifetimes. The only way to escape this seemingly endless cycle of rebirth and enter a higher consciousness is through salvation, or *moksha*—the goal of the yogi or ascetic. Chief among Hinduism's many gods are Brahma, Vishnu, and Shiva, together known as the Hindu Trinity. They represent the cosmic functions of creation, preservation, and destruction.

IN THE KNOW

The word yoga comes from the Sanskrit (ancient Indian) word meaning "to yoke" and is applied to a series of mental and physical exercises. Practiced in its highest form, yoga is intended to lead to *moksha*, or the release from earthly bonds. There are many different yogic "paths," including Bhakti-yoga (the way of devotion or selfless love), Raja-yoga (contemplative yoga), and Hatha-yoga (physical yoga).

Brahma

Also called Prajapati (Lord and Father of All Creatures), Brahma is the creator god and the wisest of all sages. Traditionally, Brahma is depicted with four heads and four arms. Legend says he originally had five heads, but one was cut off by the fire of Shiva's third eye because Brahma had shown him disrespect. He is usually shown holding a scepter, a bow, an alms bowl, and the Rig Veda (ancient scripture).

Vishnu

Vishnu is regarded as the pre-server and restorer of the universe and as a god who pervades all things. His benevolent character makes him one of the most popular gods in Hindu worship. He is usually represented as a dark blue four-armed god wearing a crown. He also wears a holy jewel called the Kaustaubha around his neck, and in his hands he carries a conch shell, a discus, a mace, and a lotus flower.

The symbol Om represents Brahma and is found in shrines and temples. It is a form of adornment and is the sacred and eternal syllable believed to represent the past, present, and future.

His vehicle is the great eagle, Garuda. Vishnu is believed to have 10 incarnations or avatars, forms in which the god appears on Earth to save the world at a time of great need. Kalki, the tenth avatar, is yet to come; when he does, he will be riding a white horse and holding a flaming sword.

Shiva

Shiva personifies the power of destruction and is usually surrounded by demons and evil spirits. He has a more peaceful side to him, however, and he is sometimes represented as a great yogi meditating alone on the slopes on Mount Kailasa.

Shiva is commonly depicted with a third eye and a garland of serpents or skulls around his neck. His matted hair is worn in a topknot sometimes threaded with a crescent moon. His wife is the beautiful goddess Parvati, and his mount is Nandi, the bull. He is often worshipped in the form of a *lingam* (a phallic symbol).

Conversation Starter When seeking success, Hindus ask the god Ganesh to remove obstacles. But why does Ganesh have the head of an elephant? Told as a boy by his mother to guard her door, he blocked the god Shiva, who smashed his head into a thousand pieces. The only head found to replace his own was that of an elephant. To soothe the mother's sorrow, Shiva gave Ganesh his special powers.

Buddhism: Religion or Philosophy?

Buddhism is a major world religion and is estimated to have around 350 million followers. It is based on the teachings of Siddhartha Gautama, a prince who lived in northern India in the sixth century BCE.

Siddhartha Gautama was born a prince, and shortly after his birth, it was prophesied that the child would either be a great sovereign or a great ascetic. His worldly father was reluctant for him to become a holy man and kept Siddhartha within the confines of the palace to shelter him from all of life's pain and suffering.

The young prince eventually disobeyed his father, however, and went to see for himself what life was like beyond the palace compound. In the nearby villages, Siddhartha encountered four sights, known as the Four Signs: an old man, a sick man, a corpse, and a homeless sadhu, or holy man. For the first time, Siddhartha had encountered old age, pain, and death; he also saw the holy man as a sign that he should renounce his life of luxury to seek the answers to the suffering he had seen all around.

The Moment of Enlightenment

Siddhartha shaved off his long hair, gave up his worldly possessions, and spent many years seeking the answers through the teachings of religious men. Siddhartha finally decided he should lead the life of a solitary ascetic in the hope that he might find the truth. Years of extreme self-denial and discipline followed. Siddhartha was near death from starvation when he realized he was no closer to finding the answer to suffering

In Fact...

The Four Noble Truths were given in a sermon by the Buddha after his enlightenment. They are:

Dukkha—All life is suffering.

Samudaya—Suffering is caused by craving or desire.

Nirodha—To eliminate suffering, it is necessary to eliminate craving or desire.

Magga—To eliminate craving or desire, it is necessary to follow the stages of the Eightfold Path: right thought, right understanding, right speech, right action, right livelihood, right effort, right concentration, and right contemplation.

than when he started out as an ascetic. The realization that he should follow The Middle Way, or path of moderation—of neither extreme self-indulgence nor self-denial—came to Siddhartha. He began to accept food again and sat beneath a Bodhi (fig) tree, and three days later he felt freed from the fear of suffering. He also learned the Four Noble Truths. From this time, he became known as Buddha, The Enlightened One.

Spreading the Word

To spread his teachings, Buddha established the Sangha (community) of monks and nuns. Life in the Sangha is austere. Members take daily walks in nearby villages, carrying empty alms bowls in which villagers place food. It may look like begging, but monks and nuns teach and advise the laypeople in return. Filling the alms bowls also cultivates generosity in the giver.

Buddhism's Main Branches

Scholars identify three main branches of Buddhism: Theravada, which evolved in Southeast Asia and India; Mahayana, from

China and Japan; and Tibetan, from high in the Himalayas. Known as "yanas," or vehicles, all three are now practiced worldwide. As people adapt Buddhism to their own needs and cultures, they will often blend the three vehicles into a variety of new forms.

Theravada Buddhism, the oldest branch, is called the "small vehicle" because it is seen as the religion for monks. It places great importance on the teachings of the Buddha himself, found in scriptures known as the Tipitaka.

Mahayana Buddhism centers more around family life. Translated as "large vehicle," Mahayana sees itself as suitable for everyone. This branch reveres the so-called bodhisattvas, people who reach enlightenment but lead ordinary lives. When they die and are reborn, they return to the community to help enlighten others.

In Tibet—since 1950, an Autonomous Region of China—Buddhism finds its noisiest and most colorful expression. Tibetan Buddhists are encouraged to openly express emotions. They also share the thread of meditation, or disciplining of the mind.

Other Faiths of the Eastern World

Many Asians practice long-standing faiths outside of the global religions. Though their ranks have been reduced in the Middle East and other places where the influence of Abrahamic religions have risen, the faithful still hold firm their age-old beliefs.

Jainism

Some 8,000,000 Jains, most of whom live in India, are followers of ancient sages known as Jinas ("victorious ones"). The most important of these sages was a contemporary of Buddha—Mahavira, born around 540 BCE. Mahavira taught that the way to liberate oneself from the rounds of reincarnation was to practice severe asceticism.

Another aspect of Indian religion the Jains took to an extreme was the emphasis on non-violence—a principle that holds all life as sacred. Accordingly, Jain monks wear masks and sweep the paths before them to avoid killing any living creature.

Zoroastrianism

Monotheistic Zoroastrianism was founded by the prophet Zarathusthra in Persia (now Iran) around 1200 BCE and survived as a major religion in that region until the Muslim conquest in the seventh century CE.

The supreme god Ahura Mazda (Wise Lord) created the universe and was responsible for all that was good. He was also engaged in unending conflict with Angra Manyu, the chaotic evil spirit.

Zoroastrianism holds that humanity must play an active role in keeping the forces of evil at bay. Participants can worship either at home or at the temple, where sacred fires symbolizing Mazda burn constantly.

Shintoism

Shintoism is a Japanese faith based on the worship of the spirits of nature, or *kami*. In fact, the word "Shinto" means the "Way of the Spirits."

Shintoism has no founder, no canonical scriptures, and no gods. The focus of Shintoism is concentrated wholly on humanity's place in this world rather than on any transcendental afterlife. There are said to be 8,000,000 Shinto shrines in Japan, often in gardens, on mountainsides (Mount Fuji is a notable example), and in other places of great natural beauty. The most commonly worshipped spirit is Amaterasu, the sun spirit, and her Grand Shrine at Ise is the most visited shrine in Japan.

In Japan, Shintoism is seen more as a way of life than a religion. As such, it provides an ethical framework but no commandments. Nor does Shinto demand that its adherents follow only one religion.

In fact, the Shintoists of today often also practice Buddhism, from which Shinto separated in the late nineteenth century.

Confucianism

Confucianism can be traced back to the life and teachings of the Chinese sage Confucius, or K'ung-fu-tzu (551–479 BCE). It is generally considered as a moral and ethical system rather than a religion, and it isn't based on the worship of a god or gods. Nor is the religion concerned with matters of the soul or the afterlife, though it does encourage the worship of ancestors.

Little is known about the life of Confucius, but his impact on the development of East Asian philosophy is indisputable. His teachings can be found in the *Analects*, a work that was completed by unknown scholars many years after his death.

Confucius emphasized the importance of Li, or proper conduct, as a means of maintaining moral order. His version of the Golden Rule, the ethic of reciprocity and the fundamental moral principal, was "What you do not want done to yourself, do not do to others."

He also believed that morality was "contagious" and that moral rulers would result in moral subjects.

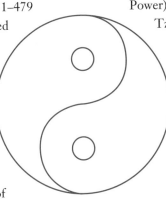

The Yin Yang symbol expresses the Taoist belief that two opposite yet complementary forces operate within the world. Yin represents all that is feminine, light, and calm, while Yang represents all that is male, dark, and active.

Taoism

Taoism, or Daoism, originated in China in the fourth century BCE. It was founded by the philosopher Lao Tzu, whose name translates as Old Master.

The main teachings of Taoism can be found in the *Tao Te Ching* (the Way and its Power). According to legend, Lao Tzu tired of the ways of men in his homeland and tried to leave China but was persuaded by a border guard to write down his teachings. After he did so, he vanished.

His book, which contains around 5,000 Chinese characters and is divided into 81 brief chapters, speaks of "active inaction"—that is, accepting the natural flow of universal energy. The principal idea in Taoism, the Tao (Way), is seen as the creative force in the universe through which all things are unified and connected.

Tao is not a god and is not worshipped. Rather, the meaning of Tao is explained in the Tao Te Ching:

The Tao that can be told is not
the eternal Tao;
The name that can be named is not
the eternal name.
The Nameless is the origin of
Heaven and Earth;
The Named is the mother of
all things.

Mythologies of the Ancient World

Faced with the unknown and the unknowable, humankind has, for as long as history records, peopled the Heavens and the Earth with beings greater and more powerful than ourselves. It is these immortals whose actions govern events in this world and the next and who must be placated if their wrath is to be averted.

Ancient Egypt

Worship of the gods and goddesses played a central role in life in ancient Egypt. Some of the Egyptian gods have animal forms, including Anubis, the jackal-headed god, who was protector of the dead, and Horus, the falcon-headed Sun god. Belief in the afterlife was fundamental to the Egyptian people, and many of the prominent gods were associated with the cult of the dead. Mythological beliefs underpinned the authority of the pharaohs, gods themselves, who stood above the common law.

In ancient Egyptian belief, a dead person faced judgment by the god Osiris, the god of afterlife who triumphed over death. The goddess Ma'at, who personified justice, morality, truth, and order, weighed souls in the underworld; a heart that was heavy with guilt meant eternal damnation.

Ancient Greece

Although the gods and goddesses of ancient Greece resembled humans, they were of greater beauty and strength. Their intellect, too, was far superior. The gods, however, were not above the petty feelings of jealousy, deceit, and revenge that beset humankind, and their actions were frequently motivated by these all too human passions.

The gods fell in love, married, had children, and quarreled with one another. They could also assume the form of humans and animals. Zeus, the Lord of the Sky who ruled over the gods on Mount Olympus, resorted to all kinds of trickery to hide his rampant philandering from his wife. At one point he took the form of a swan and made love to Leda, who gave birth to Helen of Troy. Helen later married the king of Sparta, then ran off with another man, sparking the Trojan War.

The Parthenon, on the Acropolis in Athens, dates from classical times and was built for the worship of the city's patron, Athena.

Some Greek gods were believed to have great wisdom. In Delphi, the god Apollo answered questions through a prophetess or oracle who spoke in riddles, and her words were interpreted by a priest. The Delphic oracle was consulted on matters of state as well as minor personal problems.

In Greek mythology, heroes like Achilles and Heracles (Roman name Hercules) were almost the equivalent of gods. Some heroes even claimed gods as ancestors.

Ancient Rome

To the Romans, an "old group of three" ruled the universe: Jupiter, the god of the heavens; Mars, the god of war; and Quirinus, the god of the common folk.

There were literally hundreds of gods, who between them governed events and every aspect of daily life of ancient Rome; some were of Greek origin, but most were not. The mythical founders of Rome, Romulus and Remus, were believed to be the twin sons of Mars and a mortal mother.

Norse

In Norse mythology, heaven (Asgard) is devoid of joy. The gods know that their struggle against evil is hopeless. Heroism is the highest aspiration, and it depends on battling for lost causes. The Eddas, by Icelander Snorri Sturluson (1179–1241), outline the somber saga of the gods. Among the Norse deities were Odin, god of war and intelligence; Thor, god of thunder; and the fire god Loki, a shape-shifter and trickster known as the "contriver of all fraud." He could even turn from a man into a woman.

In Fact...

Many Greek gods were assimilated into the Roman Pantheon but became known under a different name.

Greek	Roman	Power
Aphrodite	Venus	Goddess of love and beauty
Ares	Mars	God of war
Artemis	Diana	Goddess of hunting
Athena	Minerva	Goddess of wisdom
Demeter	Ceres	God of agriculture
Hephaistus	Vulcan	God of the forge and fire
Hera	Juno	Protector of women
Hermes	Mercury	Messenger of the gods
Hestia	Vesta	Goddess of the hereafter
Poseidon	Neptune	God of the sea
Zeus	Jupiter	King of the gods

Apollo, the god of lightness, poetry, and medicine, is known by the same name in both cultures.

The Four Branches of Philosophy

The term philosophy derives from the Greek for "love of" and "wisdom." In short, philosophy is the practice of asking questions and seeking answers about the nature of all things. If that sounds vague and rarefied, the study of philosophy has important applications in everything from scientific inquiry to business dealings to parenthood.

Simply put, philosophy is our search for an understanding of our world. So it's hardly surprising that such a huge subject is divided into four principal branches: epistemology, logic, metaphysics, and ethics, or moral philosophy. The distinctions are seen most clearly in the kinds of questions asked in each branch.

Epistemology: Knowledge

From the Greek, the word epistemology means "the study of knowledge." Epistemology has also been called the "door to philosophy." After all, we can reason only on the basis of what we know—and without an understanding of knowledge, how could philosophy proceed?

The subject matter of epistemology, then, is the nature, scope, and limits of human knowledge. The kinds of questions that it poses include: What can we believe? Does God exist? How can we be certain of anything? Can we trust our senses? Can we prove that the world exists? What is truth? Are there different kinds of knowledge? Epistemology also covers subjects such as doubt, paradox, and intuition.

Logic: All About Reasoning

Although reasoning must depend on what we can know, it is also the means by which we extend our knowledge. The branch of philosophy called logic (sometimes considered a part of epistemology) deals with the rules by which reasoning must be governed if it is to be valid.

Logic is the science of good argument and the means by which invalid arguments can be identified. It asks what is sound reasoning and what is unsound. It suggests that if the premises of an argument are valid, the conclusion, too, will be valid.

An example of logic at work: "If all gods are Greek and Zeus is a god, then Zeus must be Greek" is a valid argument. But "If all gods are Greek and Theseus is Greek, then Theseus must be a god" is an invalid argument because not all Greeks were gods.

Metaphysics: Thought in Toto

Metaphysics (meaning "transcending physics") concerns itself with nothing less trivial than the nature of reality as depicted in thought. It tries to establish a system explaining all human thought as a rational whole.

Metaphysics is divided into two fields: cosmology, or the study of universal order and the real in the world around us; and ontology, or the study of existence. The study of metaphysics leads to questions such as these: Who are we and how did we come to be here? What is real? Is there a god? Is there an ultimate cause? Can we experience reality directly, or does our own experience shape our sense of reality? Do we have free will or is everything predetermined?

Metaphysics examines such things as the nature of time and space, mind versus matter, certainty versus possibility, and the properties of objects (in the last case, overlapping with science). Metaphysics also asks whether things happen for a purpose.

IN THE KNOW

Are we born with innate knowledge or only the propensity to acquire knowledge? The philosopher and linguistic expert Noam Chomsky, for one, has argued that we must have innate knowledge when it comes to language; otherwise, we wouldn't be able to master the rules of such a complex system so quickly. Other linguists see the mastery of language as evidence that the structure of the human predisposes us to learn language.

Ethics: Right vs. Wrong

Variously known as value theory and moral philosophy, ethics asks what is right and what is wrong—in effect, what kind of life we should lead. It also asks what creates a just society and whether individuals are obliged to make society just.

Moral philosophy also hones in on questions as weighty as the purpose of our lives and the societies in which we live. Do our obligations to the state outweigh those to our family? Which forms of government are legitimate, and which aren't?

Such subjects as good versus evil, freedoms and responsibilities, human rights, animal rights, virtue, dignity, beauty, and happiness are also part of the sphere of ethics.

Conversation Starter The study of philosophy poses many questions, not least of which are questions about rights. However, while rights may exist in principle, they don't exist in fact—that is, you can't see, hear, smell, taste, or touch a right. You may read a right that has been written down, but this is still the work of the writer, not the right itself. How, then, do we know what rights are, and is it possible to argue that there are fundamental rights—or do rights that we take for granted depend on a specific situation?

Great Thinkers, Ancient to Modern

Sometimes certain thoughts change not just the world around us but also resonate through the ages. Most of these great thoughts have come from sages and intellectuals who in their time advanced the discipline of philosophy. Here are seven such figures.

Socrates

Philosophy is indebted to Socrates (c. 470–399 BCE) for his dialectic method of inquiry, which examines the world by seeking answers to deliberate questions. It remains central to political and moral philosophy and forms the basis of the scientific method, asking, How do you know? Socrates became an outspoken critic of Athenian society and exposed the ill-founded, often contradictory nature of its citizens' beliefs and opinions. His uncompromising quest for truth and virtue eventually brought him into direct conflict with the state, and he was sentenced to death by poisoning.

"The unexamined life is not worth living."—Socrates

Plato

Arguably the most influential philosopher of all time, Plato (c. 428–348 BCE) founded the world's first academic institution in Athens. He wrote extensively on a broad range of subjects. His *Dialogues* (including *The Republic*) discussed Socrates's work—a great favor to humanity, given that Socrates left no writings behind. Plato put forward the theory of forms, writing that the material world we experience is not the real world, but only a fleeting impression of the real world. Our only real knowledge, he said, can be of everlasting qualities such as beauty and truth.

Aristotle

A student of Plato, tutor to the young Alexander the Great, and founder of the Lyceum school of philosophy in Athens, Aristotle was one of the most knowledgeable men of his time. More of a down-to-earth investigator than Plato, Aristotle believed that the universal essence of things was to be found not in some other realm but in examples in the real world; he thereby invented the notion of science.

St. Thomas Aquinas

Thomas (1225–1274 CE)—an Italian who pursued a religious education, became a Dominican monk, and attended the universities of Naples, Paris, and Cologne—was

both a theologian and a philosopher. He was deeply influenced by Aristotle, whose works had recently been translated into Latin, and he wrote several commentaries on these. Recognizing the difference between knowledge that springs from faith (sacred doctrine) and that of the natural world (natural theology), he proposed a five-stage intellectual argument to "prove" the existence of God.

Immanuel Kant

The work of the Prussian-born philosopher Immanuel Kant (1724–1804) had an impact on several areas of philosophy. In his *Critique of Pure Reason* (1781), Kant said our limited powers of reasoning give us knowledge of things only as they appear to us; we thus have no knowledge of the things as they are in themselves. In the *Critique of Practical Reason* (1788), he held that absolute moral law exists and that obeying moral law is a "categorical imperative" for all people at all times and in all circumstances. In his *Critique of Judgment* (1790), he reduces aesthetic judgments to only four possible kinds: the agreeable, the beautiful, the sublime, and the good.

"By a lie, a man... annihilates his dignity as a man."
—Immanuel Kant

Ludwig Wittgenstein

Recognized as one of the great thinkers of the twentieth century, Wittgenstein (1889–1951) brought a whole new approach to philosophy, pointing out that many of the problems in philosophy had to do with language rather than the nature of the world.

He investigated the relationship between language and the world, and in his *Tractatus Logico-Philosophicus* concluded that the structure of language mirrored that of reality and that the limits of our ability to make sense of the world are determined by the limits of language itself.

Wittgenstein wrote this influential book during World War I, starting it in the trenches as an artillery officer in the Austro-Hungarian army and completing it in an Italian prisoner-of-war camp.

Karl Popper

Popper (1902–1994) was born in Vienna but left because of the rise of Nazism. He then spent most of his life in England, where he was a professor at the London School of Economics.

Best known as a philosopher of science,

"Our knowledge can only be finite, while our ignorance must necessarily be infinite."—Karl Popper

Popper took a stand against the infallibility of the scientific method. He argued that pseudoscientific theories could be verified by virtually anything and everything. The legitimate test for a truly scientific theory, he said, was whether it risked predictions that could later be found false. "Critical rationalism" was the term Popper used to describe his philosophy.

From the ancient to the modern, in every corner of the globe, humankind has sought wisdom in the world of religion and thought. This chapter has posed some of life's eternal questions, but do you have the answers?

The Religions of the World

1 What is the world's largest religion?

a) *Christianity*   b) *Hinduism*

c) *Islam*   d) *Judaism*

2 Which city has the largest proportion of Jewish population in the world?

a) *Jerusalem*   b) *London*

c) *New York*   d) *Tel Aviv*

Judaism and the Children of Abraham

1 True or False: Judaism is the most recent of the three largest "Abrahamic" religions.

2 Name the three main branches of Judaism.

3 In which city will you find the Wailing Wall?

Christianity: The Path of Christ

1 In which year is Christ widely held to have been crucified?

2 Who was the Roman emperor who converted to Christianity in 312 CE.

3 To the door of which church did Martin Luther nail his 95 Theses in 1517?

Islam and the Prophet Muhammad

1 In which year was the prophet Muhammad born?

2 Name the Five Pillars of Islam.

Hinduism: The Eternal Law

1 What is the name of the symbol that Hindus believe represents the past, present, and future?

2 Name the Hindu Trinity.

Buddhism: Religion or Philosophy?

1 What was the name of the man who became the Buddha, whose teachings Buddhists follow?

2 What are the Four Noble Truths that are at the core of Buddhist teachings?

3 Under what name was the Dalai Lama born?

Other Faiths of the Eastern World

1 In which nation will you find the majority of the 8,000,000 Jains?

a) *India* b) *Indonesia*
c) *Iran* d) *Iraq*

2 What is the name of the supreme god that Zoroastrians believe in?

3 What does the word "Shinto" mean?

a) *Way of breathing*
b) *Way of living*
c) *Way of the spirits*
d) *Way of thinking*

4 What do the two halves of the Yin Yang symbol represent?

5 In which century was Taoism, or Daoism, founded?

a) *third century* b) *fourth century*
c) *fifth century* d) *sixth century*

Mythologies of the Ancient World

1 What was the name of the god who weighed the souls of the dead in the Egyptian underworld?

2 In ancient Greece, where would you find the oracle of the god Apollo?

3 Which of the following pairs of Roman and Greek gods is not correct?

a) *Aphrodite and Venus*
b) *Hera and Juno*
c) *Hermes and Vesta*
d) *Zeus and Jupiter*

The Four Branches of Philosophy

1 What are the four principal branches of philosophy?

2 Which branch of philosophy deals with issues such as good versus evil?

Great Thinkers, Ancient to Modern

1 Who said that the "unexamined life is not worth living"?

a) *Aristotle* b) *Plato*
c) *Popper* d) *Socrates*

2 True or False: Plato was a student of Aristotle.

3 Which of these titles is not a work by Immanuel Kant?

a) *Critique of Ethics*
b) *Critique of Judgment*
c) *Critique of Pure Reason*
d) *Critique of Practical Reason*

Chapter Nine

Artistic Endeavor

Human history is intertwined with artistic endeavor. From the earliest cave paintings and stone carvings, the development of artistic expression has mirrored the development of humankind. The goals of artists, writers, musicians, composers, and architects are many and varied, and amid this diversity there occasionally emerges a titan of the arts whose works are universally acclaimed.

Cave and Rock Painting: The Birth of Art

Scholars can only speculate about what motivated early humans to create the astonishing paintings at Altamira, Lascaux, and other Stone Age sites. We don't know how these prehistoric people achieved such expressive sophistication—but before there were towns or cities or civilizations, these paintings tell us there was art.

The initial finds were made in 1879 by Marcelino Sanz de Sautuola, who came across a series of paintings in underground caves at Altamira in Cantabria, northern Spain. At the time, the paintings seemed too good to be true and were initially dismissed as frauds. However, further discoveries in Spain and France established their authenticity, and the Altamira paintings are now dated to the late Magdalenian period, around 15,000 BCE.

The Lascaux Caves

An even more incredible discovery was made at Lascaux in the Dordogne region of France on September 12, 1940. Four teenagers—Marcel Ravidat, Jacques Marsal, Georges Agnel, and Simon Coencas—decided to explore a hole they had come across. To their amazement, they discovered what proved to be the most exciting find in Paleolithic art. The Lascaux caves contained a number of "rooms"—now known as the Great Hall of the Bulls, the Painted Gallery, the Lateral Passage, the Shaft of the Dead Man, the Chamber of Engravings, and the Chamber of Felines—decorated with nearly 2,000 images. Many are too faint to make out, but over 900 clearly represent horses, bison, cattle, stags, felines, and bulls. There are also many geometric shapes.

The most memorable images are found in the Great Hall of Bulls and the Painted Gallery. The Great Hall includes a large fresco composed of three groups: horses, bulls, and stags. One of the bulls is 17 feet (5 m) long. The Painted Gallery is a continuation of the hall; the upper reaches of the wall and the ceiling are covered with fine examples of Paleolithic cave art, including three horses, known as the Chinese Horses, similar in style to paintings found in China.

These painted animals in the Lascaux caves are probably aurochs, an extinct wild ox and the ancestor of domesticated cattle.

The skill of execution and energy of the animal paintings is extraordinary even to twenty-first-century eyes. Our ancestors had less success depicting human figures, which often appear stiff and sticklike in surviving Paleolithic art.

The Persistence of Art

The Lascaux paintings are in black, browns, ochers, yellows, and reds that have retained much of their brightness. To make the paint, the artists used crushed ocher (a naturally occurring mineral) and powdered charcoal. Archaeologists have discovered that the images were first engraved in the rock walls or drawn on with thin lines of paint.

The paintings were in a remarkably good state of preservation when they were first discovered. In the following years, as many as 1,200 tourists a day visited the caves, increasing carbon dioxide levels and causing the paintings to deteriorate. The caves were closed to the public in 1963 to prevent further damage, and the paintings were restored to their former glory.

A replica of the Great Hall of the Bulls and the Painted Gallery was created in Lascaux II, a short distance from the original cave, enabling visitors from far and wide to experience this extraordinary art.

IN THE KNOW

Much has been written about the spiritual or other significance of cave art, but nothing can be said for certain. The caves do not show signs of habitation, and archaeologists have suggested that this is an indication that they were reserved for religious or ceremonial purposes. The Stone Age peoples who lived at this time were hunters, and the animal drawings may have been intended to provide a magical link between hunter and hunted.

The Bradshaw Paintings

Bradshaw paintings refer to a style of rock art first discovered by Joseph Bradshaw in 1891 when he got lost on an expedition in the Kimberley region of northwest Australia. There are now known to be at least 1,000 examples, and many more are believed to exist in this vast, sparsely inhabited region. To the local aboriginal people, they are known as *Gwion Gwion*.

The aboriginal people believe that the paintings are not of human origin. According to legend, birds made the paintings by pecking at the rocks until their beaks bled, and then using their tail feathers to apply the "paint."

The paintings are difficult to date because no pigment remains on the etched rock. In 1996, a fossilized mud-wasp nest was found covering one painting, and the nest has been dated at around 17,000 years of age. Many scientists believe that the paintings may be much older.

In contrast to the European cave paintings, which generally depict animals, the Bradshaw images are mostly human. The slender, reddish colored figures have elaborate hairstyles and ornamentation and appear to be taking part in ceremonial events and hunting. The Bradshaw images also include birds, fish, and reptiles.

A Brief History of Western Art

Western art is a progression of periods when certain styles and interests predominated. Periods overlap, however, and there will always be artists who march to a different beat.

Medieval Art

"Medieval Art" encompasses several phases between 300 CE and the mid-1300s, including the Gothic. The subject matter is overwhelmingly Christian. Favored media were illuminated manuscripts and mosaics as well as sculpture and painting. The Byzantine Empire (capital Constantinople, now Istanbul) had its own distinctive style, one that heavily influenced the development of Gothic art and architecture.

The Renaissance

Artists of the Italian Renaissance rejected medieval tradition in favor of the classical realism of Greece and Rome, aided by refinements in portraying depth and perspective. Artists looked to the world of science in their quest for realism; a prime example is Leonardo da Vinci, who made detailed anatomical drawings.

The Italian Renaissance had a great effect on northern Europe in the sixteenth century, and many painters from the North traveled to study under the Italian masters.

Northern Renaissance painting retained a uniquely Gothic style and was influenced by the Protestant Reformation. Notable northern artists include Hieronymous Bosch (c. 1450–1516), Jan Van Eyck (c. 1390–1441), and Hans Holbein (1460–1524).

Mannerism

Mannerism developed in Italy out of the High Renaissance style and lasted from around 1520 to 1600. Mannerist paintings are elegant, emotional, and show a high degree of artificiality.

1498	1498	1504	c. 1506	1579	c. 1611	1638	1642
Jan Van Eyck paints the *Arnolfini Portrait*.		Michelangelo completes the statue of *David*.		El Greco completes *The Disrobing of Christ*.		Poussin paints *Rape of the Sabine Women*.	
	Da Vinci paints *The Last Supper*.		Da Vinci paints the *Mona Lisa*.		Rubens paints *The Massacre of the Innocents*.		Rembrandt paints *The Night Watch*.

The Mannerists rebelled against the "rules" of Renaissance art, favoring human figures in distorted poses and often with exaggerated features. Artists of this style include Francesco Parmigianino (1503–1540) and El Greco (1541–1614).

Baroque and Rococo

Baroque art is emotional in character and realistic in style, and its spirit suited the Counter-Reformation. The genius of Baroque was Rembrandt (1606–1669), a Catholic in mostly Protestant Holland; ambitious but isolated, he never achieved the fame he wanted in his lifetime. Other Baroque masters include Caravaggio (1571–1610) and Peter Paul Rubens (1577–1640).

The term rococo applies to a short-lived style of interior decoration and painting popular in early eighteenth-century France. Its use of shell- and scroll-work and playful themes was a reaction against the excessive splendor of the court of Louis XIV.

Neoclassicism and Romanticism

The Neoclassical movement began in the mid-eighteenth century and reflected a renewed interest in the classical style of Greece and Rome. Neoclassicist artists such as Nicolas Poussin (c. 1593–1665) wished to convey serious ideas and believed the fine arts should be used to spread knowledge.

Romanticism looked to its own time for inspiration, rejecting traditional values and placing emphasis on emotions and intuition. Noted artists include Francisco Goya (1746–1828) and Eugene Delacroix (1798–1863).

Impressionism and Post

In the late 1870s, in response to the formalities of studio-bound art, a group of artists who had met as students in Paris began to portray the reality of life in a new and immediate form. Strongly influenced by Manet and Degas, artists such as Claude Monet (1840–1926) and Auguste Renoir (1841–1919) developed a loose style of painting that explored natural light, color, and the vibrancy of the landscape. Jeered at at the time, Impressionism became the most popular style in Western art.

Post-impressionism applies to the work of artists such as Vincent Van Gogh (1853–1890), who took Impressionism in more personal directions.

François Boucher, a leading French Rococo artist, paints *The Breakfast.*		Goya paints *The Third of May 1808: The Execution of the Defenders of Madrid.*		Delacroix paints *Liberty Leading the People.*		Van Gogh paints *Sunflowers.*	
1739	**1749**	**1814**	**1821**	**1830**	**1882**	**1888**	**1899**
	English rococo furniture maker Thomas Chippendale moves to London.		The English Romantic artist John Constable paints *The Hay Wain.*		Manet paints *A Bar at the Folies-Bergère.*		Monet paints *Bridge over a Pool of Water Lilies.*

Western Painting in the Twentieth Century

Two world wars and constant upheaval compelled artists of the twentieth century to make a near-total break with the forms and styles of the past.

Fauvism

The Fauves (wild beasts) were a loosely connected group of artists including Parisians Henri Matisse (1869–1954), André Derain (1880–1954), and Maurice de Vlaminck (1876–1958). The Fauves painted in bold, harsh, non-naturalistic colors and distorted images in a way that critics of the time reviled as primitive. Fauvism was most influential on German Expressionism.

Expressionism

"Expressionism" generally describes work that reflects the artist's emotions rather than a subject. The movement arose simultaneously in various countries beginning about 1905. German Expressionists dominated the movement, in particular Die Brücke (The Bridge) group. Emotionally, Expressionism was an angst-ridden movement, dwelling on the darker aspects of life. Leading Expressionist artists included Max Beckmann (1884–1950) and Russian-born Wassily Kandinsky (1866–1944).

Cubism

European art was changed forever by the works of Spaniard Pablo Picasso (1881–1973) and Frenchman Georges Braque (1822–1963). Inspired by post-Impressionist Paul Cézanne and the cultures of Africa, Micronesia, and the Americas, the two artists produced works of such originality that they're considered the forerunners of all abstract art. Dubbed Cubism by critics, this dynamic style fractures reality into angles and planes, as if the viewer were seeing through all sides of a prism at once.

1905	1906	1910	1916–20	1922	1937	1942	1947–50
Matisse paints *Woman with Hat.*		Braque paints *Violin and Candlestick.*		Kandinsky paints *On White II.*		American artist Edward Hopper paints *Nighthawks.*	
	Derain paints *Charing Cross Bridge, London.*		The Dada movement flourishes in Europe.		Pablo Picasso paints *Guernica.*		Abstract expressionist Jackson Pollock's "Drip Period."

Dadaism

Dadaism, a brief, intellectual anti-war movement, was established in 1916 in Zurich, Switzerland. Dada exponents blamed World War I on bourgeois society and saw their "anti-art" movement as a rejection of cultural and political norms. Meant to scandalize and provoke, Dada focused on the nonsensical.

Surrealism

Surrealism is art "free from the exercise of reason," in the words of proponent André Breton. Objects are distorted and appear in random places or in fantastic settings, and scenes appear dreamlike. The Surrealists, including Salvador Dali (1904–1989), Joan Miró (1893–1983), and René Magritte (1898–1967), relied on the subconscious and were no longer restrained by the "rational" and "normal."

Key Player

Georgia O'Keeffe
1887–1986

O'Keeffe, a gifted Kansas farm girl, became an icon of Modernist art. Her close-up paintings of plants, flowers, bones, and shells seem austere and anatomical but soon reveal her passion for the natural, her observational skill, and a strong current of sexual symbolism.

Abstract Expressionism

An attitude more than a specific style, its artists valued spontaneity and instinct over realistic forms. Jackson Pollock (1912–1956) was the main exponent of "Action Painting," literally pouring and dripping paint over his canvases.

Minimalism

Minimalist paintings tried to strip away all non-essential elements. As an aesthetic, minimalism continues to influence fine art, music, film, design, architecture, and literature. Prominent minimalists include Ad Reinhardt (1913–1967) and Agnes Martin (1912–2004).

Pop Art

Pop Art emerged in Britain and reached its zenith in New York in the 1960s in the work of Andy Warhol (1928–1987). With consumerism as its inspiration, Pop took art to the masses.

Abstract expressionist Mark Rothko exhibits his first "multiform."	Belgian surrealist René Magritte paints *Golconda*.		Canadian-American minimalist Agnes Martin is "discovered."		English pop artist David Hockney paints *A Bigger Splash*.		
1949	**1949**	**1953**	**1954**	**1963**	**1967**	**1967**	**1968**
	Surrealist Joan Miró paints *Upside Down Figures*.		Salvador Dali paints *The Disintegration of the Persistance of Memory*.		American cartoon pop artist Roy Lichtenstein paints *Whaam!*		Andy Warhol paints *Campbell's Soup I*.

Great Architecture: Three Iconic Buildings

Architecture is the one fine art in which practicality is more important than artistic expression. Yet from the simplest hut to the grandest cathedral, humans have always had the impulse and vision to build impressively. Each of these three iconic structures represents an artful and innovative response to practical necessity.

The Sydney Opera House

The Sydney Opera House in New South Wales, Australia, was the brainchild of Danish architect Jørn Utzon (b. 1918). Work on the project began in 1959 and was expected to take four years to complete at an estimated cost of $7 million (U.S.). Construction problems, however, led to delays, and the project wasn't finished until 1973, at a cost of $102 million (U.S.).

The multiple roofs of the Sydney Opera House, covered in millions of white and cream tiles, recall ships under full sail at its site on Sydney Harbour.

The building is supported on 580 concrete piers sunk up to 80 feet (25 m) below sea level. Its series of shell-shaped roofs, however, define the structure. Made from precast concrete panels supported by precast concrete "ribs," the roofs are covered with white ceramic tiles that almost seem to glow from within in the Sydney sunlight. In 2007, the Opera House was declared a UNESCO World Heritage Site.

The Empire State Building

New York City's Empire State Building is located in the heart of Manhattan. The 102-story building rises 1,454 feet (443 m) to the top of the lightning rod and was the world's tallest building from 1931 to 1954. On a clear day, visitors to the observation decks can see for 80 miles (130 km).

The skyscraper was designed by the firm of Shreve, Lamb, and Harmon. Construction began in early 1930 and was finished just 410 days later.

IN THE KNOW

Denmark's Jørn Utzon won an international contest to design the Sydney Opera House. Work began in 1959. Frustrated by political pressures and budget cuts, Utzon resigned in 1966; his work was completed by a committee. He has never seen his building in person, though in 2004 a hall restored to his original design was dedicated to him. His iconic building is the home of Opera Australia, the Sydney Theatre Company, and the Sydney Symphony.

In Fact...

All great buildings aren't grand in size. Arkansas native and architecture professor E. Fay Jones (1921–2004), a former student of Frank Lloyd Wright, was commissioned in 1980 to design a chapel on a wooded site in the Ozark hills. Thorncrown Chapel— 24 feet (7.32 m) wide, 60 feet (18.29 m) long, 48 feet (14.63 m) high—is a small wonder of glass, diamond-shaped pine trusses, and natural light. Named one of the four best twentieth-century American buildings by the American Institute of Architects, the little chapel is regarded internationally as a classic of "organic architecture."

The domed Taj Mahal appears to float suspended from the red sandstone minarets at the four corners of its supporting platform on the riverside.

The Taj Mahal

The Taj Mahal, meaning "Crown Palace," stands on the banks of the Jamuna River in Agra, India. Its origins are romantic: It was commissioned by the Mogul Emperor Shah Jahan (1592–1666) on the demise of his queen, Mumtaz Mahal, who died in 1631 giving birth to their fourteenth child.

The Taj Mahal was constructed by 20,000 men over a period of 22 years. Documents indicate that the Indian Muslim architect Ustad Ahmad Lahauri played a key role in designing the building, though Shah Jahan was closely involved.

Over 1,000 elephants brought materials from all over India and other parts of Asia, including marble from Rajasthan, turquoise from Tibet, and carnelian from Arabia. The mausoleum is decorated with inlaid flower designs and calligraphy of Qu'ranic quotations, all using 28 types of precious and semi-precious stones.

Other buildings in the complex include a gateway, a mosque, and a guesthouse, all of which are set in a formal garden with reflecting pools. Red sandstone walls stand on three sides of the complex.

It is estimated that 3,400 workers worked on the construction for a total of 7,000,000 man-hours.

The Empire State Building, like the nearby Chrysler Building constructed at the same time, is a good example of the streamlined art-deco style popular in the 1920s and 1930s. In 1945, the building was hit by a B-25 bomber flying in thick fog. The accident killed 14, but the structure survived. The Empire State Building is also a "movie star," featured in over 100 films, including three versions of *King Kong*, the tale of a giant gorilla who meets his end on the skyscraper.

Great Architecture: Buildings of Washington

When Pierre-Charles L'Enfant, a veteran of the American Revolution, laid out the future city of Washington, D.C., in 1790, he envisioned a grand Baroque tribute to freedom. The capital was, after all, to be built from scratch—a revolutionary symbol of the struggle that had so recently created the first modern democracy.

President George Washington selected, and Congress approved, the site for the capital city: a swampy patch of land on the Potomac River between Maryland and Virginia. The Native Americans called it Conegocheague.

Washington is one of the few international seats of government constructed from the ground up. The early going was rough, characterized by argument, jealousies, and political interference. But the result was a collection of public buildings and monuments unique among world capitals.

The Capitol Building

The Capitol, at the eastern end of the National Mall, commands a westward view across the Capitol Reflecting Pool to two other iconic buildings: the Washington Monument and the Lincoln Memorial.

During the War of 1812, the original structure, designed by self-taught architect Dr. William Thornton, was burned down by the British in 1814 before it was finished. It wasn't until 1826 that work was completed by Charles Bullfinch, a Boston architect. In the 1850s, architect Thomas Ustick Walter, of Philadelphia, supervised further additions and the replacement of the original, low central dome with the soaring 287-foot (87-m) cast iron dome. This completed major construction until the east front entrance was added in 1959–1960.

The White House

It is often said that the White House, in its elegant simplicity, is the perfect symbol for a government of, by, and for the people. It was designed by Irish-born James Hoban, inspired by a villa in his native land; Hoban oversaw the rebuild-

Key Player

Pierre-Charles L'Enfant
1754–1825

French-born architect L'Enfant first surveyed the site for the capital city and developed the gridiron street plan.

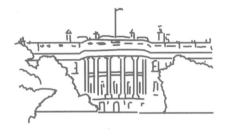

In Fact...

Other great buildings of America's capital city, one of them very famous, and a couple less so.

The Washington Monument

was first planned as an equestrian statue. The final design, based on Egyptian obelisks, was that of Lt. Col. Thomas Casey. The Corps of Engineers constructed the monument, which was dedicated in 1885.

The original Smithsonian

museum—the Castle—faces the Capitol Mall. The symbol of the Smithsonian Institution, it contains the crypt of James Smithson, the British scientist who became the first benefactor of the great repository of knowledge in 1846.

St. John's Episcopal

Church on Lafayette Square has been attended by every president since James Madison. For services or special events, pew 54 is traditionally reserved for the sitting chief executive. The classical structure was designed by Benjamin Latrobe in 1816.

The White House, as seen from the South Lawn, includes the magnificent South Portico, which, with the North Portico, was built in 1829 by architect James Hoban. The Truman balcony was added in 1947.

The United States Supreme Court was designed by Cass Gilbert in neoclassical style. The words "Equal Justice Under Law" are inscribed above the front (west) entrance. The building took only three years to complete and came in $94,000 (U.S.) under budget.

The United States Capitol boasts a dome topped by the bronze Statue of Freedom cast by Thomas Crawford, who saw it as "Freedom triumphant in war and peace." The 19-foot-tall (5.8-m) statue pushes the height of the dome to 188 feet (57.3 m).

ing after the house was razed in 1814 by the British. President Theodore Roosevelt remodeled the residence in 1909, adding the Oval Office. The last major renovation, during Harry Truman's presidency, included replacing the wood frame with steel and adding the south balcony.

Great Architecture: Buildings of Europe

Any list of great European architecture would be very long and controversial, because everyone has their favorites. So the three structures here were chosen for uniqueness. Each is one of a kind, with dedicated fans and detractors alike.

Neuschwanstein Castle

Neuschwanstein Castle is the ultimate fairy-tale castle, paying homage to Lohengrin, the Swan Knight of Richard Wagner's opera. Located in southern Germany, it sits high on a crag above the Alps.

This nineteenth-century fantasy was commissioned by King Ludwig II of Bavaria in honor of Wagner, his favorite composer; Ludwig was a keen opera enthusiast and a generous patron of Wagner. Wall art in chambers throughout the castle are themed to specific Wagnerian epics: *Lohengrin* in the great parlor, *Parsifal* for the Singers' Hall, *Tannhäuser* in the study. Neuschwanstein was designed by theatrical set maker Christian Jank to look like a medieval castle, complete with gatehouse, knight's house, and a citadel. The battlements and towers give the building its spiked silhouette. Inside is a large throne room, a singer's hall, a grotto, and many private rooms. The castle was never fully completed because the king was declared legally insane and was forced to give up his throne.

Neuschwanstein is perched above spectacular Pöllat Gorge in the Bavarian Alps.

Conversation Starter Ludwig II died mysteriously in 1886. He asked the psychiatrist who had declared him insane to walk with him to the lake, and their bodies were later found floating in the water. Ludwig supposedly drowned, but an autopsy was inconclusive. The cause of the eccentric king's death remains uncertain to this day.

The all-glass exterior of the Pompidou Center is key to the sense of openness.

The Pompidou Center

Renzo Piano and Richard Rogers stunned the world of architecture with their design for the Pompidou Center, located in the Beaubourg area of Paris. The post-modern building was the idea of French president Georges Pompidou, who wanted to create a contemporary cultural center for the visual arts.

The building's defining characteristics include glass walls, exterior escalators, and a series of exposed color-coded ducts that are part of the center's infrastructure—all part of the architects' attempt to link the exterior world of the city to the interior world of the arts center.

When the center opened in 1977, the reaction was largely negative, but the center has since become one of the most visited buildings in Paris.

In 2007, British architect Rogers received the prestigious Pritzker Prize for projects including the center. Spaniard Piano was likewise honored in 1998.

La Sagrada Família

Barcelona is home to the Roman Catholic basilica of La Sagrada Família (The Holy Family) designed by the brilliantly eccentric architect Antoni Gaudi (1852–1926).

Construction work began in 1882. The building remains unfinished and isn't expected to be completed until 2026 (a century after Gaudi's death) at the earliest.

Intended by Gaudi to be the "last great sanctuary of Christendom," the church is an ornate glorification of the Christian faith. Particularly striking are the 18 spindle-shaped towers representing the 12 apostles, the four evangelists, the Virgin Mary, and Jesus Christ.

The basilica has three façades—the Nativity, Glory, and Passion façades, the last arrayed with Joseph Subirach's gaunt sculpted figures, seen by some visitors as unorthodox.

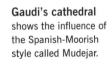

Gaudi's cathedral shows the influence of the Spanish-Moorish style called Mudejar.

Who's Who: Great European Artists

Beginning with the Renaissance, the visual arts in Europe not only flourished at home but also traveled to distant places. The works of the following six European artists continue to affect the evolution of artistic endeavor worldwide.

Michelangelo Buonarroti

Michelangelo (1475–1564) was an Italian Renaissance painter, sculptor, architect, poet, and engineer. He gained fame with his sculpture of the Pietà when he was 25.

The ceiling fresco of the Sistine Chapel was commissioned by Pope Julius II. Michelangelo took four years, working alone, to complete this fresco of the biblical creation. At age 37, he was now widely regarded as the greatest artist of his era. A man of volatile temperament, he frequently quarreled with his patrons, including popes, over the years but was never short of important commissions.

Among his best-known works are *The Last Judgment* fresco, his sculptures of *David* and *Moses*, and his powerful though unfinished *Rondanini Pietà*.

Titian (Tiziano Vecelli)

Titian (c. 1488–1567), the greatest of the Venetian painters, is regarded as the forefather of modern art. After the death of his teacher Giovanni Bellini in 1516, Titian succeeded him as official painter to the republic and began his *Assumption of the Virgin*, an altarpiece for Venice's Basilica of Santa Maria dei Frari.

Titian's fame spread throughout Europe. In 1533 he painted a portrait of Austrian emperor Charles V, who ennobled Titian and appointed him court painter. Charles's successor, Philip II of Spain, became Titian's greatest patron. The expressive multilayered brushwork and impressionistic patches of color in Titian's later work revolutionized oil painting.

Diego Velázquez

The paintings of royalty and court life by Velázquez (1599–1660), who was born in Seville of Portuguese Jewish parents and in 1623 became the court painter to King Philip IV of Spain, are among the finest works to come out of Spain. His most famous painting is *Las Meninas* (1656), a group portrait of the young infanta (princess) Margareta and her handmaidens, her dog, the dwarf court jester, and the artist himself. Velázquez's realistic style facilitated his depiction of character in this otherwise complex and enigmatic portrait.

Rembrandt van Ryn

Born in Leyden, Holland, Rembrandt (1606–1669) was the son of a miller. Today, he is regarded as the grand master of high Baroque style. After studying with the painter Pieter Lastman for a short but crucial period, Rembrandt moved to Amsterdam, where he became a successful professional portraitist. His group portrait of the Amsterdam Guild of Surgeons, *Anatomy Lesson of Dr. Tulp,* established his talent and boosted his business.

Rembrandt's portraits show a fascination with the human face and human psychology. These portraits reject the formality of earlier portrait artists and herald a realistic style. His numerous self-portraits throughout his life (totaling more than 90) provide a unique insight into the maturing artist and bequeathed to posterity what could be called an autobiography in art.

He also painted a number of biblical scenes, including *The Blinding of Samson* and *Joseph Accused by Potiphar's Wife,* and produced brilliant etchings and drawings.

Paul Cézanne

Born in Aix-en-Provence, France, Cézanne (1839–1906) is often called the "father of modern art." His very personal paintings bridge the gap between Impressionists and the developments of the twentieth century, particularly Cubism. Pablo Picasso called Cézanne "my one and only master."

Cézanne, a visionary ahead of his time, believed art should be an emotional as well as a visual experience, and that paintings should be respected for their internal integrity rather than as mere subject matter.

Vincent van Gogh

Vincent van Gogh (1853–1890) was a prolific Dutch painter, almost as well known for being an anguished artist as for the astounding quality of his work.

After jobs as a clerk, salesman, teacher, and missionary, Van Gogh took up painting in 1880 at the age of 27. His early works show a strong sense of form and an astute eye for light and shade, yet they are dark and heavy, as exemplified in *The Potato Eaters.*

After moving to Paris, Van Gogh brightened his colors at the behest of his brother Theo, the director of an art gallery, and went on to develop a vivid and energetic style. He also met the artists Pissarro and Gauguin. Moving to Arles in Provence, he suffered the first of the mental breakdowns that led to his suicide in 1890, at age 37.

Van Gogh's use of strong primary and complementary colors, simplified forms, and thick, impasto brush-

work would influence the German Expressionists in particular and Abstract Expressionists the world over.

Who's Who: Great Western Writers

Most of us have our favorite novelist, poet, or playwright. With so many great writers to choose from, how can we select the best? We can't. The following seven represent all writers whose works endure beyond a particular time and place and continue to enthrall, entertain, and influence new generations of writers and readers.

William Shakespeare

Lauded as the greatest writer in the English language, playwright and poet William Shakespeare (1564–1616) was born in Stratford-upon-Avon in England. Not much is known of his early life, but public records show he married Anne Hathaway in 1582.

He began his theatrical career as an actor in London, and by 1592 he had established a name as a playwright in the capital. His fame and wealth grew, and by 1598 he was a co-owner of the Globe Theatre, home to the King's Men, the most famous acting company at the time.

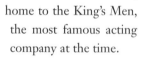

Shakespeare's plays reveal his mastery of language and his ability to create complex and believable characters; he has been called the "poet of human nature." His plays can be divided broadly into three categories: the histories (for example, *Henry IV* and *Richard III*); the comedies (including *Taming of the Shrew* and *A Midsummer Night's Dream*); and the tragedies (such as *King Lear*, *Othello*, and *Macbeth*). Shakespeare also wrote a number of sonnets and other poems.

Leo Tolstoy

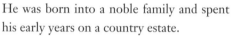

Count Leo Nikolayevich Tolstoy (1828–1910) was a Russian novelist, essayist, reformer, and philosopher. He was born into a noble family and spent his early years on a country estate.

Tolstoy's early works were autobiographical, and his experiences in the Crimean War gave him material for the battle scenes in *War and Peace* (1862), an epic novel that took him some seven years to complete. In his old age, Tolstoy renounced his former life and devoted himself to social reform in accord with his Christian asceticism.

Mark Twain

Mark Twain is the pen name of American novelist, humorist, lecturer, and raconteur Samuel Langhorne Clemens (1835–1910). When Sam was four years old, the Clemens family moved to Hannibal, Missouri, on the banks of the Mississippi River. Twain later worked as a steamboat pilot on the Mississippi, and the great

river plays an important role in his best writing. *The Adventures of Huckleberry Finn* (1885) is an American classic, acclaimed for its warmth, wit, and imagination.

Ernest Hemingway

An icon among twentieth-century American writers, Ernest Hemingway (1899–1961) is known for his spare, straightforward style, which conveys the joys and terrors of what it is to live with love and war.

Nicknamed "Papa," Hemingway began his writing career as a journalist, and his experiences as a reporter during the Spanish Civil War inspired his most successful novel, *For Whom the Bell Tolls* (1940). Other notable works include *A Farewell to Arms* (1929) and *The Old Man and the Sea* (1952). He received the Nobel Prize in Literature in 1954. Hemingway later suffered from severe depression and committed suicide in 1961.

Günter Grass

Günter Grass was born in 1927 in Danzig (now Gdansk), Poland. He is best known for his Danzig Trilogy: *The Tin Drum* (1959), *Cat and Mouse* (1961), and *Dog Years* (1963), satires dealing with Germany in the early twentieth century and the rise of Nazism.

His literature belongs to the Vergangenheitsbewältigung, an artistic movement concerned with "coming to terms with the past." In 1999, Grass was awarded the Nobel Prize in Literature.

Gabriel García Márquez

Born in Colombia, Márquez (b. 1927) began work as a journalist and spent much of his life in Europe and Mexico. His fiction is written in the "magical realism" style, integrating fantastical elements into realistic situations.

Considered a giant among twentieth-century novelists, his work *One Hundred Years of Solitude* (1967) is the best-selling Spanish language book of all time. García Márquez was awarded the Nobel Prize in Literature in 1982.

Toni Morrison

Morrison, born Chloe Anthony Wofford in Ohio in 1931, was captivated by stories from early childhood on. Her father regaled her with black folk tales, and she devoured novels by Austen and Tolstoy. After marrying, she earned degrees in English and became a professor and part-time writer. In the 1960s, Morrison brought African-American literature to a larger audience as a senior editor at a New York publishing house.

Her first novel, *The Bluest Eye* (1970), foreshadowed the vivid characterization and dialogue that she is known for. *The Song of Solomon* (1977) garnered awards, and *Beloved* (1988)—which was based on the heartbreaking true story of an escaped female slave—won critical acclaim worldwide. Morrison was awarded the Nobel Prize in Literature in 1993.

Who's Who: Great European Composers

The world might well have yet to hear from its greatest composer, who could burst upon the scene at any time. Still, the six composers profiled here represent a stunning and still influential flowering of the musical realm in pre–twentieth century Europe.

Johann Sebastian Bach

At least 60 members of the Bach family were musicians, but Johann Sebastian Bach (1685–1750) was the genius.

Music played an important part in both court and church life during his lifetime, and Bach held posts as a court violinist, town church organist, chief court musician, and cantor of the St. Thomas Church and School in Leipzig, Germany. Bach composed many pieces for the organ and harpsichord and is known for his church music. The six *Brandenburg Concertos* are among his most performed compositions.

Franz Joseph Haydn

Haydn (1732–1809) was born in Rohrau on the Austrian-Hungarian border. He was the son of a wheelwright, and his peasant upbringing and exposure to folk music influenced his work. He began his career as a choirboy at age six and later became a musical director for a Bohemian nobleman.

In 1761, Haydn entered the service of the music-loving Esterhazy family, giving him the opportunity to work with one of the

best ensembles of that time. He was a prolific composer, writing 104 symphonies, 83 string quartets, 52 piano sonatas, and many other concertos and chamber pieces. *The Creation*, *The Seasons*, and his *Emperor's Hymn* are perhaps his most famous compositions. Many music scholars hold that in Haydn's hands, the symphonic, string quartet, and piano sonata forms reached near perfection. He is considered by many to be the father of modern music.

Wolfgang Amadeus Mozart

Mozart (1756–1791) was one of the most naturally gifted musicians of all time. Richard Wagner called him "the greatest and most divine genius." A child prodigy, Mozart began to play the clavier at the age of three and by five had started to compose small pieces. He was performing in the courts of Europe at the age of six, and by 14 had received a knighthood from the pope. In his later youth, Mozart spent some time at the

court of the Archbishop of Salzburg, but it proved to be an unhappy stay. He later moved to Vienna, where he flourished as a pianist and composer. He was appointed chamber composer to Emperor Joseph II in 1787.

Mozart produced an enormous amount of work during his brief life, including nearly 50 symphonies and 20 operas and operettas. Among his most famous works are the operas *Figaro*, *Don Giovanni*, and *The Magic Flute*, which made its debut shortly before Mozart's death at age 35.

Ludwig van Beethoven

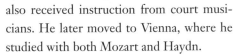

Born in Bonn, Germany, Beethoven (1770–1827) was introduced to music by his father, a singer, and also received instruction from court musicians. He later moved to Vienna, where he studied with both Mozart and Haydn.

Unlike other composers of the day, Beethoven did not become a court musician but relied upon the support of enthusiastic aristocrats. When he was about 30, Beethoven began to lose his hearing, which became progressively worse until he was totally deaf. But Beethoven did not allow his disability to affect his musical output. Many of his finest works, including the Ninth Symphony and the mass Missa Solemnis were composed after his loss of hearing.

Beethoven is considered to be the first of the Romantic composers. His music is both passionate and powerful, and his influence in the world of music remains profound.

Richard Wagner

Born in Leipzig to a theatrical family, Wagner (1813–1883) became interested in music and the stage at an early age.

Like Beethoven, Wagner belongs to the nineteenth-century German Romantic Movement. Among his compositions, it is undoubtedly the operas that stand out as his best works. Wagner's greatest and most famous operas, based on German myth and legend, include *Tannhäuser*, *Tristan and Isolde*, and the Ring Cycle (*Rhinegold*, *The Valkyrie*, *Siegfried*, and *The Twilight of the Gods*).

Wagner designed and supervised the construction of a theater in Bayreuth, Germany, to showcase his operas, and a festival of his works is still held there annually.

Peter Ilich Tchaikovsky

One of the world's most enduringly popular composers, Tchaikovsky (1840–1893) was the first Russian composer to enjoy fame outside his home country, though he had a harder time earning critical approval.

Tchaikovsky is particularly known for three ballets—*Swan Lake*, *The Sleeping Beauty*, and *The Nutcracker*. His other popular works include the opera *Eugene Onegin*, the Pathétique symphony, and the well-known perennial crowd pleaser, *The 1812 Overture*. Tchaikovsky died suddenly after contracting cholera at the age of 53.

Test You

From primitive, albeit beautiful, daubs on cave walls, art in its many forms has come a long way. This chapter has examined great paintings and painters, architecture, authors, and composers. But how much can you remember?

Cave and Rock Painting: The Birth of Art

1 How old are the cave paintings of Altamira in northern Spain estimated to be?

a) *13,000 years old*
b) *15,000 years old*
c) *17,000 years old*
d) *19,000 years old*

2 What is the name of the cave system in France that contains nearly 2,000 cave paintings?

A Brief History of Western Art

1 In which year did Da Vinci paint *The Last Supper*?

a) *1398*   b) *1498*
c) *1598*   d) *1698*

2 In which century did Mannerism develop?

a) *1400s*   b) *1500s*
c) *1600s*   d) *1700s*

3 With which movement would you associate Rembrandt?

Western Painting in the Twentieth Century

1 After which war did Dadaism briefly flourish?

a) *The American Civil War*
b) *World War I*
c) *The Spanish Civil War*
d) *World War II*

2 Which artist painted *Guernica*, a painting inspired by the aerial bombardment of the city in the Spanish Civil War?

3 What was the name of the movement that included artists such as David Hockney, Roy Lichtenstein, and Andy Warhol?

Great Architecture: Three Iconic Buildings

1 True or False: The Sydney Opera House is a UNESCO World Heritage site.

2 How many days did it take to build the Empire State Building?

a) *410*   b) *510*
c) *610*   d) *710*

Great Architecture: Buildings of Washington

1 What was the Native American name for the site on which Washington, D.C., was built?

2 Who was the French-born architect responsible for the capital city's gridiron street plan?

Great Architecture: Buildings of Europe

1 Who was the supposedly mad king of Bavaria who commissioned the fairy-tale Neuschwanstein Castle?

2 In which city would you find the Pompidou Center?

   a) *Geneva*   b) *Marseilles*
   c) *Paris*   d) *Toulouse*

3 True or False: The Sagrada Família was completed in 1882.

Who's Who: Great European Artists

1 In which decade was the Renaissance artist Michelangelo born?

   a) *1440s*   b) *1450s*
   c) *1460s*   d) *1470s*

2 For which king of Spain was Diego Velázquez the court painter?

3 Which artist is considered to be the "father of modern art"?

4 True or False: Vincent van Gogh committed suicide.

Who's Who: Great Western Writers

1 Of which theater in London did William Shakespeare become the co-owner in 1598?

2 By what name is Samual Langhorne Clemens better known?

3 During which war did Ernest Hemingway gain experience as a reporter?

Who's Who: Great European Composers

1 Which composer created the opera Figero?

   a) *J. S. Bach*   b) *Mozart*
   c) *Beethoven*   d) *Wagner*

2 True or False: Over the course of his career, Mozart slowly became deaf.

3 Name the four works that make up Wagner's Ring Cycle.

4 Who composed *Swan Lake*, *Sleeping Beauty*, and *The Nutcracker*?

Chapter Ten

?

The
Quizzes

You've read the book, and now it's time to take
the tests. But with so much new information, can
you still remember who, what, where, when, why,
or how? And can you tell the truth from the lies in
True or False? Over the next few pages you'll find
plenty of questions to challenge you, along with
some illustrations to help prompt your memory when
the going gets tough. As well as attempting the
quizzes yourself, why not challenge your friends and
family to see who really does know it all?

The history of the world is populated by amazing characters, from charismatic leaders to ingenious inventors, and from the brainiest of scientists to famous wordsmiths. But can you remember *who* they were, what they did, and what they said?

1 Who wrote the *Principia Mathematica* and what country was he from?

2 Who won the Nobel Prize in 1922 for his work on the orbits of electrons within an atom?

3 Name the German geologist who gave his name to a scale that defines the hardness of minerals.

4 Can you name the two American scientists whose work simulating the conditions of the early Earth showed how the building blocks of life may have arisen?

5 Who was the scientist responsible for suggesting a new system of mammalian classification?

6 Name two of the three scientists who collaborated on the discovery of DNA.

7 Who was the historian and philosopher who wrote *The Prince*, and in what period did he come to prominence?

8 Three famous inventors, three famous quotes; but who said what?

a) *Da Vinci*
b) *Thomas Edison*
c) *Alfred Nobel*

I) *If I find 10,000 ways something won't work, I haven't failed. I am not discouraged, because every wrong attempt discarded is another step forward.*
II) *I intend to leave after my death a large fund for the promotion of the peace idea, but I am skeptical as to its results.*

III) *Iron rusts from disuse; stagnant water loses its purity and in cold weather becomes frozen; even so does inaction sap the vigor of the mind.*

9 This Italian physicist made a telling contribution to splitting the atom, but who is he?

10 Who is this twentieth-century Spanish dictator, and in what years did he reign?

11 Who was the first person to walk through the Brandenburg Gate after the fall of the Berlin Wall?

12 Who is this Russian leader whose policies spurred the fall of the USSR?

13 Who are the economist authors of *Das Kapital; The General Theory of Employment, Interest, and Money;* and *The Quantity Theory of Money.*

14 What is the name of the pope who launched the first Crusade, and in what year did it take place?

15 Four famous painters, four famous paintings—but who painted what?

   a) *Da Vinci*   b) *Delacroix*
   c) *Rembrandt*   d) *Van Eyck*

   I) *The Arnolfini Portrait*
   II) *The Last Supper*
   III) *Liberty Leading the People*
   IV) *The Night Watch*

16 Four famous authors, four famous books—but who wrote what? ?

   a) *Günter Grass*
   b) *Ernest Hemingway*
   c) *Gabriel Garcia Márquez*
   d) *Toni Morrison*

   I) *A Farewell to Arms*
   II) *Beloved*
   III) *One Hundred Years of Solitude*
   IV) *The Tin Drum*

17 Which famous composer created the operas *Figaro, Don Giovanni,* and *The Magic Flute?*

Do you know what type of galaxy we live in or what type of rock you're standing upon? Perhaps you can remember what the name of a great artwork or important city is. Test yourself now to see if you know what's *what* in the world of knowledge.

1 What are these four different types of galaxies known as?

2 What are the two different fates that await a red giant, depending on its mass?

3 Starting with the closest to the Sun, what is the order of the planets in the solar system?

4 What is the most common type of rock?

   a) *Igneous*
   b) *Metamorphic*
   c) *Sedimentary*

5 Can you remember what the gemstone is for each month of the year?

6 Can you name what types of volcanoes these are?

 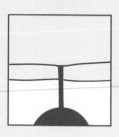

7 What are the four chemical letters that make up the structure of DNA?

   a) *ABCD*   b) *ABXY*
   c) *ACGT*   d) *ACNX*

8 What are the four divisions of seed plants?

9 What invention was nicknamed "The Gadget"?

   a) *The first cinema projector*
   b) *The first computer*
   c) *The first fission bomb*
   d) *The first cell phone*

10 Name the British liner carrying American passengers that was sunk by a German submarine, hastening the entry of the United States into World War I?

a) SS *Central America*
b) *Lusitania*
c) *Titanic*
d) *Wilhelm Gustloff*

11 Name two of the eight U.N. Millennium Development Goals.

12 What was the capital of Nigeria prior to its replacement by the purpose-built city of Abuja in 1991?

a) *Ibadan* b) *Kaduna*
c) *Kano*   d) *Lagos*

13 Nelson Mandela was active within the ANC, leading the party to power in 1993—but what does ANC stand for?

14 What important religious text was published in 1611?

a) *The Book of Common Prayer*
b) *The Gutenberg Bible*
c) *The King James Bible*
d) *Wycliff's Bible*

15 What name for a branch of philosophy derives from the Greek for "the study of knowledge"?

16 What was the great artwork painted by Edward Hopper in 1942?

17 What is the name of the art movement that emerged in Britain and reached its peak in New York in the 1960s and whose stars included Roy Lichtenstein, David Hockney, and Andy Warhol?

18 What is the literal translation of "Taj Mahal"?

a) *Crown Palace*   b) *King's Palace*
c) *Queen's Palace* d) *Royal Palace*

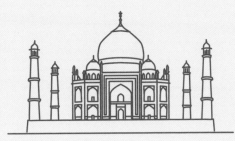

19 What prize did British architect Richard Rogers receive in 2007 for his work that included the Pompidou Center in Paris?

a) *the Booker*   b) *the Nobel*
c) *the Pritzker* d) *the Pulitzer*

20 At what age did Vincent van Gogh commit suicide?

a) *27*   b) *37*
c) *47*   d) *57*

From the tallest mountains to the most bustling metropolis, *Know It All* has taken you on a grand tour of the globe. But can you remember what happened *where*? We give you some hints on the map below.

1 Where in the Milky Way (hint: on which of the galaxy's spiral arms) would you find the Sun?

2 Where in the Earth's atmosphere would you find the Ozone layer?

    a) *the troposphere*   b) *the stratosphere*
    c) *the mesosphere*   d) *the thermos-phere*

3 Where would you find the Franz Josef Glacier?

    a) *Argentina*   b) *France*
    c) *Italy*   d) *New Zealand*

4 Where was the most powerful earthquake ever recorded?

5 Where would you find a hydrothermal vent?

6 What is the name given to the area marked on the map in which agriculture first began?

7 To where did the *Jules Verne* cargo ship make its first voyage in April 2008?

8 What were the names of the two key naval battles that turned the course of World War II in the Pacific?

9 What is the name of the capital city of Afghanistan, pictured below?

10 In which nation was the term fascism first used?

   a) *Germany*   b) *Italy*
   c) *Japan*   d) *Spain*

11 In which city in Europe did the Solidarity Movement take form?

12 Where would you find the world's fastest growing population according to a 2004 United Nations report?

13 To which city in the Middle East does the annual Islamic pilgrimage, the Hajj, take place?

   a) *Jerusalem*   b) *Mecca*
   c) *Medina*   d) *Tehran*

14 In which historical city would you find the ruins of the Parthenon?

15 In which cave system would you find the prehistoric art shown below?

16 In which South American country was the great writer Gabriel García Marquez born?

17 In which U.S. state was the author Toni Morrison born?

Having looked back as far as the beginning of time itself *Know It All* has guided you through the ages to meet the first life on Earth, the earliest civilizations, and even the first humans in space along the way. But can you remember *when* it all happened?

1 When was the Hubble space telescope launched?

   a) *1990*   b) *1991*
   c) *1992*   d) *1993*

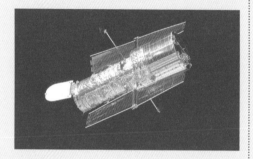

2 When are the Andromeda Galaxy and our own galaxy, the Milky Way, expected to collide?

3 When did the Sun begin to burn?

4 When did the Earth begin to form from spinning space dust?

5 When was the Kyoto Protocol agreed upon?

   a) *1977*   b) *1987*
   c) *1997*   d) *2007*

6 When did the HMS *Challenger* undertake the first worldwide oceanographic survey?

7 All birds can trace their roots back to a common ancestor, but when did this common ancestor live?

   a) *1.5 billion years ago*
   b) *150 million years ago*
   c) *15 million years ago*
   d) *1.5 million years ago*

8 The dodo went extinct after cats, dogs, and rats brought by Western explorers reached its native island of Mauritius, but in which century?

   a) *fourteenth century*
   b) *fifteenth century*
   c) *sixteenth century*
   d) *seventeenth century*

9 When did the Aztecs found their capital city, Tenochtitlán, on an island in Lake Texcoco?

10 When was the last recorded gladiatorial contest held in the Colosseum?

11 Below are four inventions that were crucial to the progress of the Industrial Revolution. Which date matches which invention?

a) *ball bearings* b) *circular saw*
c) *electromagnet* d) *plastic*

I) *1777* II) *1794*
III) *1825* IV) *1862*

12 When did the first horror film premiere and what was its title?

13 During the American Civil War, on what date did General Robert E. Lee surrender his troops?

a) *April 12, 1861*
b) *September 17, 1862*
c) *April 9, 1865*
d) *April 12, 1865*

14 In which year did Lyndon B. Johnson succeed assassinated U.S. president John F. Kennedy?

15 In which year did the Suez Crisis take place?

16 Below are four key moments in the history of European communism. Can you name the years in which they occurred and place them in order?

a) *the Berlin Wall is built*
b) *the Cuban Missile Crisis occurs*
c) *the Strategic Arms Limitation Treaty is signed*
d) *the Warsaw Pact is signed*

17 This graph shows share values on the New York Stock Exchange over the course of 100 years. Which infamous date predicated the crash shown?

18 When was the Eastern religion of Zoroastrianism founded in Persia?

a) *around 1200* BCE
b) *around 200* BCE
c) *around 200* CE
d) *around 1200* CE

19 When did President Theodore Roosevelt remodel the White House, adding the now famous Oval Office?

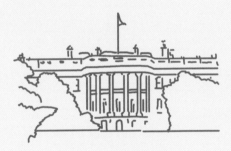

There's a difference between knowing and understanding, and while *Know It All* has given you plenty of facts and figures, that's not the end of the story. Sure, you might know what happened, but can you remember *why*?

1 Why does the gravity vary slightly all over the planet?

2 Why do some stars go supernova while others do not?

3 Why does the Red Sea have such a high salt content?

  a) *because the rate of evaporation is low, while the flow of water is low*
  b) *because the rate of evaporation is low, while the flow of water is high*
  c) *because the rate of evaporation is high, while the flow of water is low*
  d) *because the rate of evaporation is high while the flow of water is high*

4 Why is it thought that, beginning in 2007, hundreds of thousands of honey bee colonies suffered from "colony collapse disorder"?

5 Why are flying insects so important to the reproduction of some plants?

6 Why did the Aztecs hold the jaguar in particular esteem?

7 Chang Ch'ien is considered by many as the father of the Silk Road, but why was his journey westward delayed by 10 years?

8 Why did the Medici family of Florence play a key role in the development of Renaissance art?

9 Why did the city of Petra remain hidden to the Western world until it was "discovered" by Johann Ludwig Burckhardt in 1812?

10 Why did Alfred Nobel bequeath the funds to found the Nobel Prize?

11 Why did the first Battle of Marne mark a turning point in World War I?

a) *it was the first battle in which tanks were used to good effect*

b) *it was the bloodiest battle of the war*

c) *it marked the start of the German advance*

d) *it marked the start of a period of stalemate*

12 Why did the government of Afghanistan request Soviet assistance in 1979?

13 Why was Sir Thomas More, the author of the political work *Utopia*, tried, found guilty, and beheaded?

14 Why was China the first country to sign the United Nations Charter?

15 Why was the capital of Brazil relocated to the newly built city of Brasilia in the 1950s?

16 Why is the UBS trading floor in Stamford, Connecticut, particularly noteworthy?

17 Why are the Bradshaw Paintings found in the Kimberley region of Western Australia particularly noteworthy?

18 Why did architect Jørn Utzon resign from the project to build his design for the Sydney Opera House?

a) *because of ill health*

b) *because of dangerous working practices*

c) *because of political pressures and budget cuts*

d) *because of a fear of heights*

19 Why were the battle scenes in Tolstoy's *War and Peace* especially realistic?

How much have you learned from *Know It All*? How many trips did Columbus make to the Americas? How would you find the celestial South Pole? How does the Fibonacci sequence run? Just *how* much or *how* little do you know about the world around you?

1 How could you find the celestial South Pole with the help of a constellation?

2 How did the Danish physicist Neils Bohr win his Nobel Prize in 1922?

3 How many tons of material are added to the Earth every year as cosmic dust and meteorites fall to the ground?

α) *10,000*   b) *20,000*
c) *30,000*   d) *40,000*

4 How are the different natural shapes of crystals known?

α) *classes*   b) *groups*
c) *species*   d) *types*

5 How deep is the deepest ocean trench in the world?

6 How did Julius Caesar's reign as Roman dictator come to an end in 44 BCE?

α) *he was assassinated*
b) *he went mad*
c) *he was forced to retire*
d) *he died of natural causes*

7 How many voyages to the "New World" did the Italian explorer Christopher Columbus make?

α) *1*   b) *2*
c) *3*   d) *4*

8 The Fibonacci mathematical sequence starts 0, 1, 1, 2, 3, 5, 8... how should it continue?

α) *12*   b) *13*
c) *14*   d) *15*

9 How did the surgeon Joseph Lister decrease the rates of post-surgical mortality in his patients?

10 How many of the Group I elements in the Periodic Table can you name?

11 How much is work on the International Space Station expected to have cost when it is completed?

a) *$700 million (U.S.)*
b) *$28 billion (U.S.)*
c) *$92 billion (U.S.)*
d) *$130 billion (U.S.)*

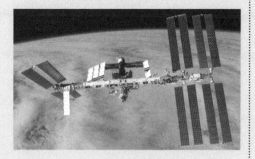

12 How were the units of foreign volunteers that fought for the Republicans in the Spanish Civil War known?

13 The American government justified intervention in anti-communist conflicts such as the Vietnam War as an effort to prevent a succession of states becoming communist. How was this fear known?

14 Once a single nation, Yugoslavia has splintered into a number of independent states. How many, and what are their names?

15 How is the form of government in countries such as Sweden, France, and Germany often described?

16 How does the following quote from Vladimir Ilyich Lenin finish?

"Freedom in capitalist society always remains about the same as it was in ancient Greek republics…"

17 How are goods and services that would not be provided if it were left purely to market forces known?

a) *marginal goods*   b) *private goods*
c) *public goods*   d) *social goods*

18 How many followers does Christianity have around the world?

a) *1.1 billion*   b) *2.1 billion*
c) *3.1 billion*   d) *4.1 billion*

19 How high is the U.S. Capitol, and how tall is the Statue of Freedom that stands upon it?

20 How did the composer Richard Wagner describe the child prodigy Wolfgang Amadeus Mozart?

a) *the greatest composer of all time*
b) *the greatest and most divine genius*
c) *the greatest musical genius*
d) *the greatest genius of all*

It's one thing being able to pull a date from the recesses of your mind, or the name of an ancient philosopher, but things start to get tricky when people put ideas into your head. Can you tell the truth from the lies?

1 True or False: If you drop a hammer and a feather at the same time in the absence of air resistance, they will reach the ground at the same time.

2 True or False: Saturn is the biggest planet in the solar system.

6 True or False: Hammurabi, the sixth king of Persia, is famous for setting out a set of laws known as *The Code of Hammurabi.*

7 True or False: The guillotine was invented as a more humane method of execution.

3 True or False: All of the oceans in the world are interconnected.

4 True or False: Panspermia is the idea that life arose on Earth independently.

5 True or False: Squamata, the order of reptiles that includes snakes and lizards, is the largest of the reptile orders, with over 20,000 species.

8 True or False: The only one of the Seven Wonders of the Ancient World that is still standing is the Great Pyramid at Giza, in Egypt.

9 True or False: In 1938 a television broadcast of Orson Welles's *The War of the Worlds* was mistaken by thousands for a live news broadcast, causing widespread panic.

10 True or False: Sally Ride was the first woman in space.

11 True or False: Before his election, Abraham Lincoln did not propose the abolition of slavery; he only opposed its extension into the western territories.

12 True or False: The Viet Minh "Tet offensive" during the Vietnam War was an unqualified success.

13 True or False: The basis for English common law was laid down in the Magna Carta of 1215.

14 True or False: China, France, Germany, the Russian Federation, the United Kingdom, and the United States together form the permanent members of the U.N. Security Council.

15 True or False: The earliest equities market was in ancient Rome.

16 True or False: The symbol Om is sacred to Hinduism and represents the creator god Brahma.

17 True or False: The Yin Yang symbol is sacred to the Japanese faith of Shintoism.

18 True or False: The early twentieth century art movement of Expressionism was dominated by German artists.

19 True or False: King Ludwig II commissioned his fairy-tale castle in homage to the character of the Swan Knight from Wagner's opera *Lohengrin*.

Answers:

Understanding the Universe

The Cosmos: An Explosive Birth?
1. a) radiation left over from the Big Bang
2. 100 million years
3. the Planck time
4. 1929
5. 90 percent

Newton's Laws: Why Things Move as They Do
1. gravity
2. three
3. optics
4. Newton's third law

The Milky Way: Billions of Stars Strong
1. stars, dust, gas
2. spiral, barred, elliptical, irregular
3. true
4. d) 100,000 million

Constellations: Ancient Legends in the Stars
1. Sirius, Alpha Canis Majoris, the Dog Star
2. the Great Bear

The Science of the Stars
1. b) a light-year
2. hydrogen
3. a white dwarf or a supernova (depending on size)

The Sun: Our Own Star
1. 100 times
2. the northern lights

The Solar System: Our Planetary Neighborhood
1. Venus
2. a) Jupiter
3. Mars
4. dwarf planets

Comets, Meteors, and Other Celestial Visitors
1. 3.3 years
2. c) an asteroid

Time and Space: It's All Relative
1. c) 186,000 miles per sec. (299,792 km.p.s.)
2. b) younger
3. 1955

The Amazing Atom: Protons Plus
1. electrons, neutrons, protons
2. the number of protons it has

The Story of the Earth

The Formation of Planet Earth
1. a) 4,540,000,000 years ago
2. the rotation of its liquid metal outer core
3. iron and nickel

Water World: The Earth's Oceans
1. b) 70 percent
2. Atlantic, Pacific, Indian
3. true
4. desalination

Earth's Atmosphere: A Coat of Many Layers
1. troposphere, stratosphere, mesosphere, thermosphere, exosphere
2. atmospheric pressure
3. c) nitrogen and oxygen
4. by destroying the ozone layer

On Shifting Ground: Plate Tectonics
1. a convergent or destructive boundary
2. a destructive boundary
3. Pangaea

Rocks and Fossils: Earth's Upper Crust

1 sedimentary rock

2 heating and compression

Earth's Climate: What Gives?

1 c) 4

2 2 billion years ago

3 the Ward Hunt Ice Shelf

The Never-ending Water Cycle

1 3 percent

2 burning fossil fuels releasing sulfur dioxide and other oxides

3 c) evaporation from plants

Minerals and Gems: Treasures of the Earth

1 icy cold

2 32

3 c) South Africa

Volcanoes: Builders and Demolishers

1 Herculaneum and Pompeii

2 composite, shield, cinder cone, fissure

3 Indonesia

The Destructive Power of Earthquakes

1 a tsunami

2 strange animal behavior

3 Shensi, China

The Story of Life

The Birth of Life on Earth

1 3.5 billion years

2 Panspermia

Insects and the Diversity of Life

1 head, thorax, abdomen

2 d) 80 percent

3 a) 20 percent

Insects and the Diversity of Life

1 epipelagic (sunlight), mesopelagic (twilight), bathypelagic (midnight), abyssopelagic (abyss), hadopelagic (trenches)

2 the Marianas Trench

3 true

Reptiles: On Land to Stay

1 squamata, testudines, crocodilia, sphenodontia

2 false—they can only be found in the Americas

Birds and Life on the Wing

1 150 million years ago

2 a) the air pressure above it is reduced

3 c) 40,000 miles (32,000 km)

Mammals: A Class of Their Own

1 the blue whale

2 the bumblebee bat

3 herbivores, carnivores, omnivores, insectivores

Homo Sapiens and the Origins of Us

1 *A. Afarensis*

2 false—Neanderthals were a related, but parallel species, rather than an ancestor of *Homo Sapiens*

3 c) 200,000 years

Charles Darwin and the Story of Evolution

1 the nineteenth century (1800s)

2 HMS *Beagle*

3 *On the Origin of Species by Means of Natural Selection*

DNA and Genetics: The Stuff of Life

1 a double helix

2 1953

The Kingdom of Plants

1 the stamen (male) and stigma (female)

2 oxygen

The Ecological Balancing Act
1 producers, primary consumers, secondary consumers, decomposers

3 one third

Lost Forever: A Guide to Extinction
1 1796

2 b) 1914

Exploring the World

Out of Africa: A Guide to Human Migration
1 the Omo river basin in Ethiopia

2 b) 17,000 years ago

The First Civilizations: Three Giant Leaps
1 the Sumerian

2 Menes

3 Mohenjo-daro and Harappa

Great Empires of the Ancient World
1 Macedon

2 Marathon (490 BCE), Salamis and Plataea (480 BCE)

3 Romulus and Remus

Great Civilizations of Ancient America
1 d) the Olmecs

2 a plumed serpent

3 the Andes

Ancient Trade Routes: The Road to Riches
1 d) 4,000 miles (6,440 km)

2 Chang Ch'ien

3 gold

The Renaissance: A Rebirth in Europe
1 Florence, Italy

2 the Medicis

3 b) *The Prince*

4 that the planets revolved around the Sun, not around the Earth

Global Explorations by Land and Sea
1 c) 17

2 false—he died during the voyage

3 the *Victoria*

4 180°

Three Great Modern Revolutions
1 c) Louis XVI

2 c) St. Petersburg

3 the KMT (Chinese Nationalist Party)

The Seven "New" Wonders of the World
1 c) Rio de Janiero

2 Petra in Jordan

3 Mexico

Invention and Discovery

Agriculture: The Endless Quest for Food
1 the Fertile Crescent

2 a) 1862

3 c) Mexico

The Written Word and the Printed Page
1 the *Diamond Sutra*

2 Johannes Gutenberg

3 c) 1884

The Written Word and the Printed Page
1 true

2 Leonardo Fibonacci

The Fight For Life: A History of Medicine
1 c) 1628

2 Edward Jenner

The Periodic Table: Order out of Chaos

1. Dmitri Ivanovich Mendeleev
2. true
3. hydrogen

Great Inventors: Da Vinci, Nobel, Edison

1. the *Vetruvian Man*
2. dynamite

The Industrial Revolution: No Going Back

1. Luddites
2. Tsar Nicholas I

Communication: From Telegrams to Email

1. semaphore
2. Mr Watson, come here, I want to see you.

The Moving Image and the Silver Screen

1. 24 frames per second
2. true

Radio and Television Bring the World Home

1. 1938
2. a) 1960s

Splitting the Atom: The New Atomic Age

1. the Manhattan Project
2. New Mexico

The International Space Station

1. Yuri Gagarin
2. c) 1963
3. true

☮ Conflicts of the Modern Age

Warring States: The American Civil War

1. b) 1861
2. Alabama, Florida, Georgia, Louisiana, Mississippi, South Carolina

World War I: Death on a Grand Scale

1. a) June 28, 1914
2. the Battle of Cambrai

The Spanish Civil War: A Bloody Preview

1. the Popular Front
2. Paris
3. c) 36 years

World War II: The World at War

1. the Treaty of Versailles
2. b) 1933
3. false—"Little Boy" was dropped on Hiroshima

The Cold War: A Four Decade Standoff

1. Winston Churchill
2. the Warsaw Pact
3. a) 1989
4. d) remodeling
5. the cover of the *Bulletin of Atomic Scientists*

The Vietnam War: A Futile Intervention

1. France
2. Saigon

Arab–Israeli Conflicts: Fight for a Homeland

1. a) Israel and Egypt
2. the Camp David Accords
3. true

War in Afghanistan: The Soviet Quagmire

1. Jimmy Carter
2. 1989
3. a) the Northern Alliance

War in the Balkans: Europe's Hot Spot

1. Bosnia-Herzegovina, Croatia, Kosovo, Macedonia, Montenegro, Serbia, Slovenia
2. Slobodan Milosovic

⚖️ The Structure of Society

Forms of Government: Democracies
1 Athens
2 *The Social Contract*
3 d) 1789

Three More Forms of National Government
1 c) Russia
2 *Utopia*

The Rise and Fall of European Communism
1 1917
2 Bolsheviks
3 Solidarity
4 c) 500 days

The World as One: The United Nations
1 c) New York
2 China
3 United Nations Educational, Scientific, and Cultural Organization
4 2015

World Population: A Visual Guide
1 d) 1800s
2 a) 6.8 billion

Centers of Power: Capitals of the World
1 Peter the Great
2 Rio de Janiero
3 d) Paris

Iconic Leaders of the Modern World
1 African National Congress (ANC)
2 Pope John Paul II
3 Law

The Father of Modern Economics
1 Adam Smith
2 *An Inquiry into the Nature and Causes of the Wealth of Nations*
3 Milton Friedman

World GDP: A Visual Guide
1 Gross Domestic Product
2 the United States

Buy, Buy, Buy: The World of Stock Markets
1 b) 1929
2 the dot com boom

📖 Religion and Thought

The Religions of the World
1 Christianity
2 d) Tel Aviv

Judaism and the Children of Abraham
1 false—it is the oldest
2 Orthodox, Conservative, Reform
3 Jerusalem

Christianity: The Path of Christ
1 33 CE
2 Constantine I
3 Wittenburg Castle Church

Islam and the Prophet Muhammad
1 c. 570 CE
2 Shahadah (testimony of faith), Salah or Sadat (prayer), Zakat (giving alms), Sawm (fasting), Hajj (pilgrimage)

Hinduism: The Eternal Law
1 Om
2 Brahma, Vishnu, Shiva

Buddhism: Religion or Philosophy?
1 Siddhartha Gautama

2 Dukkha (all life is suffering), Samudaya (suffering is caused by craving or desire), Nirodha (to eliminate suffering it is necessary to eliminate craving or desire), Magga (that it is necessary to follow the eightfold path)

3 Tenzin Gyatso

Other Faiths of the Eastern World
1 a) India
2 Ahura Mazda
3 c) Way of the Spirits
4 Yin represents feminine, light, and calm; Yang represents masculine, dark, and active
5 b) the fourth century

Mythologies of the Ancient World
1 Ma'at
2 Delphi
3 c) Hermes and Vesta

The Four Branches of Philosophy
1 epistemology, logic, metaphysics, ethics
2 ethics

Great Thinkers: Ancient to Modern
1 d) Socrates
2 false—Aristotle was a student of Plato
3 a) *Critique of Ethics*

Artistic Endeavor

Cave and Rock Painting: The Birth of Art
1 c) 17,000 years old
2 Lascaux

A Brief History of Western Art
1 b) 1498
2 b) 1500s
3 Baroque

Western Painting in the Twentieth Century
1 b) World War I

2 Pablo Picasso
3 Pop Art

Great Architecture: Three Iconic Buildings
1 true
2 a) 410

Great Architecture: Buildings of Washington
1 Conegocheague
2 Pierre-Charles L'Enfant

Great Architecture: Buildings of Europe
1 King Ludwig II
2 c) Paris
3 false—it was begun in 1882, it remains incomplete

Who's Who: Great European Artists
1 d) 1470s
2 King Philip IV
3 Cézanne
4 true

Who's Who: Great Western Writers
1 the Globe
2 Mark Twain
3 the Spanish Civil War

Who's Who: Great European Composers
1 b) Mozart
2 false—it was Beethoven who became deaf
3 *Rhinegold, The Valkyrie, Siegfried, The Twilight of the Gods*
4 Tchaikovsky

The Quizzes

Who?
1 Sir Isaac Newton, Great Britain
2 Neils Bohr

3 Friedrich Mohs

4 Stanley Miller and Harold Urey

5 Gaylord Simpson

6 James Watson, Francis Crick, Maurice Wilkins

7 Niccolo Machiavelli, the Renaissance

8 a), III; b), I; c), II

9 Enrico Fermi

10 Francisco Franco, 1939–1975

11 West German Chancellor Helmut Kohl

12 Mikhail Gorbachev

13 Karl Marx wrote *Das Kapital*; John Maynard Keynes wrote *The General Theory of Employment, Interest, and Money*; Milton Friedman wrote *The Quantity Theory of Money*

14 Pope Urban II, 1095 CE

15 a), II; b), III; c), IV; d), I

16 a), IV; b), I; c), III; d), II

17 Wolfgang Amadeus Mozart

What?

1 clockwise: spiral, barred, irregular, elliptical

2 it either becomes a white dwarf, or, if it is large enough, it goes supernova

3 Mercury, Venus, Earth, Mars, Jupiter, Saturn, Uranus, Neptune

4 a) igneous

5 January = garnet; February = amethyst; March = aquamarine; April = diamond; May = emerald; June = pearl; July = ruby; August = peridot or carnelian; September = sapphire; October = opal; November = topaz; December = turquoise

6 clockwise: composite, shield, fissure, cinder cone

7 c) ACGT

8 cycads, ginkgo, conifers, gnetophytes

9 c) the first fission bomb

10 b) Lusitania

11 eradicate poverty and hunger; achieve universal primary education; promote gender equality and empower women; reduce child mortality; improve maternal health; combat HIV/AIDS, malaria and other diseases; ensure environmental sustainability; create a global partnership for development

12 d) Lagos

13 African National Congress

14 c) The King James Bible

15 Epistemology

16 *Nighthawks*

17 Pop Art

18 a) crown palace

19 b) the Pritzker

20 b) 37

Where?

1 the Orion arm

2 b) the stratosphere

3 d) New Zealand

4 Chile

5 on the ocean floor

6 the Fertile Crescent

7 the International Space Station

8 Coral Sea, Midway

9 Kabul

10 b) Italy

11 Warsaw, Poland

12 Liberia

13 b) Mecca

14 Athens, Greece

15 Lascaux, France

16 Colombia

17 Ohio

When?

1 a) 1990

2 in 3 billion years

3 4.57 billion years ago

4 4.54 billion years ago

5 c) 1997

6 1872–1876

7 b) 150 million years ago

8 d) seventeenth century

9 1325 CE

10 404 CE

11 a), ii; b), i; c), iii; d), iv

12 1908, *Dr. Jekyll and Mr. Hyde*

13 c) April 9, 1865

14 1963

15 1956

16 d), 1954; a), 1961; b), 1962; c), 1971

17 September 11, 2001

18 a) around 1200 BCE

19 1909

Why?

1 because the Earth is not a perfect sphere

2 because some have insufficient mass

3 c) because the rate of evaporation is high, while the flow of water is low

4 Israeli Acute Paralysis Virus

5 they transfer pollen between plants

6 because they believed that the animal was a link between the living and the dead

7 because he was captured and imprisoned

8 because they commissioned many works

9 because it is located in a deep gorge

10 because he was concerned that his discovery of dynamite would be used for evil ends

11 d) it marked the start of a period of stalemate

12 to fight against an insurgency

13 he refused to support Henry VIII's claim to be the head of the Church of England

14 because it was the first of the Allies to be attacked

15 to populate the interior and create jobs

16 it is the largest in the world

17 because the figures are human rather than animal

18 c) because of political pressures and budget cuts

19 because Tolstoy drew on his experiences from the Crimean War

How?

1 the constellation the Southern Cross points to it

2 by investigating the atomic orbits of electrons

3 c) 30,000

4 a) classes

5 35,798 feet (10,911 m)

6 a) he was assassinated

7 d) 4

8 b) 13 (add the previous two numbers)

9 by introducing antiseptic procedures

10 hydrogen (H), lithium (Li), Sodium (Na), Potassium (K), Rubidium (Rb), Cesium (Cs), Francium (Fr)

11 d) $130 billion (U.S.)

12 International Brigades

13 as the "domino effect"

14 7: Bosnia-Herzogovina, Croatia, Kosovo, Macedonia, Montenegro, Serbia, Slovenia

15 social democracy

16 ...freedom for slave owners."

17 c) public goods

18 b) 2.1 billion

19 the Capitol is 188 feet (57.3 m) high, while the statue is 19 feet (5.8 m) tall

20 b) the greatest and most divine genius

True or False?

1 true

2 false—Jupiter is the biggest planet in the solar system

3 true

4 false—it is the idea that life was "seeded" from space

5 false—it is the largest reptile order, but with just under 8,000 species

6 false—he was the sixth king of Babylon

7 true

8 true

9 false—it was a radio broadcast

10 false—she was the first American woman; Russian Valentina Tereshkova was the first woman, in 1963

11 true

12 false—it was a military failure, but a political success

13 true

14 false—Germany is not a member

15 true

16 true

17 false—it is a symbol in Taoism

18 true

19 true

Index